'In *Life Beyond Murder*, Dan Gabriel Rusu accompanies a group of convicted murderers as they attempt to rebuild their lives after leaving prison. Searching for new tools that might aid them in the task of reconstruction, they wrestle with guilt and frustration, try to overcome the practical impediments that litter the path towards social reintegration, and look back thoughtfully at everything they've left behind. Ambitious, intelligent and full of honesty and pathos, this is an outstanding contribution that deserves to be widely read'.

Simon Winlow, *Professor of Social Sciences at Northumbria University*

'Dan Gabriel Rusu is the most gifted young Criminologist working in the UK today, and this book shows the academy why'.

David Wilson, *Emeritus Professor of Criminology at Birmingham City University*

'Unlocking profound insights into post-homicide life, this groundbreaking book explores subjectivities within a social context, reshaping our understanding of its long-term aftermath. Essential for criminal justice professionals and graduate students, it blends criminology and psychology in a compelling narrative, documenting the complexities of rebuilding after a homicide conviction'.

Elizabeth Yardley, *Professor of Criminology at Birmingham City University*

Life Beyond Murder

Detailing the resettlement narratives of five men who have committed different types of murder (confrontational/revenge, financial gain, random, intimate partner femicide, and family feud), this book counters narratives of neoliberal, 'responsibilizing' messages of individualism to investigate what informs their experiences of resettlement.

Life Beyond Murder: Exploring the Identity Reconstruction of Mandatory Lifers After Release explores the impact of mandatory lifers' institutionalisation, families, consumer culture, emotions, and supervision, considering how these factors hamper or assist with their transition from the stigmatising identity of being 'dangerous murderers'. The book's discussion is guided by the men's narratives, employing a 'tug of war' metaphor to elucidate the 'push-pull forces' that influence the men's efforts to reconstruct their lives in the years following their release.

To be successful, the book argues, these men have to reconcile a paradoxical situation, and the most skilled mandatory lifers manage to relativise their involvement in murder whilst concomitantly showing remorse. This situation is achieved through a Splitting Narrative that ultimately defends against anxiety, contains internal stigma, and often showcases self-flagellant remorse, as they move towards positive social identities such as philanthropists, family men, wounded healers, and pious members of the church.

Dan Gabriel Rusu, PhD, is a lecturer in criminology at Birmingham City University, a graduate member of the British Psychological Society, and a fellow of the Higher Education Academy.

International Series on Desistance and Rehabilitation
General Editor: Stephen Farrall, *University of Nottingham*

Editorial Board:

Ros Burnett, *University of Oxford*
Thomas LeBel, *University of Wisconsin-Milwaukee, USA*
Mark Halsey, *Flinders University, Australia*
Fergus McNeill, *Glasgow University*
Shadd Maruna, *Queens University, Belfast*
Gwen Robinson, *Sheffield University*
Barry Godfrey, *University of Liverpool*

Comparing Pathways of Desistance
An International Perspective
Ruwani Fernando

Gender, Prison and Reentry Experiences
A Matter of Time
Silvia Gomes and Dixie Rocker

The Unmaking of Crime
Contexts, Pathways and Representations of the Processes of Desistance on the Parisian Ground
Valerian Benazeth

Peer Support in Prison
How Incarcerated People make Meaning through Active Citizenship
Christian Perrin

Life Beyond Murder
Exploring the Identity Reconstruction of Mandatory Lifers After Release
Dan Gabriel Rusu

For more information about this series, please visit: www.routledge.com/criminology/series/ISODR

Life Beyond Murder
Exploring the Identity Reconstruction
of Mandatory Lifers After Release

Dan Gabriel Rusu

LONDON AND NEW YORK

First published 2025
by Routledge
4 Park Square, Milton Park, Abingdon, Oxon OX14 4RN

and by Routledge
605 Third Avenue, New York, NY 10158

Routledge is an imprint of the Taylor & Francis Group, an informa business

© 2025 Dan Gabriel Rusu

The right of Dan Gabriel Rusu to be identified as author of this work has been asserted in accordance with sections 77 and 78 of the Copyright, Designs and Patents Act 1988.

All rights reserved. No part of this book may be reprinted or reproduced or utilised in any form or by any electronic, mechanical, or other means, now known or hereafter invented, including photocopying and recording, or in any information storage or retrieval system, without permission in writing from the publishers.

Trademark notice: Product or corporate names may be trademarks or registered trademarks, and are used only for identification and explanation without intent to infringe.

British Library Cataloguing-in-Publication Data
A catalogue record for this book is available from the British Library

ISBN: 978-1-032-54197-6 (hbk)
ISBN: 978-1-032-54198-3 (pbk)
ISBN: 978-1-003-41564-0 (ebk)

DOI: 10.4324/9781003415640

Typeset in Sabon
by KnowledgeWorks Global Ltd.

Contents

Acknowledgements	*viii*
General Editor's Introduction – Stephen Farrall	*ix*
1 Introduction	1
2 Desistance, identity, and mandatory lifers	28
3 Barriers to resettlement: Exploring new pathways for mandatory lifers	52
4 Initial release transition: Family formation, employment	70
5 Negotiating the prison voice	89
6 Pursuing identities of success: Mandatory lifers and consumer culture	101
7 Experiencing supervision	112
8 Living in the shadow of guilt: Performing remorse	132
9 Life beyond murder: The splitting narrative	150
10 Managing shame: Hierarchies of moral abomination	174
11 Conclusion	187
Index	*205*

Acknowledgements

This book represents the culmination of several years of research and teaching about crime, penology, and offender rehabilitation. During these years, I have met many people who were instrumental to the completion of the book and who are deserving of my deepest gratitude.

To all participants who shared their life stories with me; without your contribution this book could have never existed. Thank you! To Emeritus Professor David Wilson who has been my mentor ever since I moved to the United Kingdom as an undergraduate student. You have guided and supported me at each step of my journey and have been a truly remarkable figure in my life. Thank you for everything. To my gatekeepers, especially Jackie Malton who has put me in contact with some of the men as well as the staff at HMP Springhill where I used to work during the first two years of my PhD. Your assistance was indispensable. To Dr. Sarah Pemberton, Professor Elizabeth Yardley, and Professor Michael Brookes OBE. Thank you for your help and support. Liz, you have always been very kind and generous. Thank you. To my friend Emma Winlow who supported my academic journey since day one. You have impacted my life in truly positive ways, and for this, I thank you. Also, to Professor Simon Winlow who took the time to read my work and engage me in challenging and fruitful discussions. To my good friend Dr Liam Brolan. Thank you for our innumerable conversations, some of which were about our PhDs and all the support with this book. To my parents, Mihaela Rusu and Daniel Rusu for your unconditional support throughout the years. To my brother, Mihai Rusu who has always trusted my academic potential. Thank you for proof-reading my work over the last 10 years. Also, to my sister-in-law, Adelina for your kindness, optimism, and for always giving me a sense of perspective. Also, to Maria Cojocaru, my grandmother who always loved to ask me whether I have 'now' submitted my book. Also, to my niece Victoria, who is now six months old. I am wishing you a lovely life.

To lovely Andreea who has put up with me in the later stages of my research. Thank you for staying by my side and for supporting me during the darkest moments of my life when my health deteriorated. Your optimism and resilience are contagious. I would also like to thank you for your dedication to our relationship and continuous support with writing this book. You are an amazing person.

General Editor's Introduction

The *International Series on Desistance and Rehabilitation* aims to provide a forum for critical debate and discussion surrounding the topics of why people stop offending and how they can be more effectively reintegrated into the communities and societies from which they came. The books published in the series will be international in outlook, but tightly focused on the unique, specific contexts and processes associated with desistance, rehabilitation, and reform. Each book in the series will stand as an attempt to advance knowledge or theorise about the topics at hand rather than being merely an extended report of a specific research project. As such, it is anticipated that some of the books included in the series will be primarily theoretical, whilst others will be more tightly focused on the sorts of initiatives which could be employed to encourage desistance. It is not our intention that books published in the series be limited to the contemporary period, as good studies of desistance, rehabilitation and reform undertaken by historians of crime are also welcome. In terms of authorship, we would welcome excellent PhD work, as well as contributions from more established academics and research teams. Most books are expected to be monographs, but edited collections are also encouraged.

As Dan Rusu correctly notes, studies of murderers have not been widespread in studies of desistance. In part, this is a fault of those of us who have studied desistance from crime in the past and our insistence that one cannot desist from a one-off (or even very short or limited offending career). The simile which is often used relates to smoking; if a person smokes a cigarette and never has another one, can they really be seen as 'an ex-smoker'? Surely, a more entrenched degree of smoking is needed? For this reason, and perhaps some others too, those studying desistance have focused on those sorts of offences which are commonly repeated (drug-use, theft, burglary, violence, fraud and the like) where we can be more certain that an entrenched offending career existed. Rusu does not chastise earlier desistance researchers for these choices, but his work does show how that the operationalisation of the variable(s) *prior* to the variable of central concern in the study of desistance has encouraged a blind-spot in our studies. Only, to my knowledge, Catherine Appleton's now quite old *Life After Life Imprisonment*, 2010, OUP) deals with lifers, and not all of her sample had committed murder, and her focus is on processes of resettlement more broadly. Rusu then pushes our thinking along a new dimension, and in so doing touches on some areas of offending careers, former-offenders' lives and processes of release and re-settlement which few have explored in such depths. As someone who has used what is sometimes referred to as 'N=1 studies', I appreciate the insights and depth of understanding, which can be generated by small-N studies, and Rusu is able to show this off wonderfully well. He also takes seriously earlier claims for accounts which draw upon both psycho-social explanations and those which seek to account for crime using macro-logical considerations. This is a book which shows the author's ability to interview men about some of the most difficult experiences of their lives with real maturity and sensitivity, and I hope that he is able to repeat this in his future studies – criminology needs that sort of depth of vision and understanding. It is with great pleasure that I welcome *Life Beyond Murder* into the series.

Stephen Farrall,
Sheffield,
March 2024.

1 Introduction

One evening, in November 2022 standing before a lecture full of criminology and psychology students, I announced with a mixture of enthusiasm and anxiety that we will soon be hosting a session with a guest speaker who has received a life sentence for a very serious crime. His name is Raul, and he was convicted of murder after stabbing a fellow teenager during a gang-related altercation in London over 15 years ago. As the day of Raul's visit approached, a myriad of emotions washed over me. Would my students feel intimidated by his past? Would Raul be able to effectively discuss with a lecture hall full of students despite his lack of public speaking experience? I felt the weight of this decision heavy on my shoulders and for a few weeks, I ruminated about the potential implications of the event. The moment arrived – Raul enters the lecture hall and sits on one of the two chairs I carefully placed at the front of the room. I could feel the collective gaze of the anticipating students fixed on him. I was surprised to notice that not a single student was using their phone; the air was filled with deafening silence, which was revealing the gravity of the encounter. I started by introducing Raul as one of my friends. I had known him for over four years at the time. Soon after the introductions, he nonchalantly disclosed that he had committed murder, saving students from the embarrassment of their hesitant question. Raul spoke of the criminal justice system, life on probation, prison hierarchies, and his difficulties of re-building his life post release. When asked whether he had ever internalised the stigmatising label 'murderer' by one of the students, his response sent ripples of surprise through the room: "I do not consider myself a real murderer; I've been in prison with real murderers, people that have killed children or women. I killed someone who lived the same life as me". The room fell silent.

Imbued with the newly found courage, several months later, I extended an invitation to Peter. He had murdered an elderly man during a robbery, which was driven by what seemed to be his need to feed his drug addiction. He had spent 12 years in prison and was in his fourth year of release at the time. During his guest lecture, Peter gravitated around a poignant exploration of his remorse, shame, and overwhelming guilt. He disclosed that he had committed murder but decided to withhold any details about the victim or

DOI: 10.4324/9781003415640-1

the circumstances surrounding their death. He was reserved to saying that he was not 'particularly fond of what he has done'. Paul's guilt was being publicly portrayed; his shame was apologetically acknowledged, evidencing that "relationally speaking, intense shaming is a conferral of guilt and a death sentence for identity" (Stein, 2007: 45). Nevertheless, Peter spoke at length about his children, his wife, and his dedication to his family.

Although my research project had been completed by that time, the men's visit to the university opened up a series of debates with my students, prompting them to reflect upon the ways in which everyday understandings of 'murder' are socially constructed (May, 1999). Raul's 'othering' of different types of murderers as the truly despicable types was presented as an attempt at constructing a moral self (Ugelvik, 2015) in interaction with the students. We discussed how we attach different levels of moral blameworthiness to different types of murders and the context in which they occurred (Mitchell, 1998). The perceived 'innocence' of victims was found to be very important in this process (May, 1999). Indeed "the experience of stigma for perpetrators of homicide cannot be separated from their social context" (Ferrito et al., 2020: 15), and this is ultimately relevant to the conditions of their release. Paul did not neutralise his crime (Sykes and Matza, 1957), nor did he project it externally, onto his victim (Gobodo-Madikizela, 2022). We started exploring some theoretical questions: What could explain the difference between Raul and Peter's discourse? Are the resettlement experiences of different types of murderers comparatively unique based on the type of murder they committed or their criminal careers (Farrall, 2019)? I suggested this as a possibility given existing power dynamics between dominant and competing discourses (Hollway, 1984) around 'appropriate' violence in our society. These would perhaps provide a set of 'ready-made excuses' (Gadd and Jefferson, 2007: 44) for these men to draw from when upon release.

We ended up discussing offenders' remorse and its role in the criminal justice system. We decided that the significance of this emotion lies precisely in its capacity to publicly convey a genuine willingness to abstain from similar behaviours in the future (Gobodo-Madikizela, 2022). We often expect remorse to be performed publicly, perhaps as reassurance through its visible display of regret.

Without question, releasing someone who has committed murder can elicit emotive responses in our society due to public fear that they might 'do it again' (Liem and Weggemans, 2018: 474). This is understandable given the high profile of such cases and the enormity and irreparability of their crime. Perhaps this is one of the most important lessons that the release and recall of Colin Pitchfork has taught us not too long ago. On 7 June 2021, Colin Pitchfork – the first person to have been caught with DNA fingerprinting analysis – and a convicted double murderer, was granted release on life licence. This event marked the recollection of a murder case that had captured national attention three decades earlier when he was first put in prison. Pitchfork had raped and strangled 15-year-old victims Lynda Mann and Dawn Ashworth in 1983 and 1986, respectively. Both the type of murder committed and his age at the time of killing emerged as significant factors in his public denunciation. The sexual nature of his murders alongside the fact that he was 'mature' when he had killed the two young girls secured him a special place on the public's hierarchy of moral abjection. In the wake of the public scandal, the print media reminded their readers of an incident, which would stand as proof of his capacity to deceive and manipulate (BBC, 2021). The story details that while he was held in an open prison and waiting for his release, Pitchfork had lied to a female shop worker about his marital status, telling her that he was married when he was not, while on a temporary release from prison. Of course, marital status confers one a sense of identity, even more so, the appearance of credibility and stability. A few months after his release, Pitchfork was recalled to prison; he had started approaching women while on walks from his bail hostel, thus violating the terms of his release. While his recall may be justified, it exemplifies an institutional focus on 'risk elimination', prompting an important discussion about the inherent tension between public protection and the prospects of rehabilitation that lie at the heart of the probation system in England and Wales (Barry, 2021).

The three cases, while inherently distinct, draw our focus to the exceptional experiences of a group of individuals who have seldom been the subject of criminological or psychological research. These men also direct our focus towards the significance of the specificities of the type of murder they committed in shaping the nature of their post-release experience and accessible avenues of identity reconstruction. Furthermore, they offer a pathway for reflecting on the degree to which formal and informal support and surveillance mechanisms impede or facilitate the process of pro-social identity reconstruction for individuals sentenced to life for murder, following their release.

Following this line of thought, this book explores the ways in which people who have committed murder reconstruct and talk about their lives post-release. It draws from longitudinal narrative research that closely followed the journeys of five men, some over a period of four years. The men are at different stages of the resettlement process and have all received a mandatory life sentence (MLS) or 'Custody for Life' for different types of murder. Typically, sentences of this kind are directly imposed on individuals who have committed murder and, therefore, serve to differentiate these men from those who have committed other forms of homicide. The book is not principally concerned with aetiologies of murder (Doctor, 2015; Hyatt-Williams, 1999; Stein, 2007), but rather, it explores the ways in which these five men reconstructed and negotiated identities after their prison sentences and constructed desistance narratives (Maruna, 2001). Before delving into the book's content and the rich narratives that informs its analysis, we need to make sense of the specificities of the MLS, as a form of unlawful homicide in England and Wales.

Exploring the mandatory life sentence

'Homicide' is an umbrella term, which is used in much criminological literature. As Brookman (2022) stated, the term 'homicide' refers to the killing of another human being, irrespective whether this is lawful or unlawful. As this book is focused on an unlawful form of homicide, a crucial distinction needs to be made at this point. Under English and Welsh jurisprudence, the principal distinction made is between infanticide, murder, and manslaughter (Brookman, 2022) and a conviction of murder requires proof that there was intent to kill. Manslaughter, on the other hand, refers to instances of unlawful homicide where there was intent to kill but a range of mitigating circumstances were also present (voluntary manslaughter), or there was no intent to kill (involuntary manslaughter) (Brookman, 2022). These distinctions are important for the main arguments of this book. As I will argue later, most criminological research on the resettlement of homicide offenders have not considered these distinctions in their analyses (Appleton, 2010 in the United Kingdom, Liem, 2016, 2017; Liem and Garcin, 2014 in the United Sates).

Life imprisonment is understood as "a sentence, following a criminal conviction which gives the state the power to detain a person for life, that is, until they die there" (Van Zyl Smit and Appleton, 2019: 35). However, as it will be discussed below, this is not necessarily always the case across European jurisdictions, and it is certainly simplistic in reference to current life sentencing in England and Wales. In fact, the laws that govern life sentencing practices in England and Wales originated in 1957. Before the salient Homicide Act 1957, the verdict for murder was an automatic death sentence, usually by hanging (Mitchell and Roberts, 2012). Later, section 1 of the 1965 Death Penalty Act suspended capital punishment for all those convicted of murder. The death penalty was replaced with imprisonment for life.

The nature of the MLS has since been further considered by politicians. In 1983, the Home Secretary of the time, Leon Brittan, explained that an initial fixed term in the management of the life sentence is passed for retribution and deterrence. This period is known as 'the tariff'. It simply represents a minimum term of imprisonment that the individual needs to serve before being considered for release. The tariff would be based on the seriousness of the offence alongside any aggravating or mitigating factors. After the tariff is spent, individuals would be eligible for parole and then released on a life licence (although this does not mean they would be automatically paroled). Specific types of murders would attract distinct tariffs. For example, for "murdering a police or prison officer, terrorist murders, sexual or sadistic murders of children, murders by firearm in the course of robbery, the tariff would be at least 20 years" (Mitchell and Roberts, 2012: 37). The remainder of the life sentence is aimed at protecting the public and can be maintained for as long as it is necessary.

Currently, when a person is convicted for murder, the judge is required to impose a sentence for mandatory life imprisonment. There are some exceptions. For example, section 259 of the Sentencing Act 2020 states that those offenders who commit murder when under 18 are detained at Her Majesty's Pleasure (UK Public Acts, 2020). Alternatively, where the offender was between 18 and 21 at the time of the murder, the sentence received is 'Custody for Life'. In fact, the perpetrator's age is significant in sentencing guidelines. Schedule 21 of the Criminal Justice Act 2003 sets out the basic starting points for tariffs: adults aged 21 years or older can receive a whole life order (they spend their whole natural life in prison), 30 years, 25 years, and 15 years tariffs. For those aged 18–20, there are three starting points: 30 years, 25 years, and 15 years. Lastly, for youths there is a 12-year starting point (Crown Prosecution Services, 2019), but where aggravating factors are present it can be greatly exceeded. After serving their minimum term, the offender can apply for parole, but release is not guaranteed; it is subjected to the scrutiny of a Parole Board. The average tariff has been increasing ever since the imposition of MLS. For example, tariff length for murder in England and Wales has increased from an average of 12.5 years in 2003 to 21.3 years in 2016 (Prison Reform Trust, 2021). The significant increase is due to several factors, chiefly amongst these – a new discourse of risk and punitiveness which started to legitimise punishment and sentencing (Feeley and Simon, 1992; Hallsworth, 2002; Nash, 2005; Pratt, 2000; Werth, 2011, 2013).

According to a House of Commons Library's Briefing Paper (2023) as of 30 June 2022, there were 6,731 individuals imprisoned for homicide. Of these, 5,857 committed murder, and 874 committed manslaughters. Only 351 were female. According to the Office for National Statistics (2023), there were 696 victims of homicide in 2022, representing a 23% increase from 2021 when government restrictions led to a decreased social contact between individuals. Most perpetrators and victims of homicide are male. Brookman (2022) found that for the 11 years period between 2008 and 2019, males comprised 91% of offenders and 68% of victims of homicide in England and Wales. Male victims tended to be killed more commonly by a friend or stranger, whereas female victims by their partner or ex-partner (ONS, 2023). On average, two women per week are killed by a current or former partner in England and Wales. Age is also an important demographic in making sense of homicide. Young men aged 20–29 are the most common age group to commit homicide, followed by those aged 30–39 (Brookman, 2022). Most tend to be unemployed at the time of the homicide (54%), and the majority of those employed were manual workers.

Reconviction and recall

Once released, the mandatory lifer is bound by several release conditions. These are targeted as a means for further monitoring and provide "after release assistance that offers adequate social support to all former life sentence prisoners" (United Nations, in Van Zyl Smit and Appleton, 2019: 275). The Council of Europe reinforces the requirement for attention to be placed upon the needs these individuals have in the community to ensure successful resettlement (Van Zyl Smit and Appleton, 2019: 275).

The Recall, Review, and Re-release of Recalled Prisoners Policy Framework sets out the recall process and criteria for indeterminate sentenced prisoners, including mandatory lifers in England and Wales. In this sense, mandatory lifers are subject to licensed supervision and can be recalled to prison by the probation service in certain situations: (a) they have breached a specific condition of their licence or (b) the behaviour being exhibited is sufficiently concerning to indicate that the risk they pose is assessed as no longer safely manageable in the community (Ministry of Justice, 2021). It is the responsibility of the National Probation Service to initiate the recall, where Community Offender Managers must evidence a 'causal link' in current behaviours, which were also exhibited at the time of the index offence (Ministry of Justice, 2021: 6). Remember the case of double murderer Colin Pitchfork presented at the beginning of the chapter? He was subjected to an extensive set of licence conditions including GPS tracking, polygraph testing, and a direction that he resided at an approved premise (Parole Board Note Paper, 2023).

Data suggests that life-sentenced individuals do not pose a significantly higher threat to the community than most offenders once they are released (Bjørkly and Waage, 2005; Liem et al., 2014; Neuilly et al., 2011; Prison Reform Trust, 2021; Roberts, Zgoba, and Shahidullah, 2007). The trend is thought-provoking, given the implicit connection being made between long-term sentences and risk and may be seen as a "reaction to the stigmatised 'other' [which] is arguably about imposing a morality script rather than about protecting the social body from imminent physical harm" (Munn and Bruckert, 2013:117). Between 2011/2012 and 2021/2022, a total of 28 individuals were convicted for having killed again. The majority of those were convicted after release (61%) while the rest were convicted while serving a sentence for homicide (House of Commons Library's Briefing Paper, 2023). Other figures show that 4% of released life-sentenced prisoners end up committing a further offence (Prison Reform Trust, 2021), and the increasing recall rates are mostly due non-compliance with licence conditions (HMIP, 2020). Recall rates are on an ascending trend, with a 21% increase of recall rates amongst life sentence prisoners in 2023 compared to the previous year (Ministry of Justice, 2023; Rennie and Crewe, 2023).

Coker and Martin's (1985) pioneering study followed up two samples of lifers consisting of 239 individuals between 1960 and 1974. They found a recidivism rate of 29% overall, with two individuals having committed a further homicide. The reconviction rates for serious offences were over 10%, out of which 6% included violence. The authors reported no significant differences in rates between homicides and non-homicides (92% of the sample committed homicide). Interestingly, irrespective of the group of offences, over half of the men committed their further offence within two years of release. Later, McCarthy et al. (2001) followed up 53 (46 men, 5 women) individuals who committed parricide (a term used to describe fatal violence exerted by children of all ages against their parents) and 71 stranger killers (66 men, 5 women), who were discharged from Broadmoor. All were subject to restrictions orders under the Mental Health Act 1983. Overall, the reoffending rate was low, with 8% and 15% of the parricide and stranger group respectively being convicted of a further crime. None committed a further homicide upon release. Interestingly, although not statistically significant, acquaintance with the victim influenced the eventual life course of the participants. In her analysis of risk factors associated with the recall of discretionary lifers, Appleton (2010) reported that 37% of those discretionary lifers convicted of a sexual index offence had been recalled to custody, while for all other cohorts was less than 23%. Importantly, she has found closeness to the victim (meaning how well they knew each other) as an important indicator of recidivism, with 39% success rate compared to 64% where the victim was not a stranger.

Although studies and official statistics often failed to differentiate between various forms of lifers in their analyses, they altogether indicate that homicide offenders are more likely to be recalled for violating their licence conditions and other offences, rather than for committing additional homicides. Nevertheless, to quote Young (2011: 218), these figures are the 'datasaur' in the room. In the absence of homicide offenders' experience of life post-release, these figures display the atrophied narrative of a creature that is always on the move, "without any clear direction, purpose, or meaning". We need to turn to these individuals' subjective experience of life post-release if we are to ever attach meaning to these figures. Stein (2007: 8) reminds us that it is no accident that we refer to murder as the 'taking of a life' – the act leads to the death of the victim as well as the birth of a new identity – that of the murderer who has taken the life and merged with their own self. The irreparability of the act deems it difficult to imagine that one can become an ex-murderer post-release in the same way that an ex-bank robber often does. The label 'murderer' is a spoiled identity (Goffman, 1963; Tyler, 2021) that needs to be negotiated successfully post-release for a successful resettlement; unfortunately, we have little understanding of this process.

Life after life imprisonment: What do we know?

There is a paucity of studies on the resettlement experiences and desistance of long-term prison sentenced individuals generally, and those who committed murder in the United Kingdom. With few exceptions (Appleton, 2010 in the United Kingdom, Liem and Colleagues in the United States), literature did not consider people who committed murder in their resettlement and desistance-oriented analyses. Further, most research on the experience of people who have killed is confined to prison (Adshead, 2011; Adshead, Ferrito, and Bose, 2015; Brookman, 2015; Crewe, Hulley, and Wright, 2020;

8 *Life Beyond Murder*

Ferrito et al., 2012, 2020; Sapsford, 1978, 1983; Wright, Crewe, and Hulley, 2017) open prisons (Clifford, 2010), or have not considered this group of individuals as distinctive in their own right post-release (Appleton, 2010 in the United Kingdom; Liem and Richardson, 2014; Liem, 2016; Liem and Garcin, 2014 – for US-based studies). Other accounts were journalistic (Heinlein, 2013; Parker, 1990). Also, much of the research which explored the resettlement experiences of homicide offenders (for example Appleton, 2010 in the United Kingdom; Liem, 2016, 2017 in the United States) tended to be retrospective studies (Nugent and Schinkel, 2016) where identity reconstructions could not be captured 'in the now' (Brookman, 2015) and followed up in a qualitative longitudinal design (an exception is Liem and Garcin, 2014 in the United States, but the study explored the narratives individuals convicted for second-degree murder or (in)voluntary manslaughter). Although existing research hints at a distinct re-entry pathway for mandatory lifers, no research has considered the type of murder committed as bearing on any importance on the re-entry experience. This book fills attempts to fill in this crucial gap.

Some thoughts on theory

My interest in narratives and whole life stories emerged out of an affinity to several theoretical frameworks. The concepts of narrative identity and narrative reconstruction resonate with narrative psychology (Bruner, 1986, 1991; Polkinghorne, 1988); narrative criminology (Presser, 2008, 2009), socio-narratology (Frank, 2010), desistance research (King, 2013a, 2013b; Maruna, 2001; Vaughan, 2007) and rehabilitation theory, especially the Good Lives Model (Ward and Stewart, 2003). The latter posits that the rehabilitation of offenders is dependent on the construction of a more adaptive, prosocial narrative identity (Ward and Marshall, 2007).

At the heart of the narrative conceptualisation of identity is the idea that we make sense of our experiences and constitute social selves by organising experiences in narrative self-conception (Schechtman, 1996: 134 in Krueger, 2011: 37; Frank, 2010). Narratives are not simply used to record or describe the past but are constitutive of our action and future (Presser, 2009). They guide, enable, or simply discourage our actions (Harding et al., 2017). To echo narrative criminologists: "we make sense of ourselves and our relationships with others by sharing stories and through our on-going inner narrative" (Sandberg and Ugelvik, 2016: 129). Some narrative criminologists draw from ethnomethodology (Verde and Knechtlin, 2019) to explore how stories are used by offenders to perform better selves, or identities, to an audience. Stories should not be understood as merely portals into people's internal worlds, but rather as actors that do things for people (Frank, 2010). For example, in the socio-narratological tradition storytelling is ultimately a moral action: it does something for the storyteller.

Given the book's interest in the ways in which mandatory lifers reconstruct their narrative identities post-release, the study is located within a narrative paradigm (see Spector-Mersel, 2010). I draw from socio-narratology (Frank, 2010) as the main theoretical framework. This means, as was previously discussed, that the stories gathered do not merely 'reveal something about who we are' (Spector-Mersel, 2011: 173) but are in fact guiding our action (Frank, 2010). Narratives are seen as constituting our senses of selves and identities.

Socio-narratology conceptualises stories as actors in the sense that it explores what stories do to individuals rather than conceptualising them as portals into people's minds (Frank, 2010). Stories teach people who they are. Individuals do not make up stories out of thin air, but these are always made from other stories which surround the storyteller. When an individual tells a story, they "draw from the menu of narrative resources that culture and social relations make available" (Smith and Monforte, 2020:2). In this sense, stories are seldom entirely original – they draw from culturally and institutional dominant stories and resources (Hammack, 2008; Loseke, 2007; McLean and Syed, 2015; Plummer, 2019; Sandberg and Fondevila, 2022). This is not to say that storytellers have no agency; a narrative subject can negotiate with master narratives (see McLean and Syed, 2015) and resist dominant cultural narratives by telling counter-narratives.

Socio-narratology conceptualises narrative resources as paramount in the construction and maintenance of narrative identity. Caddick (2015: 232) suggests that "narrative resources are linked to narrative identity in that resources are required for sustaining identity performances". In the absence of narrative maps, to use Frank's (2010) term, a sense of direction is lost. Some of the tools used by socio-narratologists are employed in this book. For example, the concept of Interpellation (which derives from Althusser's 1971 work on ideology) is specifically important to explore the ways in which formal supervision (for example by the probation service) enables or constrains mandatory lifers to construct pro-social identities post-release. In his book, *Letting Stories Breathe*, Frank (2010) suggested that stories 'interpellate' or hail people to take on certain identities. This theoretical tool is appropriate to explore the 'pulling and pushing' forces which invite mandatory lifers to take on a series of identities post-release. Importantly, some people seem more likely to respond to such invitations and to take on identities than others. The narrative habitus, or "the collection of stories in which a life is formed" (Frank, 2010: 49) of the individual is crucial in deciding the force and success of the invitation. Frank drew from Bourdieu's theory to suggest that "narrative habitus is the unchosen force in any choice to be Interpelled by a story" (Frank, 2010: 53). It involves a narrative repertoire that one has mastered and uses, a disposition and openness to hear some stories and not others and takes the form of an inner library. There is an obvious strength to taking on this approach as it allows the research to explore stories as personal as well as culturally derived. Taking on a socio-narratological approach is also useful as it allows us to consider the ways in which mandatory lifers accumulate narrative resources to perform new identities post-release.

Thus, post-release identities are not reconstructed in a vacuum: "it's not as if we had on the one hand an individual equipped by nature with certain drives and on the other, society as something apart from him" (Fromm, 1941: 12). This is particularly true today – in a society based on consumption 'have nothing is to be nothing' (Presdee, 2004: 280). As such, the fabric of these stories is imbued with the complex interaction between existing socio-economic systems, structures, psycho-social pressures, and available ideals of success. Moreover, people's access to 'narrative resources' is contingent upon their social connections and location (Frank, 2010). This refers to the stories most often shared in specific organisations, the family, or wider communities. Ultimately, 'stories summon up whole cultures' (Frank, 2010: 37). Special interest is paid to organisationally embedded stories (Loseke, 2007) without losing track of the wider picture as, "the objective of narrative interviews is not only to reconstruct the life history of the informant, but to understand the context in which these biographies were constructed and the factors that produce change and motivate the actions of informants" (Muylaert et al., 2014: 187). Given the heavy emphasis on the relational and cultural the book pays specific attention importance of the type of murder (identity of victim and motivation) committed in shaping post-release trajectories.

Importantly, I also draw from some psychoanalytic theory to bridge a subjectivity gap present in much narrative theory (Frosh and Baraitser, 2008; Gadd and Jefferson, 2007; Hollway, 1984; Hollway and Jefferson, 2005; Jefferson, 2008; Parker, 1992; Verde, 2021) as well as ultra-realism thought (Hall and Winlow, 2015) and further provide an explanatory framework for the experiences of my participants. In line with the resurge in criminological 'emotion research' (Jacobsen and Walklate, 2019; Jones, 2019), the book also takes the affective states of the mandatory lifers (especially shame and guilt) seriously and theorises about their relevance in the resettlement process.

The mandatory lifers

As mentioned previously, this book is informed by a longitudinal narrative study that was carried out between 2019 and 2023. The longitudinal approach enabled a nuanced understanding of the men's narratives as they evolved over time. In deciding on this approach, I was influenced by the work of Harding et al. (2017) who explored stability and change of ex-prisoners' narratives in the face of structural constraints in Michigan. This was important as it allowed me to capture developments and changes in the men's lives as they resettled as well as to explore the modality in which the men engaged with 'pains and snares' of life post-release (Klaus, 2023) and reconstruct their identities in this process.

In total, 13 interviews were conducted with five released mandatory lifers over a period of four years. Two of the men were interviewed four times and two were interviewed twice. Only one participant was interviewed once. The homicide classification below is based on Brookman's (2022) and Dobash and Dobash's (2020) systems. See Table 1.1.

Table 1.1 Number of participants, murder motivation, interviews, and format

Name	Murder motivation	Reported ethnicity	Time since release (first interview)	Second interview (since no. 1)	Third interview (since no. 2)	Fourth interview
Raul	Confrontational/ Revenge	East Asian	18 months (in person)	11 months (phone)	12 months (phone)	2 years after the third interview (in person)
Peter	Financial gain homicide	White Caucasian	6 months (in person)	4 months (video call)	12 months (video call)	1.5 years after the third interview (in person)
Nathaniel	Random homicide	White Caucasian	6 years (phone)	7 months (phone)	N/A	N/A
Richard	Intimate Femicide	Black	20 years (in person)	12 months (phone)	N/A	N/A
Jacob	Financial Gain/ Family Feud	White Caucasian	20 years (phone)	N/A	N/A	N/A

Meet the men

Raul killed a young man by stabbing him when he was 17. The murder occurred in the context of an arranged fight in London. He was released 12 years later. He now works in various gyms across London as a personal trainer (a continuation of what he used to do in prison) and as a gym manager. His murder can be classed as a 'Confrontational Fighter Murder' (Dobash and Dobash, 2020) as it was a group related conflict which ultimately involved Raul's protection of his masculine honour and reputation. Based on Brookman's (2022) typologies this may also be considered a 'revenge homicide' given the history between the two groups and the planned nature of the attacks. I met Raul face-to-face in June 2019 and our first interview was rather unusual, having taken place in the waiting area of Cineworld in West London. He was released for over 18 months at the time. Two of our follow-up interviews took place over the phone during COVID-19 lockdowns, and our fourth and last interview was in person in my university office in March 2023.

Peter killed an elderly man during a robbery when he was in his early 20s. He used to be a crack cocaine addict and argues that the robbery was carried out in the context of his drug use. Peter initially entered the house to rob an elderly man who he ended up killing. Peter cut his throat with a knife and proceeded to steal a small amount of money before leaving the crime scene. This can be considered a 'murder for money' (Dobash and Dobash, 2020), or 'financial gain homicide' (Brookman, 2022) but as it will be shown later in the book, this is a rather simplistic explanation. I have met Peter in February 2020 and have conducted our first interview face to face at a train station in South England. He had been released for over six months at the time. We then proceeded with two online video calls during the COVID-19 pandemic lockdowns. Our fourth and last interview took place in person in my university office in November 2022.

Richard killed his girlfriend when he was 19 as a refusal to accept that she wanted to break up with him. He describes his murder as a 'crime of passion' and is disappointed when people do not accept his construction of what happened. His murder is classed as Intimate Partner Femicide and is characteristic of this category to include issues around control, jealousy, and possessiveness at the aetiology of the killing (Daly and Wilson, 1988; Radford and Russel, 1992 in Brookman, 2022). He was released 20 years ago and now works for a known broadcasting network, as well as in a non-governmental agency dedicated to assisting with the re-entry of people who have been incarcerated. I have met Richard in person and conducted our first interview in my university office. We then proceeded with a follow-up interview over the phone during one of the COVID-19 lockdowns.

Jacob tied, gagged, and shot a man when he was 20. He describes his murder as being classed as an 'execution'; he believes that it was callous, brutal, and ruthless. Jacob's motivation for the murder was difficult to ascertain. Murders do not always fit into neat categories and this particular case followed an 'unusual scenario' (Brookman, 2022). Initially, Jacob mentioned that he killed a man because he witnessed him stealing a car. Later, he remarked that the man he had killed looked identical to his father, which triggered the psychological constellation that precipitated the murder. The initial reading of this case moved from a potential financially motivated murder to something much more psychological when considering the paternal transference (Polnay et al., 2023) that allegedly had taken place at the time. In this sense, the murder could also be classed as a 'family feud' (Dobash and Dobash, 2020) although this can be debated. Jacob and I spoke over the phone for over three hours during our only meeting. He currently runs a successful IT business and lives an isolated life with his wife. He has been released for over 20 years.

Nathaniel went to prison for murder when he was 17. He said that he decided to 'go out and kill somebody' after an argument with his girlfriend. Based on this description, his murder was classed as a random homicide. Brookman (2022) categorised random homicides those acts of killing that fall under unusual scenarios and which defy typical explanations. Nathaniel kept silent about the details of the murder and chose to disclose very little about anything to do with the crime. His silence can be analysed as acts of 'not-saying' (Presser, 2019: 410), which may explain some exceeding anxiety or simply a matter of identity work, which will be explored in the chapters that follow. We had spoken twice and what was extraordinary about these encounters had been his performance of hyper-normality. Much of his narrative was used to provide a description of a banal, normal, even boring, typical family life. He is currently married, has one child, and works in a local factory in Birmingham.

The longitudinal narrative interview

Participants were initially subjected to a modified version of the Life Story Narrative Interview (McAdams, 2008) – this represented an initial unstructured, passive approach that aimed at eliciting participants' full life stories. They gave me the opportunity to step inside the intimate world of the storyteller and 'discover larger worlds' (Atkinson, 2012: 115). My approach was of course predicated on the notion that identity and our sense of self are narratively constructed. McAdams (2008) proposed a life story interview schedule that closely resembles that of the chapters of a book (which means that they have a beginning, a middle, and an end). In McAdams' work, participants are asked to think of their lives as if they were a book, or novel, complete with chapters, characters, themes, and scenes (McAdams and Guo, 2015). Although I have flirted with this idea, on a closer inspection, I have decided to adopt a more passive approach at the start. The decision was premised upon Mishler's (1986) observation that allowing participants to freely express themselves without any interruption is crucial for uncovering stories. Each participant was asked a simple question at the start of the interview: "please tell me your life story, in whatever order you want". This was meant to provide the space for a full narration to start. I then listened carefully and passively as participants narrated their life stories. Most participants started with their childhoods, apart from one participant, Richard, who started with the murder scene. This meant learning how to be comfortable with short awkward silences, which are inevitable when looking for a rich description of one's life. I had to overtly renounce my turn in conversation through maintaining the silence which in turn signalled to participants that they are welcomed to continue. When there was no clear coda (Jovchelovitch and Bauer, 2000), I could proceed to asking questions; in this 'conversation phase' (Kim, 2016) I avoided asking 'why questions'. Then, in the same interview sitting, I asked each participant to narrate a low point, a high point, and a turning point since their release. This semi-structured approach was used in the second half of each interview, after the life stories had been fully narrated. This approach aimed at eliciting stories directly pertinent to the men's lives post-release. Research has found that individuals start making sense of turning points naturally, without being explicitly invited to do so (Alea, 2018; Carlsson, 2012). Further, these turning points also ensured a level of consistency across participants. I then proceeded to the next phase – 'the concluding talk'. During this phase, I made it clear to the participant that the recorder has been switched off. I then asked questions, which I had formulated during the interview, but which I could not ask as they would interrupt narration.

In this phase, 'why questions' were used. To record these discussions, I used a notebook, which also acted as my reflexive journal (Goldstein, 2017). Unfortunately, this was not possible with all the interviews, which meant that I had to either write down these discussions immediately after I had left the interview; on some occasions, I recorded myself on my way to the train station, or on my way home. I have asked all participants whether I could use this data in the research, and they all responded affirmatively.

After I finished transcribing and reading the interview, I started scheduling a second in depth interview. This allowed me to explore emergent narrative themes, and to follow up on stories. Hyden (2014) remarked that it is impossible for a participant to 'say everything' in one interview. Moreover, interviews are time specific. Although we cannot do much about the time-specificity of interviews, we can combine stories from different interviews with the same participants to reach a more complete and fuller understanding of their experiences and lives (Hyden, 2014). Also, the initial interview assisted in building trust and rapport with the participants which turned out to be important in a second meeting. Cornwell (1984) found that interviewees tend to use public accounts in initial meetings, which are mere expectations transformed into stories. However, on future occasions, when trust and rapport had already been established, private accounts started to surface (Cornwell, 1984 in Grinyer and Thomas, 2012). I found this to be true. Nevertheless, trust cannot be switched on and off. I quickly understood that if I were to maintain contact with my participants, I needed to negotiate these relationships continuously. This proved to be difficult with some of the participants, who at times, reverted to avoidant or isolating behaviours. Researchers tend to think that rapport is some form of "finite commodity that can be turned on and off by the researcher" (Darlington and Scott, 2002: 54 in Grinyer and Thomas, 2012: 221). In my case, this could not be further from the truth. Comparable to research on homicide offenders in forensic settings (Ferrito et al., 2020) on this second occasion, I discussed the ways in which my participants made sense of having committed murder, and the effect this had on their lives and transition post release. My approach throughout had been neutral, and non-judgemental (Brookman, 2015). Nevertheless, as the coronavirus pandemic was declared, I had to find other means of conducting follow up interviews with some of the participants. Two of the five men were interviewed via phone only. Phone interviews were initially identified as the alternative. Of course, this presented its own limitations; as Creswell (2007) has correctly said, in phone interviews, meaning is lost due to the absence of informal communication. This has influenced my decision to discard follow-up phone interviews and turn to online applications such as Skype, Microsoft Teams, and Zoom. A strength of using video-calls was that participants managed to showcase their progress in the community, and I was able to explore stories as embodied – participants told stories as much with their words as they did with their bodies (Smith and Monforte, 2020). However, second interviews were not possible with all participants (4/5), and this was mainly due to some of their tumultuous lives post-release. This reminded me of Brookman's (2015) point, that murderers have spent lengthy time in prison; this may not only lead to 'therapeutic lingo' when interviewed but reminds us that they are likely to be institutionalised. The first two interviews were crucial in deciding what questions I should ask during this third interview. Some initial analysis of the first two interviews led to the development of a conceptual model where I mapped narrative identities for each participant as emergent from the data alongside their value commitments and their desires that underpinned the narrative identities.

Third and fourth interviews were conducted with the most recently released mandatory life sentenced offenders (Peter and Raul). Luckily, by the time of the fourth interview, the restrictions imposed by the pandemic had been lifted and we had managed to meet face to face again. The third interview took place roughly one year after the second and the fourth a year later. These were aimed at exploring the ways in which initial narratives have been maintained or changed considering some of the structural impediments that the men encountered in their lives post-release. This decision was based on the need to explore prospective accounts of their resettlement. In this sense, in approaching the men's re-entry experience of identity management, I was influenced by Leverentz's (2014) research with short-term female offenders living in Mercy Homes in Chicago. It was suggested by Leverentz that desistance is difficult to capture, and repeated interviews with our participants allow us to see how the process unfolds in participants' lives.

The decision to focus on the most recently released lifers came from the crucial timing of their release. It was found that two in five adults (representing 42%) are reconvicted within one year of their release (Prison Reform Trust, 2023). Moreover, recall rates for mandatory lifers have continuously increased since 2017 (Rennie and Crewe, 2023). Although not all participants were within the 12-month bracket at the time of our first interview, they were at the early stages of the resettlement process and would naturally face a set of struggles that could influence their initial narratives. This is a point also made by Harding et al. (2017, np) who remarked that "a longitudinal design is necessary in a study of released prisoners due to the rapidly changing nature of their lives. Re-entry is a period of significant flux".

In total, I conducted 13 interviews with these participants over a period of four years. The men were selected with a specific interest in the type of murder committed (they committed confrontational/fighters murder, financial gain, intimate partner femicide, and random homicides; Brookman, 2022; Dobash and Dobash, 2020) as well as their stages within the resettlement process (early release, or veterans of life outside). I considered early release the mandatory lifers who had been released for up to four years, while veterans four years and above. This decision was informed by existing penological research that explored sentence stages (Crewe et al., 2020). The longitudinal narrative interview is depicted in Table 1.1. A breakdown of the sample is depicted in Table 1.2.

Table 1.2 Depiction of the longitudinal narrative interview

Interview number	Interview type	Sample	Timing
1.	Life Story Interview Semi-Structured Interview	All participants	First interview
2.	In-depth semi-structured interview	All participants (excluding Jacob)	Four months to one year after the first
3.	In-depth semi-structured interview	Peter, Raul	About one year after the second
4.	In-depth semi-structured	Peter, Raul	1.5 years to 2 years after the third

Sampling and access

As Brookman (2015) remarked, interviewing homicide offenders in the community is not an easy task, and maybe this could explain its scarcity, albeit with a few exceptions (Appleton, 2010; Liem, 2016; Liem and Garcin, 2014; Parker, 1990). I could not agree more with Brookman – one of the most challenging aspects that I encountered was obtaining access to the participants. Similarly, to Ellis' (2016) ethnographic work, I decided early in the research process that, where possible, access to participants will not be facilitated through the Criminal Justice System. This, I thought, would affect the ways in which participants would engage with the interview. Many researchers admit that having personal contacts with the study population makes access much more comfortable to negotiate (Wilkes, 1999 in Reeves, 2004; Ellis, 2016). Initially, I had no such contacts, and therefore it was difficult to find a way to build connections and rapport with gatekeepers – this would be the only way to 'break-in' (Trulson, Marquart, and Mullings, 2004). Similarly to Kay's (2016) research, I contacted those in my closest proximity – professors and fellow colleagues in the academia, whom I thought could link me with appropriate gatekeepers. Then, it would have been simple: a snowballing strategy would lead into establishing and maintaining contacts. The individuals I was looking to interview needed to have received an MLS for murder. It was also important that they had committed different typologies of murder (represented by victims/motive) knowing that each will have their own lived and statistical particularities, falling within specific hierarchies of violence legitimacy (see Skott, 2023).

The next step was to consider was the sample size. My plan was to discuss with as many mandatory lifers as I could, although I quickly recognised that theoretical saturation was an impossible desideratum. As qualitative researchers, we are encouraged to turn to consecrated qualitative 'gold standard' assurance mechanisms/systems to defend our decisions. The go-to concept in this sense in qualitative research is 'saturation'. This procedure stems from the grounded theory approach (Guest, Bunce, and Johnson, 2006) and simply refers to the fact that we should continue collecting data until nothing new or illuminating is generated (Green and Thorogood, 2004 in O'Reilly and Parker, 2012). However, as O'Reilly and Parker (2012) recognised, this cannot be applied to all qualitative research – including mine. In fact, sample size is influenced by the aims of the research and its philosophical underpinning. For example, in narrative inquiry the focus is placed on quality rather than the quantity of the interviews. Each life story is unique, and in some sense, saturation is impossible to reach (Wray, Markovic, and Manderson, 2007). For Kvale (1996: 101) the answer is simple: "Interview as many subjects (sic) as necessary to find out what you need to know". Then, transparency, heuristic value, and the epistemological underpinning of the research should influence what is seen as an appropriate number of participants.

Criminological research, especially that stemming from psychodynamic frameworks (Gadd and Farrall, 2004), has taught us about the importance of case studies (see Kvale, 1999) and richness of data in making sense of human experience. Although these approaches, as Schiff (2013: 246) said, are "slurred as mere literature, journalism, or perhaps philosophy", we have to accept that "all qualitative researchers are philosophers" (Denzin and Lincoln, 2011: 12). Conceptions of knowledge, stemming from existential, hermeneutical, or postmodern positions, although in tension with mainstream positivist assumptions and methodologies, are important in knowledge production. It is difficult to prescribe the perfect numbers of participants needed for narrative inquiry. However, Kim (2016) for example recommends five to six participants. This, of course, is discretionary, based on a multiplicity of variables and, in the end, highly speculative. Coincidence or not, I eventually ended up with five participants some of whom were interviewed repeatedly over a period of four years (as shown above). I will now move on to describe the process of finding and keeping these men interested in the research. This was not always simple.

Having decided on participant number and approach to research, I now needed to find the men. At this point, I had already started to engage with the appropriate literature around different strategies of establishing and maintaining such links (Reeves, 2004; Trulson et al., 2004). After two years of trial and error, I've managed to break in: an addiction counsellor, whom I was introduced to by a mutual friend, mentioned that she knew someone who was 'ready to talk'. Further access was granted after one of my visits to a prison where I used to work on an Enabling Environments accreditation portfolio during my first two years of doctoral research. Several other individuals who reached the inclusion criteria refused to participate straight away or postponed continuously. This made me question my capacity to conduct this research as well as my interpersonal, communication skills. On numerous occasions I blamed my initial strategy in conversation with some of the men as having been either 'too directive' or too 'soft'. I thought that directiveness would portray a sense of professionalism – I should act as someone for whom an interview with a convicted murderer is just 'another day at the office'. I would then ruminate in reverie as rejections started to pile up. However, it became clear that I had begun collecting data at the time, even though I was not aware of it. The men's evasion represented in and of itself a measure of identity work – they were negotiating their identities from the first moment we were put into contact. I realised that for some of them, to move forward they needed to forget the past.

This demanded me to look further into the issue of absence and avoidance when it came to securing interviews. On several occasions, initial eagerness, and enthusiasm to participate was doubled by an inability to meet. It was as if an obscured force would keep these potential participants away. The closer I got to organising the location/date/hour for the interview, the further away the concretisation of the meeting became – many times I compared this with the Kafkaesque sentiments pervasive in his *Castle* (Kafka, 1998). It is not unusual for the researcher to feel rejected or disillusioned in the process of conducting research. Such refusals should be read in key with the sensitivities of the 'interview society' (Silverman, 1997: 248) under study (Herzog, 2012). These individuals have spent many years inside prison; throughout their imprisonment, they have been interviewed by countless experts in positions of authority: psychologists, probation officers, parole boards, and so forth. Then, the interview society is exacerbated in captivity; evidently, there is a discrepancy in power dynamics between the interviewers and those who are subjected to the interview process (Presser, 2005). Nevertheless, to follow Briggs' (2002) point, the fundamental thing here is not counting the number of refusals that I had (which were numerous), but to contextualise and analyse the meaning of their refusal.

Location(s)

Once some level of rapport was established often via an initial phone conversation, I proceeded to conduct the first interview. These were conducted in university offices, the library, in a participant's car, over the phone, and one took place in the waiting area of a Cineworld. Whenever necessary, I would travel to specific urban locations where participants lived actively seeking interview locations that I identified online. In selecting the interview location, I have always tried to negotiate between the need for security and privacy – a compromise, which had to be navigated continuously, and participants were active in this negotiation. For example, the decision to interview in the café at Cineworld took on board the following considerations: the time would ensure that the place is not busy and therefore noise pollution is low (2 pm); enough individuals would be there, including the staff to make the place a public one. Of course, I ensured that the interviews took place in quiet places for participants' privacy – talking about one's past is seldom an easy task, especially when the one shares personal information with a stranger. To address additional ethical considerations inherent to this book, pseudonyms have been employed to protect the identity of my participants, and the locations intentionally altered to ensure confidentiality.

While this type of 'immersive fieldwork' felt exciting, I was aware it influenced the dynamics of the interview and generated data. However, this is not necessarily a limitation; I was not there to excavate 'uncontaminated data' from my participants; all interview data is co-constructed in the research process and any attempt to remove bias would inadvertently represent adherence to positivism. As qualitative researchers, we acknowledge that interviews are social processes which are integral to the data generated in the research interaction (Holstein and Gubrium, 1995). Interview situations, as Gubrium and Holstein (2012) have described, affect what is said and how it is said in fundamental ways. It is key that we maintain a reflective stance throughout the research process.

Criminological research has been interested in how interview accounts are situated within power relations (Presser, 2005; Rowe, 2014). In Presser's research, the interview location, alongside gender assumptions of the interviewer, has provided participants with opportunities to present themselves in different ways while in prison (Liebling, 2001). Unfortunately, most of these discussions are related to institutionalised dynamics, usually in prisons or forensic settings. My own identity as a neophyte Romanian researcher interviewing British released homicide offenders surfaced several times during data collection and also when accessing prospective participants. I have never been so aware of my national identity than in some encounters with my participants. Of course, English is my second language, and my strong Romanian accent is not one that I can hide. On one occasion, after the interview had been completed, Raul made a game out of identifying each Romanian on the street of Camden Town as we were walking together towards the train station. I recorded this in my diary once I got on the train:

> Only a couple of minutes ago Raul showed me every Romanian on the streets he could identify. He didn't personally know these people; so, he only guessed with complete certainty that they were Romanians. This reminds me of the conversations we had during the interview; he said that the animal he identifies with the most is the eagle. He looks down on us, flying, he knows who the Romanians are, who the Asians are; he can spot this from miles, as he said. I was on his territory, and he wanted to make this clear. I can only wonder how my 'Romanianness' has affected the interview data. Does he not like Romanians? Was this an attempt to say that he accepts me or was I being exposed as someone not worthy? (7/30/2019).

During the data collection phase, I would note down all my feelings, thoughts about the interview in my reflexive diary, and then, I would contemplate for days over the process. By re-reading the transcript, I was able to imagine how I was experienced by my participants. I would seek to experience myself as both subject and object (Aron, 2000 in Goldstein, 2017; Finlay, 2002), I had to think back to the intersecting subjectivities that create the participant-researcher relationship; these considerations were crucial for analysing the data. In doing this, I had to think about the feelings elicited by each participant, the fears, encounters, discussions, wishes, and anxieties as they occurred in the interview. Other times, interviews had to be conducted over the phone, mainly because the COVID-19 pandemic had been declared and the subsequent disruption ensued. To further manage other ethical issues relating to this book, all the names used are pseudonyms to protect the identities of the participants. To avoid any level of deductive disclosure, I have also used different geographical locations to the ones mentioned by my participants.

To anticipate potential criticism, some may say that the book is solely interested in fiction and 'language games' rather than in what has happened in reality. For example, critics could draw from Laws (2022: 6) in arguing that "without external reference points beyond the narrative it can be hard to identify the lines of demarcation between fantasy and real-life event". However, the book does not claim access to crystal clear, objectively identifiable truths. In fact, I was interested in the worlds as they made sense to my participants. However, to control for 'fantasies' presented as real life events, and to gain a degree of access to events as seen by others, I read about the men's murders in the print media after the finalisation of the data analysis, to spot any outright discrepancies. There were none.

Structure of the book

The book is comprised of 11 chapters in total. Chapters 2 and 3 provide a critical review of relevant existing literature and set the theoretical background to this book. In this sense, Chapter 2 explores a set of theories that are collectively referred to as 'desistance research'. Specifically, the chapter focuses on the agency versus structure divide, as well as their interaction in producing and maintaining prosocial identity change in individuals who are released from prison. Ultimately, it is suggested that mandatory lifers are a neglected population within this body of research. Individuals who have been imprisoned for murder require further academic attention due to the idiosyncratic pains that they experience as 'barriers post-release', stemming from adaptive responses to imprisonment and to their index offence. Chapter 3 explores barriers to reintegration in more depth. Specific attention is given to the 'offence-crime nexus', relevant to people who committed murder. In addition, the chapter explores systemic barriers to resettlement by focusing on issues around experiencing stigma and the dissolution of traditional sites of identity construction. Chapters 4–10 represent the main themes and arguments of the book.

Chapters 4–8 focus on the content of the men's stories, exploring the significance of specific factors in their identity reconstruction after release. The men are shown to negotiate their identities against a series of 'push-pull' forces which either constrain or enable the development of pro-social identities. For example, the role of prisoners' families and employment in early resettlement will be explored in Chapter 4. Chapter 5 focuses on the ways in which the men reconciled an internal 'lingering prison voice' with life in the community. The chapter critically considers the long-term effects of imprisonment as an institutionalising force as well as a necessary system of atonement, which contains unmetabolised guilt. The ways in which the men negotiate identities in the context of the post-Fordist economy and consumer culture are explored in Chapter 6. Further, the role of the probation service in interpellating (Althusser, 1971; Frank, 2010) the men as risky is outlined in Chapter 7, and issues around guilt, 'complicated redemption' and generativity in Chapter 8.

Chapters 9 and 10 draw from ethnomethodology to explore the ways in which the men reconstructed their identities in the interview context. In other words, these chapters focus on the function of the stories rather than solely on their content. Chapter 9 suggests that despite the remorse shown by some of the men for what they had done, they relativise their involvement in the murder scene through employing a 'Splitting Narrative' aimed at denying agency. This serves the role of solving the Murderer's Identity Paradox (to be guilty of a crime one did not fully commit). Chapter 10 further explores the ways in which the lifers negotiated ethical selves through constructing murderer hierarchies of moral abomination in the interview context. Chapter 11 concludes the main arguments of the book and provides a set of practical recommendations for the criminal justice and voluntary sector to improve the resettlement experiences of mandatory lifers.

References

Adshead, G. (2011) The life sentence: Using a narrative approach in group psychotherapy with offenders. *Group Analysis*, 44 (2), 175–195.

Adshead, G., Ferrito, M., and Bose, S. (2015) Recovery after homicide: Narrative shifts in therapy with homicide perpetrators. *Criminal Justice and Behaviour*, 42 (1), 70–81.

Alea, N. (2018) Does the life story interview make us make sense? Spontaneous and cued Redemption and contamination in life story scenes. *Imagination, Cognition, and Personality: Consciousness in Theory, Research, and Clinical Practice*, 37 (3), 271–292.

Althusser, L. (2001 [1971]) *"Lenin and Philosophy" and Other Essays*, trans. Ben Brewster. New York, NY: Monthly Review Press.

Appleton, C. (2010) *Life after Life Imprisonment*. Oxford, UK: Oxford University Press.

Atkinson, R. (2012) The life story interview as a mutually equitable relationship. In Gubrium, J. F, Holstein J. A., Marvasti A. B., and McKinney, K. D. (Eds.), *The SAGE Handbook of Interview Research: The complexity of the Craft*, second edition. SAGE: Thousand Oaks, 115–128.

Barry, M. (2021) 'Walking on ice': The future of parole in a risk-obsessed society. *Theoretical Criminology*, 25 (2), 325–342.
BBC (2021) Double child killer Colin Pitchfork sent back to prison, 19 November, 2021. Available at: Double child killer Colin Pitchfork sent back to prison – BBC News [accessed on 13/11/2023].
Bjørkly, S., and Waage L. (2005) Killing again: A review of research on recidivistic single victim homicide. *International Journal of Forensic mental Health*, 4 (1), 99–106.
Briggs, C. L. (2002) Interviewing, power/knowledge, and social inequality. In J. A. Holstein and J. F. Gubrium (Eds.). *Handbook of Interview Research: Context and Method*. Thousand Oaks, CA: SAGE, 911–922.
Brookman, F. (2015) Researching homicide offenders, offenses, and detectives using qualitative methods. In Copes H. and Miller M. J. (Eds.), *The Routledge Handbook of Qualitative Criminology*. Oxon: Routledge, 236–252.
Brookman, F. (2022) *Understanding Homicide*, 2nd edition. London, UK: SAGE.
Bruner, J. (1986) *Actual Minds, Possible Worlds*. Cambridge, MA: Harvard University Press.
Bruner, J. (1991) The narrative construction of reality. *Critical Inquiry*, 18 (1), 1–21.
Caddick, N. (2015) Doing Narrative Analysis. In Lyons E. and Coyle A. (Eds.), *Analysing Qualitative Data in Psychology*, 2nd edition. Sage Publications: London, 222–239.
Carlsson, C. (2012) Using 'Turning Points' to understand processes of change in offending. *British Journal of Criminology*, 52, 1–16.
Clifford, J. L. (2010). Managing a Murderous Identity: How men who murder experience life imprisonment and the concept of release. PhD Thesis, University of Bath.
Coker, J. and Martin, J. P. (1985) *Licensed to Live*. Oxford, UK: Basil Blackwell.
Cornwell, J. (1984) *Hard-Earned Lives: Accounts of Health and Illness from East London*. London, UK: Tavistock.
Creswell, W. J. (2007) *Qualitative Inquiry and Research Design, Choosing Among Five Approaches*, 2nd edition. Thousand Oaks, CA: SAGE.
Crewe, B., Hulley, S., and Wright, S. (2020). *Life Imprisonment from Young Adulthood Adaptation, Identity, and Time*. London, UK: Palgrave Macmillan.
Crown Prosecution Services (2019) Sentencing – Mandatory life sentences in murder cases. Available at: https://www.cps.gov.uk/legal-guidance/sentencing-mandatory-life-sentences-murder-cases [accessed on 15.04.2022].
Denzin, N. K. and Lincoln, Y. S. (Eds.) (2011) *The SAGE Handbook of Qualitative Research*, 4th edition. Thousand Oaks, CA: SAGE.
Dobash, R. P. and Dobash, R. E. (2020) *Male–Male Murder*. Abingdon, Oxon: Routledge.
Doctor, R. (2015) History, murder, and the fear of death. *International Journal of Applied Psychoanalytic Studies*, 12 (2), 153–160.
Ellis, A. (2016) *Men, Masculinities, and Violence: An Ethnographic Study*. Abingdon, Oxon: Routledge.
Farrall, S. (2019) *The Architecture of Desistance*. London, UK: Routledge.
Feeley, M. M. and Simon, J. (1992) The new penology: Notes on the emerging strategy of corrections and its implications. *Criminology*, 30 (4), 449–474.
Ferrito, M., Needs, A., Jingree, T., and Pearson, D. (2020) Making sense of the dark: A study on the identity of men who committed homicide. *Journal of Forensic Psychology Research and Practice*, 20 (2), 163–184.
Ferrito, M., Vetere, A., Adshead, G., and Moore, E. (2012) Life after homicide: Accounts of recovery and redemption of offender patients in a high security hospital – a qualitative study. *Journal of Forensic Psychiatry & Psychology*, 23 (3), 327–344.

Finlay, L. (2002) Negotiating the swamp: The opportunity and challenge of reflexivity in research practice. *Qualitative Research*, 2 (2), 209–230.
Frank, W. A. (2010) *Letting Stories Breathe: A Socio-narratology*. Chicago, IL: University of Chicago Press.
Fromm, E. (1941) *Escape from Freedom*. New York, NY: Henry Holt and Company.
Frosh, S. and Baraitser. (2008) Psychoanalysis and psychosocial studies. *Psychoanalysis, Culture & Society*, 13, 346–36.
Gadd, D. and Farrall, S. (2004) Criminal career, desistance, and subjectivity: Interpreting men's narratives of change. *Theoretical Criminology*, 8 (2), 123–156.
Gadd, D. and Jefferson, T. (2007) *Psychosocial Criminology, an Introduction*. London, UK: SAGE.
Gobodo-Madikizela, P. (2022) Remorse as ethical encounter and the impossibility of repair. In Tudor S., Weisman R., Proeve M., and Rossmanith K. (Eds.), *Remorse and the Criminal Justice: Multidisciplinary Perspectives*. New York, NY: Routledge, 243–264.
Goffman, E (1963) *Stigma Notes on the Management of Spoiled Identity*. London, UK: Penguin.
Goldstein, E. S. (2017) Reflexivity in narrative research: Accessing meaning through the participant-researcher relationship. *Qualitative Psychology*, 4 (2), 149–164.
Grinyer, A. and Thomas, C. (2012) The value of interviewing on multiple occasions or longitudinally. In Gubrium F, J., Holstein, A. J., Marvasti B. A., and McKinney D. K. (Eds.), *The SAGE Handbook of Interview Research: The Complexity of the Craft*, 2nd edition. Thousand Oakes, CA: SAGE, 219–230.
Gubrium, F. J. and Holstein, A. J. (2012) Narrative practice and the transformation of interview subjectivity. In Gubrium J. F., Holstein J. A., Marvasti A. B., McKinney, K. D. (Eds.), *The SAGE Handbook of Interview Research: The Complexity of the Craft*. Thousand Oakes, CA: SAGE, 27–43.
Guest, G., Bunce, A., and Johnson, L. (2006) How many interviews are enough? An experiment with data saturation and variability. *Field Methods*, 18 (1), 59–82.
H.M. Inspectorate of Probation (HMIP) (2020) A thematic review of probation recall culture and practice. Available at: A thematic review of probation recall culture and practice (justiceinspectorates.gov.uk) [accessed on 18.11.2023].
Hallsworth, S. (2002) The case for a postmodern penalty. *Theoretical Criminology*, 6 (2), 145–163.
Hall, S. and Winlow, S. (2015). *Revitalising Criminological Theory: Towards a New Ultra-realism*. Oxon: Routledge.
Hammack, P., L. (2008) Narrative and the cultural psychology of identity. *Personality and Social Psychology Review*, 12, 222–247.
Harding, D. J., Dobson, C., Wyse, J. J. B., and Morenoff, D. (2017) Narrative change, narrative stability, and structural constraints: The case of prisoner reentry narratives. *American Journal of Cultural Sociology*, 5 (1), 261–304.
Heinlein, S. H. (2013) *Among Murderers: Life after Prison*. Berkeley and Los Angeles, CA: University of California Press.
Herzog, H. (2012) Interview location and its social meaning. In Gubrium, J. F., Holstein, J. A., Marvasti, A. B., and McKinney, K. D. (Eds.), *The SAGE Handbook of Interview Research: The Complexity of the Craft*, 2nd edition. London, UK: SAGE, 207–218.
Hollway, W. (1984) Gender difference and the production of subjectivity. In J. Henriques, W. Hollway, C. Urwin, C. Venn, and V. Walkerdine (Eds.), *Changing the Subject: Psychology, Social Regulation, and Subjectivity*. London: Methuen, 227–263.
Hollway, W. and Jefferson, T. (2005) Panic and perjury: A psycho-social exploration of agency. *British Journal of Social Psychology*, 44 (2), 147–163.
Holstein, J. A. and Gubrium, J. F. (1995) *The Active Interview*. Thousand Oakes, CA: SAGE.

House of Commons Library (2023) Homicide Statistics, 11 July, 2023. Available at: CBP-8224.pdf (parliament.uk) [accessed on 13/11/2023].
Hyatt-Williams, A. (1999) *Cruelty, Violence, and Murder: Understanding the Criminal Mind*. London, UK: Karnac.
Hyden, M. (2014) The teller-focused interview: Interviewing as a relational practice. *Qualitative Social Work*, 13 (6), 795–812.
Jacobsen, M. H. and Walklate, S. (2019) *Emotions and Crime: Towards a Criminology of Emotions*. Abingdon, Oxon: Routledge.
Jefferson, T. (2008) What is "The psychosocial"? A response to frosh and Baraitser', psychoanalysis. *Culture and Society*, 7, 366–371.
Jones, D. (2019) *Understanding Criminal Behaviour: Psychosocial Perspectives on Criminality and Violence*. Abingdon Oxon: Routledge.
Jovchelovitch, S. and Bauer, M. W. (2000) Narrative interviewing. In Bauer, Martin W. and Gaskell, G. (Eds.), *Qualitative Researching with Text, Image and Sound: A Practical Handbook*. Thousand Oaks, CA: SAGE, 57–74.
Kafka, F. (1998) *The Castle*, trans. Mark Harman. New York, NY: Schoken.
Kay, C. (2016) *Desistence in Transition: Exploring the Desistence Narratives of Intensive Probationers Within the Context of "Transforming Rehabilitation*. University of Manchester, Unpublished PhD Thesis.
Kim, J.-H. (2016) Understanding narrative inquiry. *The Crafting and Analysis of Stories as Research*. Thousand Oaks, CA: SAGE.
King, S. (2013a) Transformative agency and desistance from crime. *Criminology and Criminal Justice*, 13 (3), 317–335.
King, S. (2013b) Early desistance narratives: A qualitative analysis of probationers' transitions towards desistance. *Punishment and Society*, 15 (2), 147–165.
Klaus, W. (2023) Snares and pains, or what stands in the path to desistance from crime. In Klaud W., Rzeplińska I., and Woźniakowska-Fajst D. (Eds.), *Criminal Careers*. Routledge: Oxon, 221–278.
Krueger, J. (2011) The who and the how of experience. In Siderits M., Thompson E., and Zahavi D. (Eds.), *Self, No-Self? Perspectives from Analytical, Phenomenological, and Indian Traditions*. Oxford, UK: Oxford University Press, 27–55.
Kvale, S. (1996). *Interviews*. Thousand Oaks, CA: SAGE.
Kvale, S. (1999) The psychoanalytic interview as qualitative research. *Qualitative Inquiry*, 5 (1), 87–113.
Laws, B. (2022) Reimaging 'the Self' in criminology: Transcendence, unconscious states and the limits of narrative criminology. *Theoretical Criminology*, 26 (3), 457–493.
Leverentz, A. M. (2014) *The Ex-Prisoner's Dilemma: How Women Negotiate Competing Narratives of Reentry and Desistance*. New Brunswick: Rutgers University Press.
Liebling, A. (2001) Whose Side are we on? Theory, practice and allegiances in prison research. *British Journal of Criminology*, 41, 472–484.
Liem, M. (2016) *After Life Imprisonment*. New York, NY: New York University Press.
Liem, M. (2017) Desistance after life imprisonment. In Hart L. and van Ginneken (Eds.), *New Perspectives on Desistance: Theoretical and Empirical Developments*. London, UK: Palgrave, 85–110.
Liem, M. and Garcin, J. (2014) Post-release success among paroled lifers. *Laws*, 3 (4), 798–823.
Liem, M. and Richardson, N. J. (2014) The role of transformation narratives in desistance among released lifers. *Criminal Justice and Behavior*, 41, 692–712.
Liem, M. and Weggemans, D. (2018) Reintegration among high-profile ex-offenders. *Journal of Developmental and Life-Course Criminology*, 4 (4), 473–490.
Liem, M., Zahn M., and Tichavsky L. (2014) 'Criminal Recidivism among Homicide Offenders.' *Journal of Interpersonal Violence*, 29(14), 2630–2651.

Loseke, D., R. (2007) The study of identity as cultural, institutional, organizational, and personal narrative: theoretical and empirical integrations. *Sociological Quarterly*, 48, 661–688.

Maruna, S. (2001) *Making Good: How Ex-convicts Reform Rebuild Their Lives*. Washington, DC: American Psychological Association [Database].

May, H. (1999) Who killed whom? Victimization and culpability in the social construction of murder. *British Journal of Sociology*, 50 (3), 489–506.

McAdams, D. P. (2008) *The Life Story Interview. The Foley Center for the Study of Lives*. Evanston, IL: Northwestern University.

McAdams, D. P. and Guo, J. (2015) Narrating the generative life. *Psychological Science*, 26 (4), 475–483.

McCarthy, L., Page, K., Baxter, H., Larkin, E., Cordess, C., and Duggan, C. (2001) Mentally disordered parricide and stranger killers admitted to high-security care. 2: Course after release. *The Journal of Forensic Psychiatry*, 12 (3), 501–514.

McLean, K., and Syed M. (2015) Personal, master, and alternative narratives: an integrative framework for understanding identity development in context. *Human Development*, 58, 318–349.

Ministry of Justice (2021) *Recall Review and Re-Release of Recalled Prisoners Policy Framework*. Ministry of Justice, 1–55.

Ministry of Justice (2023) *Offender Management Statistics Bulletin, England, and Wales*. Available at: OMSQ_Q4_2022.pdf (publishing.service.gov.uk) [accessed on 1/06/2023].

Mishler, E. (1986) The analysis of interview-narratives. In Sarbin T (ed.) *Narrative Psychology: The Storied Nature of Human Conduct*. New York, NY: Praeger, 233–255.

Mitchell, B. (1998) Public perceptions of homicide and criminal justice. *British Journal of Criminology*, 38 (3), 453–472.

Mitchell, B. and Roberts, J. V. (2012) *Exploring the Mandatory Life Sentence for Murder*. Oxford, UK: Hart Publishing.

Munn, M., and Bruckert C. (2013) *On the Outside: From Lengthy Imprisonment to Lasting Freedom*. Vancouver, Toronto: UBC Press.

Muylaert, C. J., Sarubbi, V. Jr., Gallo, P. R., Neto, M. L. R., and Reis, A. O. A. (2014) Narrative interviews: An important resource in qualitative research. *Revista da Escola de Enferm USP*, 48 (2), 184–189.

Nash, M. (2005) The probation service, public protection and dangerous offenders. In J. Winstone and F. Pakes (Eds.), *Community Justice, Issues for Probation and Criminal Justice*. Cullompton: Willan Publishing, 16–32.

Neuilly, M.-A., Zgoba, K. M., Tita, G. E., and Lee, S. S. (2011) Predicting recidivism in homicide offenders using classification tree analysis. *Homicide Studies*, 15(2), 154–176.

Nugent, B. and Schinkel, M. (2016) The pains of desistance. *Criminology and Criminal Justice*, 16 (5), 568–584.

O'Reilly, M. and Parker, N. (2012) 'Unsatisfactory Saturation': A critical exploration of the notion of saturated sample size in qualitative research. *Qualitative Research*, 13 (2), 190–197.

Office for National Statistics (ONS) (2023) Homicide in England and Wales: year ending March, 2020. Available at: Homicide in England and Wales – Office for National Statistics (ons.gov.uk) [accessed on 1/06/2023].

Parker, I. (1992) *Discourse Dynamics: Critical Analysis for Social and Individual Psychology*. London, UK: SAGE.

Parker, T. (1990) *Life After Life – Interviews with Twelve Murderers*. London, UK: Secker and Warburg.

Parole Board Note Paper (2023) Application for a Public Hearing in the case of Mr Colin Pitchfork. Available at: The Parole Board Note Paper (publishing.service.gov.uk) [accessed on 1.06.2023].

Plummer, K. (2019) "Whose side are we on?" revisited: Narrative power, narrative inequality, and a politics of narrative humanity. *Symbolic Interaction* 43, 46–71.

Polkinghorne, D. E. (1988) *Narrative Knowing and the Human Sciences*. Albany, NY: SUNY Press.

Polnay, A., Pugh, R., Barker, V., Bell, D., Beveridge, A., Burley, A., Lumsden, A., Mizen, C. S. (2023) *Cambridge Guide to Psychodynamic Therapy*. Cambridge: Cambridge University Press.

Pratt, J. (2000) *Dangerous Offenders: Punishment and Social Order*. London, UK: Routledge.

Presdee, M. (2004) Cultural criminology: The long and winding road. *Theoretical Criminology*, 8 (3), 275–285.

Presser, L. (2005) Negotiating power and narrative in research: Implications for feminist methodology. *Signs*, 30 (4), 2067–2090.

Presser, L. (2008). *Been a Heavy Life: Stories of Violent Men*. Urbana and Chicago: University of Illinois Press.

Presser, L. (2009) The narratives of offenders. *Theoretical Criminology*, 13 (2), 177–200.

Presser, L. (2019) The Story of Antisociality: Determining What Goes Unsaid in Dominant Narratives. In Fleetwood J., Presser L., Sandberg S., Ugelvik T. (Eds.), *The Emerald Handbook of Narrative Criminology*. Bingley (UK): Emerald Group Publishing, 409–424.

Prison Reform Trust (2021) Bromley briefings prison factfile: Winter 2021. Available at: Bromley_Briefings_winter_2021.pdf (prisonreformtrust.org.uk) [accessed on 13/11/2023].

Prison Reform Trust (2023) *Prison: The Facts*. Bromley Briefings.

Reeves, L. C. (2004) A difficult negotiation: Fieldwork relationships with gatekeepers. *Qualitative Research*, 10, 315–331.

Rennie, A. and Crewe, B. (2023) 'Tightness', autonomy, and release: The anticipated pains of release and life licensing. *The British Journal of Criminology*, 63, 184–200.

Roberts, A. R., Zgoba, K. M., and Shahidullah, S. M. (2007) Recidivism among four types of homicide offenders: An exploratory analysis of 336 homicide offenders in New Jersey. *Aggression and Violent Behavior*, 12, 493–507.

Rowe, A. (2014) Situating the self in prison research: Power, identity, and epistemology. *Qualitative Inquiry*, 20 (4), 404–416.

Sandberg, S. and Fondevila, G. (2022) Corona crimes: How pandemic narratives change criminal landscapes. *Theoretical Criminology*, 26(2), 1–21.

Sandberg, S. and Ugelvik, T. (2016) The past, present, and future of narrative criminology: A review and an invitation. *Crime Media Culture*, 21 (2), 129–136.

Sapsford, R. J. (1983) *Life Sentence Prisoners: Research, Response and Change*. Milton Keynes: Open University Press.

Sapsford, R. J. (1978) Life-sentence prisoners: Psychological changes during sentence. *British Journal of Criminology*, 18 (2), 128–145.

Schiff, B. (2013) Fractured narratives: Psychology's fragmented narrative psychology. In Hyvärinen, M., Hatavara M., and Hydén L-C. (Eds.), *The Travelling Concepts of Narrative*. Amsterdam: John Benjamin Publishing, 245–264.

Silverman, D. (1997) *Qualitative Research: Theory, Method, and Practice*. London, England: SAGE.

Skott, S. (2023) *Homicide: Towards a Deeper Understanding*. London, UK: Routledge.

Smith, B. and Monforte, J. (2020) Stories, new materialism, and pluralism: Understanding, practising, and pushing the boundaries of narrative analysis. *Methods in Psychology*, 2, 1–8.

Spector-Mersel, G. (2010) Narrative research: Time for a paradigm. *Narrative Inquiry*, 20(1), 204–222.

Spector-Mersel, G. (2011) Mechanisms of selection in claiming narrative identities: A model for interpreting narratives. *Qualitative Inquiry*, 17(2), 172–185.

Stein, A. (2007) *Prologue to Violence: Child Abuse, Dissociation, and Crime*. Mahwah: The Analytic Press.

Sykes, G. M. and Matza, D. (1957) Techniques of neutralisation: A theory of delinquency. *American Sociological Review*, 22, 664–673.

Trulson, R. C., Marquart, W. J., and Mullings, L. J. (2004) Breaking in: Gaining entry to prisons and other Hard-to-access criminal justice organisations. *Journal of Criminal Justice Education*, 15 (2), 451–478.

Tyler, I. (2021) *Stigma, the Machinery of Inequality*. London, UK: Bloomsbury Publishing.

Ugelvik, T. (2015) The rapist and the proper criminal: The exclusion of immoral others as narrative work on the self. In Presser L. and Sandberg S. (Eds.), *Narrative Criminology: Understanding Stories of Crime*. New York, NY: New York University Press, 23–41.

UK Public Acts (2020) UK Public General Act. Available at: https://www.legislation.gov.uk/ukpga/2020/17/section/259/enacted [accessed on 12.07.2022].

Van Zyl Smit, D. and Appleton, C. (2019) *Life Imprisonment: A Global Human Rights Analysis*. Cambridge, MA: Harvard University Press.

Vaughan, B. (2007) The internal narrative of desistance. *British Journal of Criminology*, 47 (3), 390–404.

Verde, A. (2021) Whose narrative? The self as (also) an alien – For a complex concept of 'Self' in narrative criminology. *Tijdschrift Over Cultuur & Criminaliteit*, 10 (3), 35–58.

Verde, A. and Knechtlin, N. (2019) 'Protecting and defending mummy': Narrative criminology and psychosocial criminology. In J. Fleetwood, L. Presser, S. Sandberg, and T. Ugelvik (Eds.), *The Emerald Handbook of Narrative Criminology*. Bingley, UK: Emerald Group Publishing, 395–414.

Ward, T. and Marshall B. (2007). Narrative identity and offender rehabilitation. *International Journal of Offender Therapy and Comparative Criminology*, 51 (3), 279–297.

Ward, T. and Stewart, C. (2003) The treatment of sex offenders: Risk management and good lives. *Professional Psychology: Research and Practice*, 34 (4), 353–360.

Werth, R. (2011) I do what I'm told, sort of: Reformed subjects, unruly citizens, and parole. *Theoretical Criminology*, 16, 329–346.

Werth, R. (2013) The construction and stewardship responsible yet precarious subject: Punitive ideology, rehabilitation, and 'tough love' among parole personnel. *Punishment & Society*, 15 (3), 219–246.

Wray, N., Markovic, M., and Manderson, L. (2007) 'Researcher saturation': The impact of data triangulation and intensive-research practices on the researcher and qualitative research process. *Qualitative Health Research*, 17 (10), 1392–1402.

Wright, S., Crewe, B., and Hulley, S. (2017) Suppression, denial, sublimation: Defending against the initial pains of very long sentences. *Theoretical Criminology*, 21 (2), 225–246.

Young, J. (2011) *The Criminological Imagination*. Cambridge: Polity Press.

2 Desistance, identity, and mandatory lifers

Introduction

As mentioned before, one principal domain relevant to the successful resettlement of people with offending histories generally, and mandatory lifers particularly, is whether they still reoffend after release (Leverentz, 2014). Perhaps this should be taken as a 'narrow' definition of successful resettlement and reintegration (Andersen et al., 2020), but one which is indispensable to any more complex conceptualisations that could potentially ensue. Once released, long-term ex-offenders are on a 'mission' to reconstruct their lives. At the heart of such a project is the reconstruction of their identity. In fact, criminological research has found that a process of identity change stands behind individuals' long-term movement away from crime, or 'desistance', to use the academic jargon. In this chapter, I will initially explore current debates around defining desistance, particularly by focusing on 'desistance as termination event' and 'desistance as a maintenance process'. It is argued that the latter perspective is more suitable to exploring the ways in which mandatory lifers commit to pro-social identities and thus achieve 'identity desistance' post-release (Nugent and Schinkel, 2016). Given the intimate relationship between long-term desistance and identity change, the chapter includes a 'brief exploration of identity' as imagined by philosophers and social scientists. The overview is by no means exhaustive but provides a guide to navigating the complexities present in desistance literature. Finally, the chapter will outline some of the most important theories of desistance and make the case that mandatory lifers are a neglected population that require further academic attention.

What is desistance?

Desistance is sometimes regarded as a theory, but it may be more appropriate to be considered a cluster of perspectives, or theories (Fox, 2022) stemming from different theoretical positions. Desistance scholarship has traditionally conceptualised the term as proclaiming the termination of one's criminal career, generally resembling 'an end state or an event' (King, 2014;

Roque, 2017: 55). For example, Laub and Sampson (2001: 11) distinguished between 'cessation' and 'termination' and defined desistance as the "causal process that supports the termination of offending". Initially, Maruna (2001) also imagined desistance as a 'termination event' – it involved an individual's abstinence from committing further offences. However, Maruna has questioned the actual momentum at which this can be fixed. For example, "a person can steal a purse on a Tuesday morning then terminate criminal participation for the rest of the day. Is that desistance?" (Maruna, 2001: 23). Other theorists have attempted to determine an exact time frame of abstention which would resemble desistance, and some argued that less than one year (Loeber et al., 1991) or 1 year (Warr, 1998) to be sufficient. On the other hand, it may be the case that we can confidently say that someone has desisted from crime only after their death (Klaus, 2023).

However, conceptualising desistance as a 'termination event', alongside its fixed timeframe is unsophisticated and does not acknowledge it as a process with its own setbacks, in need for a maintenance process (Gadd and Farrall, 2004). It was then considered more appropriate to consider desistance as the study of continuity as opposed to change; the 'continuity of non-deviant behaviours' (Maruna, 2001: 27). In a later article, Maruna and Farrall (2004) drew from literature on criminal aetiology, namely from Lemert's (1948: 27) concepts of primary and secondary deviation to construct a more nuanced understanding and definition of the desistance process. Rather than a 'termination event', the new conceptualisation included a two-dimensional, perpetual process, that of primary and secondary desistance. Primary desistance represents "any lull or crime-free gap in the course of a criminal career" (Maruna and Farrall, 2004: 4) while secondary desistance announces a fundamental change in the identity of the individual who becomes a 'changed person'. The individual becomes committed to activities that are at odds with criminality, for example, to a new, meaningful job or some sort of prosocial passion.

King (2014) highlighted that this seemingly smooth transition between primary and secondary desistance may be more difficult to operationalise and substantiate than initially thought. Most existing studies tend to be retrospective accounts of individuals who desisted for long periods of time which were inadequate in rigorously capturing such an elusive, subjective transition. Several authors have attempted to provide explanations for the 'scaffolding' which takes place in transitioning between primary desistance to the commitment to pro-social identities, represented by secondary desistance (Healy, 2010; Healy and O'Donnell, 2008; King, 2014). Nugent and Schinkel (2016) proposed that individuals who are 'non offending' engage in 'act-desistance' and reserved 'identity desistance' to signal the appropriation of a non-offending, pro-social identity. Relational desistance represents the public recognition of this important, new change by others (McNeill, 2012), at different levels of human interaction (Bottoms, 2014; Nugent and Schinkel, 2016). We now know that most successful desistance journeys will include 'primary', 'secondary', and 'tertiary' dimensions working in concert to produce a 'conventional citizen' (Day and Halsey, 2022: 5). To underscore, primary desistance is simply a break with offending behaviour, attributable to a myriad of reasons. It is precisely the gap that Maruna referred to in his story of the thief who stole a purse on a Tuesday morning and refrained for the rest of the day. Although a promising start, it would be naïve to take this as proof for a long-term commitment to desistance. The movement from this 'act desistance' to a more profound change is needed. Secondary desistance speaks about this subjective change in the individual, a triggering point that describes the "movement from the behaviour of non-offending to the assumption of the role or identity of a changed person" (Maruna et al., 2004: 19). Thus, secondary desistance is about identity deconstruction and reconstruction by renouncing the offender identity, perhaps through de-labelling and commitment to pro-social roles. Individual motivation as well as structural opportunities are crucial for the success of this process. Tertiary desistance draws our attention to the sense of connection one may have with the community – it is a relational perspective which extends beyond internal processes. It is about belonging to a moral community (McNeill, 2012) that validates and certifies one's 'non offending identity' and allows its public expression. Given that we construct and negotiate our identities in interaction with others, it follows that long-term commitment to identity desistance is contingent on how others perceive us. Then, the desistance process can also be perceived as "making sense of one's past through recognition of change by others" (Gålnander, 2020: 1302).

Altogether, there seems to be a consensus among desistance scholars that personal identity changes and cognitive transformations are fundamental to any serious, long-term, and perpetual commitment to conventional/non-criminal lifestyles (Aresti, Eatough, and Brooks-Gordon, 2010; Bachman et al., 2016; Giordano, Cerkovich, and Rudolph, 2002; Healy, 2013; King, 2013; Maruna, 2001; Opsal, 2012; Paternoster and Bushway, 2009; Stevens, 2012) and that rehabilitation is seldom a purely personal project (McNeill, 2010: 2012). Despite this consensus, theorists often raise the age-old conundrum of the chicken and the egg, pondering what comes first: internal motivation, or structural change, or perhaps a combination of these as the catalyst for identity change (Albertson, Philips, and Fowler, 2022; Farrall, 2019; Giordano et al., 2002; Vaughan, 2007).

A brief word on identity

Theoretical complexities evident in desistance research mirror perennial reflections around the nature of identity that intrigued philosophers, social scientists, and psychologists for centuries. One problematic aspect of research on identity stems from its theorisation. Identity is what one makes it to be. It represents 'people's conceptions of who they are', 'what sort of people they are', and 'how they relate to others' (Hogg and Abrams, 1988: 2;

Lawler, 2014: 7). A pivotal point of debate revolves around the nature of identity and its role in our daily lives. This in turn influences the ways in which we understand self-change and ultimately desistance from crime.

We can categorise identity perspectives as pertaining to realists and anti-realists (Kristjánsson, 2010) or essentialist and non-essentialist views. The former imagine identity as somehow residing within the individual as a thing 'in itself' containing some form of essence. In other words, these perspectives have a realist stance. The most 'naïve' of realists assume that the 'self' exists independent of language/culture in an inner domain (Crossley, 2000). The category of 'personality types' is such an example (Costa and McCrae, 1992; McCrae and Costa, 1987). Due to advancements in neuroimaging techniques, researchers today are mapping personality traits to specific patterns of brain (in)activity (Nostro et al., 2018). Evidently, according to this perspective identity or, rather, personality is seen as residing within the neural activity of the brain. With notable exceptions (Elder-Vass, 2012), such essentialising approaches are reducing humans to their biology. Desistance scholars have identified a series of individual factors and personality traits such as 'intelligence', 'impulse control', and 'positive attitudes' as 'protective' against criminality in women (Serin, Chadwick, and Lloyd, 2016; Slotboom, Rodermond, and Hendriks, 2022). These metaphysical considerations explored above have a direct implication to studying the lives of homicide offenders. These inform the ways in which research questions are framed. For example, some research focused on the measurable effects that long-term imprisonment has on the 'sociability', 'motivation', and 'affective flatness' of homicide offenders (Sapsford, 1978). Of course, such an approach is overly simplistic and does not uncover identity as experienced by individuals.

Some variants of non-essentialist positions accept that identity emerges through various subject positionings in ideology and discourse (Althusser, 2001 [1971]; Hollway, 1989, 1984), or positioning within day-to-day interactions, at micro-level (Davies and Harré, 1990), and generally understand the role of language as creative in the process of identity construction (Burr, 2002, 2015). For example, symbolic interactionists conceptualise the self as a social construction, shaped by symbols and linguistic exchange (Cooley, 1902; Baldwin, 1897 in Harter, 1999; Mead, 1934). Specifically, the Meadian (1934) self emerges in social interactions, where 'role-taking' is the primary mechanism that 'produces' dichotomy between the 'I' and the 'Me', with the latter having a strong social origin. Selfhood is in continuous construction, and identity then, is "never gained nor maintained once and for all … it is constantly lost and regained" (Erikson, 1959: 118). Cooley (1902) proposed that individuals internalise what 'others' believe of them, in a process summed up as the 'looking glass self'. Imagining how one is perceived and judged while acknowledging the emergent guilt, or shame stemming from these operations are all parts of the Cooley's looking glass self (Scott, 2015). This stands as confirmation for the self as a dynamic process; one does not simply have selves, but rather one is continuously constructing, or 'doing' identity through constant reflection (Scott, 2015). Criminological literature is saturated with work stemming from this tradition (Becker, 1963; Lemert, 1967; Schur, 1971). Authors writing from within a desistance paradigm have long ago acknowledged the effect of a 'Pygmalion effect' (Maruna et al., 2009) on reintegration post-release. Mead's (1934: 68) observation that "we are more or less unconsciously seeing ourselves as others see us" is particularly poignant considering that desistance is fundamentally relational and interpersonal (Gålnander, 2020; Nugent and Schinkel, 2016; Todd-Kavam and Todd-Kavam, 2022). Similar debates have been present in psychoanalytic theorisation (Frosh and Baraitser, 2008; Jefferson, 2008; Parker, 1992; Verde, 2021) with the 'relational turn' (Kuchuck, 2021: 8) and its pluralism seen as aligned with social constructionist and postmodern thought (Harris, 2018).

Increasing numbers of researchers have also been drawing from narratology to make sense of desistance. The narrative perspective is making the ontological claim that identities are narratively constructed (Smith and Sparkes, 2008). The 'Narrative Turn' (Riessman, 2008) emerged in the 1980s as a challenge to the predominant realism and positivism that has traditionally dominated social research. It was around this time that philosophers (MacIntyre, 1981; Ricoeur, 1984), and social scientists (Bruner, 1986; McAdams, 1985; Polkinghorne, 1988) underlined that people make sense of their lives through self-defining self-stories that reconstruct the past and provide expectations for the future (McAdams, 2006). It is through this mechanism that individuals provide life with identity, coherence and meaning (McAdams, 2006). Put simply, the essence of narrative approaches is that 'oneself' is created by narratives. Most such approaches agree that human experience is structured as stories and that one's individual and cultural reality is inextricably linked to narrative (Smith, 2016). Somers (1994) argued that while older interpretations of narrative were limited to that of representational form (in form of history or literature), these new approaches conceptualise 'narrativity' as concepts of social epistemology and ontology. It is through 'narrativity' that one comes to understand the social world that they navigate, the various experiences of life and how we make sense of them – "it is through narrativity that individuals constitute their social identities" (Somers, 1994: 606). Stories are not a form of representing knowledge, but rather, stories are guiding action; people construct identities by representing themselves in a plot. Individuals make sense of experience through integrating these in a coherent story (Somers, 1994). It is assumed that we behave in particular ways because not doing so would violate our very sense of existence at times and spaces (Somers, 1994).

Most narrative theorists agree with this claim, but they tend to disagree whether the individual or the social are the principal site of narrative identity construction. Some prefer a 'thick individual and thin social' view, while others prefer a 'thick social and thin individual' one (Smith and Sparkes, 2008: 7). Some suggests that people's narratives are something that people have in their minds (McAdams, 1993). This is a psychosocial perspective over narrative identity, or a 'cognitive-personality approach' (Smith, 2016). Identities are seen as situated within the individual rather than the social; the latter is still significant as personal narratives are influenced by socio-cultural matrices available at societal level. In other words, stories are not made from thin air and thus imply some level of interaction in the relational world. In contrast to this view, some understand narratives as residing outside the inner world of individuals and their complementary cognitive scripts, acting as vehicles through which selves are articulated (Smith and Sparkes, 2008). From a social constructionist perspective, narratives are 'discursive actions' and "they derive their significance from the way in which they are employed within relationships" (Gergen and Gergen, 2006: 118). In this sense, the perspective does not imagine individuals having their readily "narrated life stories in their back pockets […], waiting for a researcher to collect them" (Alasuutari, 1997: 6), but rather, narrative identities are formed to an important degree 'on the spot' and thus serve precise functions. This point has been already addressed to some degree by Somers (1994: 622) for whom "all identities […], must be analysed in the context of relational and cultural matrices because they do not 'exist' outside of these complexities". Here 'the social' is the crucial force in identity construction (Smith, 2016). Given this, it becomes evident that desistance is very much a relational process.

As the unremitting debate about the nature of identity has traversed from the critique of Cartesian western metaphysics – influencing pragmatics to the endlessly performative and fractured self of postmodernism – identity has evolved reaching 'everywhere', leading some theorists to contend that 'if identity is everywhere, it is nowhere' (Brubaker and Cooper, 2000: 1). Solving the unremitting debate is beyond the scope of this book. Nevertheless, the richness of identity theorisation has influenced desistance research, and despite theoretical debates that favour individual motivation and agency over structure, or their fruitful tandem, identity change remains indispensable to any level of long-term desistance.

On theoretical desistance

The desistance paradigm represents a 'cluster of theories' (Fox, 2022: 1), which as discussed concur on crucial points but have some points of contention. The 'scholarly tug of war' (Roque, 2017: 115) evident in the field meant that theories do not always fit within strict categorisations. Despite difficulties, research has discerned a range of desistance research categories. King (2014) found three broad theoretical categories: structural, agency-oriented, and integrated. Others refer to 'ontogenetic' (referring to age and maturation), 'social bonds (or sociogenic)', and 'narratological' (Polaschek, 2019; Roque, 2017). Those interested in the relationship between identity and desistance tend to use categories such as: 'identity transformation', 'structural', and 'narrative desistance' (Dent and Ward, 2023). One of the simplest ways to conceptualise and separate the theoretical divide between perspectives is to scrutinise the attention paid to outside forces (structure, the social world) and inside the individual (subjective sense of self, motivation, agency) that create the desisting individual.

Sociogenic approaches to desistance

Proponents of the sociogenic model argue that identity change is seen to occur within the favourable structural conditions and do not necessarily involve the individual as an active participant; rather, a process of 'desistance by default' takes place (Laub and Sampson, 2003: 278–279). For Sampson and Laub (2016: 330) 'behaviour changes identity' rather than the reverse.

Longitudinal studies in this tradition found that salient life events, such as domestic unions, employment, or military experience, referred to as 'turning points' are crucial in crime trajectories (Glueck and Glueck, 1950; Gottfredson and Hirschi, 1990; Laub and Sampson, 2003; Maruna and Roy, 2007; Sampson and Laub, 1993; Sampson and Laub, 2016; Sampson, Laub, and Wimer, 2006). In their initial theory, Sampson and Laub (1993) argued that prosocial institutions were particularly important due to their associated social costs for committing crime, providing echoes of Social Control Theory (Hirschi, 1969). Later, salient life events were seen to offer a new sense of identity and increase the social capital of desisting individuals (Albertson et al., 2022; Laub and Sampson, 2003; Sampson and Laub, 2005). Nevertheless, attention to identity change was ultimately seen as a 'distraction rather than a theoretical advance' (Sampson and Laub, 2016: 329). In this sense, this theory of desistance should be placed on the 'structure' continuum of the debate (Bersani and Doherty, 2018); subjective change is seen as 'below the surface of active consciousness' and does not involve 'purposeful identity change' (Sampson and Laub, 2016: 328).

Studies have systematically emphasised the importance of family and employment on post-release reintegration/re-entry and identity reconstruction (Aresti et al., 2010; Andersen et al., 2020; Berg and Huebner, 2011; LeBel et al., 2008; Morizot and Le Blanc, 2007; Opsal, 2012; Skardhamar and Savolainen, 2014; Tripodi, Kim, and Bender, 2010; Uggen, 2000; Visher, 2013; Visher, Debus-Sherrill, and Yahner, 2010; Visher and Travis, 2003). It is now accepted that the quality of the workplace alongside individuals' subjective attachment triggers desistance and produces social identity change, and not work in and of itself (Weaver, 2019). Family ties facilitate emotional support and identity transformation (Berg and Huebner, 2011). They can also act as a bridge to the job market (Glaser, 1964 in Berg and Huebner, 2011; Uggen, Manza, and Behrens, 2004). Investing in marriage (Laub and Sampson, 2003) may also lead to desistance (Bersani, Laub, and Nieuwbeerta, 2009). For Laub and Sampson (2003) marriage represents a control mechanism as well as a facilitator of new routine activities.

Social and structural approaches to desistance are useful in exploring the ways in which social institutions exert their influence on 'desisting' individuals but fail to seriously consider the subjects' interaction with such forces. Gadd and Farrall (2004) made the points that criminal career research disregarded the meaning attached to these social controls. These structures may be irrelevant in the absence of some motivation to change on the offenders' part (Giordano et al., 2002). In other words, as LeBel et al. (2008: 155) remarked, it may as well be that "subjective changes may precede life-changing structural events and, to that extent, individuals can act as agents for their own change". This apparent need to contain the "beast within" (Hall, 2012: 117) in the absence of which crime is imminent, as presented by Control Theorists discussed above, disregards individual agency in personal change. Also, sociogenic approaches to desistance cannot explain how individuals who have limited interactions with others, including severed ties with their families and no employment prospects continue to desist by isolating themselves from others (F.-Dufour, Brassard, and Martel, 2015; Liem and Garcin, 2014; Nugent and Schinkel, 2016). Such limited relationship with families and significant others seems to be the reality of most released homicide offenders' accounts in in available research (Liem, 2016, 2017; Liem and Garcin, 2014 in America, or Appleton, 2010 in the United Kingdom) and thus research failed to identify the factors which support such offenders in their re-entry efforts, despite their deficient social capital.

Despite the questions posed above, it seems that sustaining long-term desistance seems to be conditioned by an active engagement in non-offending networks and civic society. This ranges from micro level intimate relationships to relationships with the wider society (Albertson and Albertson, 2023). These connections are generally referred to as 'social capital', which was defined by Bourdieu (1986: 248) as "individual resources linked to possession of a durable network of institutionalized relationships of mutual acquaintance or recognition". Put simply, desistance scholars use the concept of 'social capital' to describe resources that reside in social networks (Albertson and Hall, 2020). Such resources can be used to achieve a set of goals (Kay, 2022) post-release. As shown above, the two most important social institutions which are sometimes referred to as the main correlates of desistance are family formation and stable employment (Farrall, 2011). Thus, the significance of wider relational factors in supporting individuals moving away from crime has been an important conversation in the desistance literature (Farrall, 2011; Fox, 2016; King, 2014; McNeill, 2006). Nevertheless, as Kay (2022) recognised, not all social capital is benign. In fact, the desistance process can be seen as a reorientation of anti-social capital to pro-social capital. The inability to accumulate, or access pro-social capital resources as hampering the decision process (Albertson, 2021). In their Sheffield Desistance Study, Bottoms and Shapland (2011) pointed to an interactive picture to account for the early stages of desistance for their sample of young offenders. In this sense, the complex picture includes elements such as the importance of criminal history and habits, fresh employment status and personal ties, 'all held together by the individual agent' (Bottoms and Shapland, 2011: 69–70).

For Bottoms and Shapland personal ties and employment were important building blocks to consider given the difficult life released individuals experience immediately after their return.

Often, prisoners' families are the only social capital available after release (Farrall, 2011; Mills and Codd, 2008; Wright, Cullen, and Miller, 2001). Calverley (2013, 2019) found that UK desisters from different cultural and ethnic provenances dispose of varied levels of social capital post-release. For example, Indian families were found the most potent in identifying jobs for their released children, and on numerous occasions this meant working for the family business (ibid.). Overall, as Farrall (2011) remarked, low levels of social capital are what stands at the heart of the problem facing probationers on release. Social capital may well be the personification of potential social identities which can promote the initiation in the desistance process post-release (F.-Dufour et al., 2015). These indicate that social capital can act as a 'sociological superglue' (Putnam, 2000: 23) meaning that a diverse set of relationships post-release have the potential to place homicide offenders in positions which subsequently allows them to scaffold into new identities or strengthen existing pros-social ones.

Identity change and desistance: The self and society

At the other end of the continuum, some theorists propose that individual motivation is indispensable to any level of identity change and subsequent desistance. Paternoster and Busway's (2009: 1111) theorisation purports that individuals have multiple identities – 'a sense of who one is' which ultimately dictate the ways in which people behave (Liu and Bachman, 2021). Although social processes are seen as important, the authors give primacy to an 'agentic cognitive identity transformation' (Liu and Bachman, 2021: 353). Social networks are only sought and valued only after the emergence of a new identity. More specifically, the desistance process is initiated once the individual connects current failures with a bleak future where a 'feared self' is imagined to be likely reached if criminal behaviour continues. For example, the individual is in danger of becoming like someone who they despise or find themselves at risk of dying in prison. Having reached 'rock bottom', epitomised by a 'crystallization of discontent', the process of imagining a new, possible self takes place, usually initiated by a series of epiphanies. At this point the would-be desister starts identifying opportunities to re-enter conventional society and live a pro-social life (Bachman et al., 2016; Liu and Bachman, 2021). In this sense, the individual desists from crime from their own volition, despite the absence of a job or that of a romantic partner, although these could offer further crime-inhibitory effects (Liu and Bachman, 2021). This theory is diametrically opposed to Laub and Sampson's (2003: 278–279) 'desistance by default'. In support of the theory, Bachman et al. (2016) found that female offenders, once faced with their 'feared self' (dying alone on the streets) had successfully decided to change, despite not having a good job and prosocial partners. Similarly, Thomas, Nguyen, and Jackson (2022) identified that internal changes in value orientation precede important life transitions and that these often take place independent of marriage or employment.

This perspective can be criticised on the grounds that it has focused on the internal dynamics of desistance at the expense of the social, economic, or political (Farrall, 2019). Others argued that desistance maintenance requires a specific type of interaction between individual agentic action and structural factors. For example, Farrall and Bowling (1999) illustrated how agency and structure work together to promote identity desistance. For them, "the process of desistance is one that is produced through an interplay between individual choices, and a range of wider social forces, institutional and societal practices which are beyond the control of the individual" (Farrall and Bowling, 1999: 261). In support of this argument, King (2013) remarked that most conceptualisations of agency in desistance research are too vague to account for the role of structure in conditioning agency. He argued that would-be desisters navigate institutional uncertainty and structural barriers to achieve their desired selves (which reflects their projective orientation to agency) post-release; in critical situations would-be desisters fell back onto habitual action and possibly crime. Then, the logical deduction is that social structures and changes in social situations are important because they can either enable or constrain agency (Farrall, Bottoms and Shapland, 2010). But, as Burnett and Maruna's (2004) suggested, without some initial hope, success is difficult to achieve post-release, but hope was found to shrink as the number of problems encountered after release rose for the participants.

Following a similar line of thought, Bottoms et al. (2004) warned that agency should be conceptualised within the limits of and not disembedded from social context; he employed Bourdieu's habitus to argue that the social context is indispensable in any transitions out of crime. New identities are often communicated through social roles (Healy, 2013); once released, to desist from crime, offenders decide that they would like to put a life of crime behind (LeBel et al., 2008). This would be mainly achieved through building a family or re-connect with families and therefore regaining a status of the 'family man', to get a steady job or simply to be a good person. Theorists are inclined to foreground the agent as evidenced above, but they "tended to hold constant the issue of structural variation in processes of desistance" (Farrall, 2019: 4).

More closely to the structural view, Giordano et al. (2002), underlined that individuals in the process of cognitive transformation need to attend to the structural possibilities that Sampson and Laub were alluding to. However, the change process has primacy, as opposed to occurring 'without the offenders even realizing it' (Laub and Sampson, 2003: 278–279). In this sense, there needs to be some initial openness to change to attend turning points, or 'hook for change'. These must produce a cognitive transformation and initiate a process of envisioning the future through an appealing 'replacement self'. In other words, the hooks proffer the opening or a new identity, but it is the cognitive shift, not the mere presence of the control aspect that led to desistance. Although a genuine desire to change is crucial in the desistance process, this is a very difficult path without access to social capital, opportunities, and prosocial contacts (Giordano, 2022). On the structure agency debate, the authors position agency in the middle of a continuum. The meaning attached and the cognitive transformations that the hooks attract is more important than their mere presence (F-Dufour et al., 2015). In a later refinement of their theory, Giordano, Schroeder, and Cernkovich (2007) have considered the importance of emotional factors as 'fellow travellers' alongside cognitive processes as well as the presence of 'redefinitions about crime' as a precursor to initial openness (Giordano, 2022: 795). Although Giordano's model is relying heavily upon the presence of supportive structural forces which contribute to cognitive transformation, the environment is a 'scaffold' which ultimately needs some level of motivation from the individual (Dent and Ward, 2023: 3).

Narrative criminology and desistance

The narrative field of study is closely linked to desistance research in attempting to understand the role of language and narrative identity in the construction and maintenance of desistence narratives (Fleetwood, 2016; Maruna, 2001; Presser and Sandberg, 2015; Vaughan, 2007). According to Lucius-Hoene and Deppermann (2000: 200–201) a narrative identity includes "the virtual potential of different stories a person might tell about him – or herself at different times and in different circumstances". To be able to stay away from crime, ex-criminals need to reconstruct their narrative identities and live by 'redemption scripts' (Gadd and Farrall, 2004; Harding et al., 2017; Maruna, 2001; Maruna, Wilson, and Curran, 2006; Stone, 2015). To transition to a non-offending identity people have to avoid defined by their past, find new meaning usually constituted by generativity (wanting to give back to those harmed), and acquire a sense of agency and control over their lives (Liem and Richardson, 2014; Maruna, 2001; Redondo, Padrón-Goya, and Martín, 2022). This is less about an explicit break with a past self, but more about integrating, or reinterpreting the past into a new narrative (Dent and Ward, 2023). In Maruna's (2001) seminal studies persistent offenders lived their lives by a 'condemnation script' – believing that their lives were decide by fate and misfortune. Although these stories seem entirely personal constructions, they interact with societal structure and contextual conditions – in the end, we do not construct stories out of thin air (Fleetwood et al., 2019; Healy, 2013; Villman, 2023).

In their review of narrative criminological influence on desistance research, Maruna and Liem (2020) remarked how internal narratives of desistance are important for social and psychological reasons. Firstly, desistance narratives are useful in negotiating acceptable identities with conventional society after release; ex-prisoners have the difficult role of convincing others of the legitimacy of their reform as well as to portray themselves in an empowering light. This would ultimately assist with the accrual of social capital on release as well as with 'correctional supervision' (Maruna and Liem, 2020). A series of studies have explored this phenomenon in depth (Covington, 1984; Copes, Hochstetler, and Williams, 2008; Hochstetler, Copes, and Williams, 2010; Presser, 2008, 2012; Presser and Sandberg, 2015; Scully and Marolla, 1985). Violent offenders' narratives (Hochstetler et al., 2010), and those of murderers (Brookman, 2015) have been found to be directed at creating a moral distance between authentic violent offenders and participants' good core selves, which were incompatible with such descriptions. Identities were therefore constructed synchronically (Bamberg, 2011), by comparing their authentic selves, seen as diametrically opposed and more nuanced than those of intrinsically flawed authentic violent criminals. These accounts can be seen as typical 'neutralization techniques' (Sykes and Matza, 1957) used to reinterpret the past in ways consistent with a presently non-criminal self while concomitantly preserving a positive, and coherent self (Healy, 2013; Maruna and Copes, 2005).

Nevertheless, this process seems to be significantly more difficult to certain types of offenders who have a difficult time in finding a 'suitable other' upon which to project their 'abominable character' (Verde, 2021; Victor and Waldram, 2015). Murderers may well fall under this category due to the irreparability and enormity of their crime, but very few research has seriously explored the narratives of such offender's post-release.

Warr (2019) evidenced how lifers engage in 'narrative labour' to showcase their change to authorities and secure release. Research on lifer populations in the United States (Herbert, 2019; Liem, 2016; Liem and Richardson, 2014) remarked how individuals created a fundamental difference between their current self and a criminal self, or the people who they were at the time of the homicide. These identities are discarded in favour of new, pro-social identities post-release. These techniques, then, apart from maintaining an internal narrative of desistance, perform the role of negotiating acceptability at a discursive level. The ways in which people who committed murder utilise an internal narrative of desistance to manage (or contain) internal and external stigma and perform a moral self despite the enormity of their crime upon release has not been considered by previous research. The importance of the type of murder committed remains virtually unexplored. As evidenced above, identity is a concept that runs through much criminological research, and which is especially pertinent to studies that explore individuals' movement away from crime.

The bottom line: Mandatory lifers are a neglected population in desistance research

Considering the above, there is a degree of consensus across the desistance literature that social networks, friendships, marriage, and meaningful employment all have an important role to play in 'variously constraining, enabling, and sustaining' desistance (Weaver, 2019: 650). Nevertheless, most studies discussed so far have focused on general prison populations and general offenders, incarcerated for relatively short periods of time (Liem and Garcin, 2014). This is a fundamental methodological issue: long-term offenders, and lifers generally, spend significant proportions of their lives in prison. This methodological and theoretical conundrum echoes across continents. For example, Kazemian and Travis (2015) described long-termers and lifers in the United States as a neglected population and unfortunately very little has changed since the publication of their article in 2015. The difficult reality is that the correlates of desistance which act as vehicles for identity reconstruction (such as family formation, employment, or parenthood), may not typically apply to mandatory lifers' lives post-release. The reasons for this have been captured by Flanagan (1979: 234) who remarked that "family members and friends who can (and often do) wait for three years cannot (and often do not) wait for thirteen years".

Research on homicide offenders has supported this hypothesis. Liem and Garcin (2014) explored the narratives of 64 homicide offenders who were either re-incarcerated (mainly due to parole violations) or currently out on parole in Boston. They found that interviewees did not attribute their success on release to social ties. In fact, such ties acted as negative influences rather than pro-social forces. What ensured their success was their 'self-efficacy' on release. Homicide offenders go to prison in their 20s and 30s which coincides with a time when most such social transitions into normative roles take place. In addition, they were at risk of 'missing the boat' (Liem and Garcin, 2014: 801) as their parents were deceased by the time of release, and the prospects of a new and meaningful career was not readily visible on the horizon. Some homicide offenders' families simply sever ties to avoid sharing stigma with the perpetrators (May, 2000). In fact, Goffman made the point a long-time ago: "The loyal spouse of the mental patient, the daughter of the ex-con, the parent of the cripple, […], are all obliged to share some of the discredit of the stigmatized person to whom they are related" (Goffman, 1963: 43). Ultimately, this could lead to abandonment of the offender. For example, research conducted by Liem and Weggemans (2018) found that the partners and families of high-profile ex-offenders such as homicide offenders, paedophiles, and terrorists break-up contact with the perpetrators. This is partly due to the length of ex-offenders' sentences as well as the enormity of their crime which ignites strong media coverage. Of course, the separate crimes reminded above attract different levels of social unrest; one professional participant in their study has vividly made the point:

> When a convicted murderer comes to live next door, well, people probably do not like that. But it is a whole less problematic than when someone has a history as a sex offender.
> (Liem and Weggemans, 2018: 484)

Given the above, it is surprising that research did not consider the type of murder committed as having relevance in the resettlement process of the perpetrator post-release. In fact, the ways in which homicide offenders make sense of their homicide have been considered in a handful of published work, which mainly focused on imprisoned individuals (Adshead, 2011; Adshead, Ferrito, and Bose, 2015; Clifford, 2010; Crewe, Hulley, and Wright, 2020; Ferrito, 2020; Ferrito et al., 2012; Sapsford, 1978, 1983; Wright, Crewe, and Hulley, 2017), and the type of murder committed had rarely been central to the analysis (Griffin, 2018; Sapsford, 1978, 1983).

Long-term sentences are 'dislocations in time' (Cohen and Taylor, 1972; Jamieson and Grounds, 2005) and resuming ties with children after such dislocations may be a complicating factor rather than an enabling one. Building romantic ties was constructed as a 'catching up' on lost time and was constructed negatively rather than as a positive outcome (Liem and Garcin, 2014: 808). Similarly, Liem (2016) found that for homicide offenders in the US domains typically considered representative of support such as intimate relationships and parenthood did not elicit support on release; in contrast, they symbolised areas of additional challenge. Many participants conceived children while in their teens, and thus, re-assuming a parental role was not generally applicable. Due to their situation, participants did not have pre-existing families and children did not represent a 'returning point'; they were vehicles for further marginalisation. Such issues have been systematically re-counted in criminological literature. After imprisonment a major obstacle encountered by long-term prisoners is finding and keeping a workplace (Appleton, 2010; Jamieson and Grounds, 2005 for UK context), but the 'felon label' (Liem, 2016) is a significant deterrent of employment for homicide offenders. In fact, employment has been found to be meaningful only if it offered opportunities for 'professional ex-roles' (Liem, 2016, 2017; Liem and Garcin, 2014).

This is not to say that similar effects of imprisonment have not been observed on other types of life sentenced offenders, but that they are magnified for mandatory lifers because of the stigma of their offence, media attention to the case, and the institutional arrangements that they face (Griffin and Healy, 2019). This has led Liem and Garcin (2014) to argue in favour of a purely 'intra-individual' rather than sociogenic explanation of desistance and success for homicide offenders. The difference between reincarcerated homicide offenders and those desisting in their study was related to differences in 'self-efficacy'. While both groups distanced themselves from their old selves, the non-incarcerated group believed in their powers as agentic individuals and evidenced a clear perspective of the future where they had an active role.

Nevertheless, the ways in which an internal narrative of desistance is constructed, structured, and performed by mandatory lifers given structural impediments that they face post-release remains unexplored. Such an analysis should also consider differentiating between 'homicide' as an umbrella term which includes manslaughter and mandatory life sentence, which is a sentence automatically given to people who murder under UK jurisprudence (as discussed in the introduction). Research to this date has not considered this fundamental distinction in offence type which is hypothesised to be crucial in the process of making sense of one's past and index offence as well as in interactions with others post-release. Also, much research which explored the resettlement experiences of homicide offenders (for example, Appleton, 2010 in the United Kingdom; Liem, 2016, 2017 in the United States) tended to be retrospective studies (Nugent and Schinkel, 2016) where identity reconstructions could not be captured 'in the now' (Brookman, 2015) and followed up in a qualitative longitudinal design (an exception is Liem and Garcin, 2014 in the United States but the study explored the narratives of individuals convicted for second-degree murder or (in)voluntary manslaughter).

As mentioned in the introduction to the book, as a society we have different sensibilities and emotional reactions to the constituent elements of a murder, including who the victims were and in what context the murder occurred. This was observed by Griffin (2018) in her study on parole board members constructions of different types of lifers based on the type of murder committed (including the circumstances surrounding the commission of the offence and the relationship between the offender and victim). The members considered those who committed 'crimes of passion' such as domestic murders (Brookman, 2022 for a distinction) 'low risk'. In contrast, gang-related murder, or organised criminal activity would constitute a high-risk category. The extent to which such constructions at the hand of criminal justice agencies affect mandatory lifers post-release remains unexplored.

Discussion

There seems to be a consensus among desistance scholars that identity change is fundamental to any serious and long-term cessation of criminality and successful re-entry post-release. Sociogenic approaches to desistance were invoked to highlight the importance of salient life events or 'turning points' (Sampson and Laub, 1993: 2003) such as family formation and gaining meaningful employment in individuals' pathways to desistance from crime. One potential way that turning points have such a strong influence on individuals is because they provide a 'stake into conforming' to a pro-social life. Further, salient life events provide clear opportunities to identity change. The narrative approaches explored, such as the one proposed by Maruna and colleagues present desistance in a much more agentic way where individuals choose to reconstruct their identity and then desist from crime. However, research started to explore the interplay between these salient events and the individual who needs some level of initial motivation to engage with and even contribute to emerging opportunities in their lives. In other words, the interplay at work is between the individual agent and their projection of future identities, and available opportunities within their immediate social context to achieve and perform such identities (Shapland and Bottoms, 2011). This interplay between agency and structure has received much traction in academic literature and has been generally coalesced under the banner of 'interactional approaches' (Weaver, 2019).

In considering this critical point, the chapter highlighted a series of barriers to the resettlement of long-term offenders as described in penological literature while introducing mandatory lifers as a neglected population in the field. While the concept of 'pains of imprisonment' is among the most prominent in the study of incarceration (Haggerty and Bucerius, 2020) and thus deserving of a separate chapter, a bridge between such barriers to reintegration and desistance literature was critical to be introduced at this point. This was because previous research, especially stemming from the United States had presented 'usual' correlates of desistance (Farrall, 2011) such as family formation and employment generally unadaptable to the realities of homicide offenders' lives post-release. For Liem and colleagues, what distinguished successful homicide offenders (and they were successful because they were still released) to reincarcerated homicide offenders (Liem, 2016, 2017; Liem and Garcin, 2014) was self-efficacy. The study's neo-liberal, 'responsibilizing' message of cherished individualism seems almost too good to be true. The next chapter will explore added barriers to reintegration to contextualise these gaps and justify the rationale of the book further before we delve into the narratives our participants.

References

Adshead, G. (2011) The life sentence: Using a narrative approach in group psychotherapy with offenders. *Group Analysis*, 44 (2), 175–195.

Adshead, G., Ferrito, M., and Bose, S. (2015) Recovery after homicide: Narrative shifts in therapy with homicide perpetrators. *Criminal Justice and Behaviour*, 42 (1), 70–81.

Alasuutari, P. (1997) The discursive construction of personality. In A. Lieblich and R. Josselson (Eds.), *The Narrative Study of Lives*, Vol. 5. Newbury Park, CA: SAGE, 1–20.

Albertson, K. (2021) Social capital building supporting the desistance process. Her Majesty's Inspectorate of Probation, June 2021.

Albertson, K., and Albertson, K. (2023) Social capital, mutual aid and desistance: A theoretically integrated process model. *The British Journal of Criminology*, 63 (5), 1255–1273.

Albertson, K., and Hall, L. (2020) Building social capital to encourage desistance: Lessons from a veteran-specific project. In Ugwudike P., Graham H., McNeill F., Raynor P., Taxman F.S. and Trotter C. (Eds.), *The Routledge Companion to Rehabilitative Work in Criminal Justice*. London: Routledge, 310–319.

Albertson, K., Philips, J., and Fowler, A. (2022) Who owns desistance? A triad of agency enabling social structures in the desistance process. *Theoretical Criminology*, 26 (1), 153–172.

Althusser, L. (2001) *"Lenin and Philosophy" and Other Essays*, trans. B. Brewster. New York, NY: Monthly Review Press [1971].

Andersen, T. S., Scott Deena, A. I., Bohme, H. M., King, S., and Mikell, T. (2020) What matters to formerly incarcerated men? Looking beyond recidivism as a measure of successful reintegration. *The Prison Journal*, 100 (4), 488–509.

Appleton, C. (2010) *Life after Life Imprisonment*. Oxford: Oxford University Press.

Aresti, A., Eatough, V., and Brooks-Gordon, B. (2010) Doing time after time: An interpretative phenomenological analysis of reformed ex-prisoners' experience of self-change, identity, and career opportunities. *Psychology Crime and Law*, 16 (3), 168–190.

Bachman, R., Kerrison, E., Paternoster, R., O'Connell, D., and Smith, L. (2016) Desistance for a long-term drug involved sample of adult offenders: The importance of identity transformation. *Criminal Justice and Behaviour*, 43 (2), 164–186.

Bamberg, M. (2011) Who am I? – Narration and its contribution for self and identity. *Theory & Psychology*, 21, 3–24.

Becker, H. S. (1963) *Outsiders: Studies in the Sociology of Deviance*. New York, NY: Free Press.

Berg, M., and Huebner, B. M. (2011) Reentry and the ties that bind: An examination of social ties, employment, and recidivism. *Justice Quarterly*, 28, 382–410.

Bersani, B. E., and Doherty, E. E. (2018) Desistance from offending in the twenty first century. *Annual Review of Criminology*, 1, 311–334.

Bersani, B., Laub, J. H., and Nieuwbeerta, P. (2009) Marriage and desistance from crime in the Netherlands: Do gender and socio-historical context matter? *Journal of Quantitative Criminology*, 25 (1), 3–24.

Bottoms, A. E. (2014) Desistance from crime. In Z. Ashmore, and R. Shuker (Eds.), *Forensic Practice in the Community*. Abingdon, Oxon: Routledge, 251–273.

Bottoms, A., and Shapland, J. (2011) Steps towards desistance among male young adult recidivists. In Farrall, S., Hough, M., Maruna, S., and Sparks, R. (Eds.), *Escape Routes: Contemporary Perspectives on Life after Punishment*. Oxford: Routledge, 43–80.

Bottoms, A. E., Shapland, J., Costello, A., Holmes, D., and Muir, G. (2004) Towards desistance: Theoretical underpinnings for an empirical study. *The Howard Journal of Criminal Justice*, 43 (4), 368–389.

Bourdieu, P. (1986) The forms of social Capital. In J. G. Richardson (Ed.), *Handbook of Theory and Research for the Sociology of Education*. New York, NY: Greenwood, 241–258.

Brookman, F. (2015) Researching homicide offenders, offenses, and detectives using qualitative methods. In Copes H., and Miller M. J. (Eds.), *The Routledge Handbook of Qualitative Criminology*. Oxon: Routledge, 236–252.

Brookman, F. (2022) *Understanding Homicide*, 2nd edition. London: SAGE.

Brubaker, R., and Cooper, F. (2000) Beyond "identity". *Theory and Society*, 29 (1), 1–47.

Bruner, J. (1986) *Actual Minds, Possible Worlds*. Cambridge, MA: Harvard University Press.

Burnett, R., and Maruna, S. (2004) "So 'prison Works', does it? The criminal careers of 130 men released from prison under Home Secretary, Michael Howard. *The Howard Journal*, 43 (4), 390–404.

Burr, V. (2002) *Social Constructionism*, 2nd edition. East Sussex: Routledge.

Burr, V. (2015) *Social Constructionism*, 3rd edition. New York: Routledge.

Calverley, A. (2013) *Cultures of Desistance*. London: Routledge.

Calverley, A. (2019) Exploring the processes of desistance by ethnic status: The confluence of community, familial and individual processes. In S. Farrall (Ed.), *The Architecture of Desistance*. London: Routledge, 75–95.

Clifford, J. L. (2010) Managing a murderous identity: How men who murder experience life imprisonment and the concept of release. PhD Thesis, University of Bath.

Cohen, S., and Taylor, L. (1972) *Psychological Survival: The Experience of Long-Term Imprisonment*. London: Penguin.
Cooley, C. (1902) *Human Nature and the Social Order*. New York, NY: Charles Scribner's Sons.
Copes, H., Hochstetler, A., and Williams, J. P. (2008) We weren't no regular dope fiends: Negotiating hustler and crackhead identities. *Social Problems*, 55, 254–270.
Costa, P. T. Jr., and McCrae, R. R. (1992) Four ways five factors are basic. *Personality and Individual Differences*, 13, 653–665.
Covington, J. (1984) Insulation from labelling: Deviant defenses in treatment. *Criminology*, 22, 619–644.
Crewe, B., Hulley, S., and Wright, S. (2020) *Life Imprisonment from Young Adulthood Adaptation, Identity, and Time*. United Kingdom: Palgrave Macmillan.
Crossley, M. L. (2000) *Introducing Narrative Psychology: Self, Trauma, and the Construction of Meaning*. Buckingham: Open University Press.
Davies, B., and Harré, R. (1990) Positioning: The discursive production of selves. *Journal for the Theory of Social Behaviour*, 20 (1), 43–63.
Day, A., and Halsey, M. (2022) Desistance theory and forensic practice. In Langton C. M and Worling J. R. (Eds.), *Facilitating Desistance from Aggression and Crime: Theory, Research, and Strengths-Based Practices*. Hoboken, NJ: John Wiley and Sons.
Dent, H., and Ward, T. (2023) An enactive view of identity transformation: Implications for correctional rehabilitation. *Aggression and Violent Behavior*, 69, 1–11.
Elder-Vass, D. (2012) *The Reality of Social Construction*. Cambridge: Cambridge University Press.
Erikson, E. H. (1959) *Identity and the Life Cycle*. New York, NY: international Universities Press.
F.-Dufour, I., Brassard, R., and Martel, J. (2015) An integrative approach to apprehend desistance. *International Journal of Offender Therapy and Comparative Criminology*, 59 (5), 480–501.
Farrall, S. (2011) Social capital and offender reintegration: Making probation desistance focussed. In Maruna S. and Immarigeon R. (Eds.), *After Crime and Punishment: Pathways to Offender Reintegration*. Cullompton: Willan, 57–82.
Farrall, S. (2019) *The Architecture of Desistance*. London: Routledge.
Farrall, S., Bottoms, A., and Shapland, J. (2010) Social structures and desistance from crime. *British Journal of Criminology*, 7 (6), 46–70.
Farrall, S., and Bowling, B. (1999) Structuration, human development, and desistance from crime. *British Journal of Criminology*, 39, 253–268.
Ferrito, M. (2020) Life after taking a life: The Processes of meaning reconstruction and identity for men who committed suicide. PhD Thesis, University of Portsmouth.
Ferrito, M., Vetere, A., Adshead, G., and Moore, E. (2012) Life after homicide: Accounts of recovery and redemption of offender patients in a high security hospital – a qualitative study. *Journal of Forensic Psychiatry & Psychology*, 23 (3), 327–344.
Flanagan, J. T. (1979) Long-term prisoners: A study of characteristic institutional experience and perspectives of long-term inmates in State Correctional Facilities. Unpublished Doctoral Dissertation, State University of New York, Albany, NY.
Fleetwood, J. (2016) Narrative habitus: Thinking through structure/agency in the narratives of offenders. *Crime Media Culture*, 12 (2), 173–192.
Fleetwood, J., Presser, L., Sandberg, S., and Ugelvik, T. (2019), Introduction. In J. Fleetwood, L. Presser, S. Sandberg, and T. Ugelvik (Eds.), *The Emerald Handbook of Narrative Criminology*. Bingley, UK: Emerald Publishing Limited.
Fox, K. J. (2016) Civic commitment: Promoting desistance through community integration. *Punishment and Society*, 18 (1), 68–94.
Fox, K. J. (2022) Desistance frameworks. *Aggression and Violent Behaviour*, 63, 101684.

Frosh, S., and Baraitser, L. (2008) Psychoanalysis and psychosocial studies. *Psychoanalysis, Culture & Society*, 13, 346–365.

Gadd, D., and Farrall, S. (2004) Criminal career, desistance, and subjectivity: Interpreting men's narratives of change. *Theoretical Criminology*, 8 (2), 123–156.

Gålnander, R. (2020) 'Shark in the Fish Tank': Secrets and stigma in relational desistance from crime. *British Journal of Criminology*, 60, 1302–1319.

Gergen, M., and Gergen, K. (2006) Narratives in action. *Narrative Inquiry*, 16 (1), 112–121.

Giordano, P. C. (2022) Some cognitive transformations about the dynamics of desistance. *Criminology and Public Policy*, 22, 787–809.

Giordano, P. C., Cerkovich, S. A., and Rudolph, J. L. (2002) Gender crime and desistance: Toward a theory of cognitive transformation. *American Journal of Sociology*, 107 (4), 990–1064.

Giordano, P. C., Schroeder, R. D., and Cernkovich, S. A. (2007) Emotions and crime over life course: A neo-median perspective on criminal continuity and change. *American Journal of Sociology*, 112 (6), 1603–1661.

Glueck, S., and Glueck, E. T. (1950) *Unravelling Juvenile Delinquency*. New York, NY: The Commonwealth Fund.

Goffman, E. (1963) *Stigma Notes on the Management of Spoiled Identity*. London: Penguin.

Gottfredson, M. R., and Hirschi, T. (1990) *A General Theory of Crime*. Stanford, CA: Stanford University Press.

Griffin, D. (2018) *Killing Time: Life Imprisonment and Parole in Ireland*. Cham: Palgrave Macmillan.

Griffin, D., and Healy, D. (2019) The pains of parole for life sentenced prisoners in Ireland: Risk, rehabilitation, and re-entry. *European Journal of Probation*, 11 (3), 124–138.

Haggerty, K. D., and Bucerius, S. (2020) The proliferating pains of imprisonment. *Incarceration*, 1 (1), 1–16.

Hall, S. (2012) *Theorizing Crime and Deviance: A New Perspective*. London: SAGE.

Harding, D. J., Dobson, C., Wyse, J. J. B., and Morenoff, D. (2017) Narrative change, narrative stability, and structural constraints: The case of prisoner reentry narratives. *American Journal of Cultural Sociology*, 5 (1), 261–304.

Harris, A. (2018) The relational tradition and canon. In Barsness R. E. (Ed.), *Core Competencies of Relational Psychoanalysis: A Guide to Practice, Study, and Research*. Abingdon, Oxon: Routledge, 43–63.

Harter, S. (1999) Symbolic interactionism revisited: Potential liabilities for the self constructed in the crucible of interpersonal relationships. *Merril-Palmer Quarterly*, 45 (4), 607–703.

Healy, D. (2010) *The Dynamics of Desistance: Charting Pathways through Change*. Cullompton: Willan.

Healy, D. (2013) Changing fate? Agency and the desistance process. *Theoretical Criminology*, 17 (4), 557–574.

Healy, D., and O'Donnell, I. (2008) Calling time on crime: Motivation, generativity, and agency in Irish probationers. *Probation Journal*, 55 (1), 25–38.

Herbert, S. K. (2019) *Too Easy to Keep: Life-Sentenced Prisoners and the Future of Mass Incarceration*. Oakland, CA: University of California Press.

Hirschi, T. (1969) *Causes of Delinquency*. Berkeley, CA: University of California Press.

Hochstetler, A., Copes, H., and Williams, P. (2010) That's not who I am: How offenders commit violent acts and reject authentically violent selves. *Justice Quarterly*, 27, 492–516.

Hogg, M. A., and Abrams, D. (1988) *Social Identifications: A Social Psychology of Intergroup Relations and Group Processes*. London & New York, NY: Routledge.

Hollway, W. (1989) *Subjectivity and Method in Psychology: Gender, Meaning, and Science.* London: SAGE.
Hollway, W. (1984) Gender difference and the production of subjectivity. In J. Henriques, W. Hollway, C. Urwin, C. Venn, and V. Walkerdine (Eds.), *Changing the Subject: Psychology, Social Regulation, and Subjectivity.* London: Methuen.
Jamieson, R., and Grounds, B. (2005) Release and adjustment: Perspectives from studies of wrongly convicted and politically motivated prisoners. In Liebling A., and Maruna S. (Eds.), *The Effects of Imprisonment.* Cullompton Devon: Willan Publishing, 33–65.
Jefferson, T. (2008) What is "The psychosocial"? A response to frosh and Baraitser, Psychoanalysis. *Culture and Society,* 7, 366–371.
Kay, C. (2022) Rethinking social capital in the desistance process: The 'Artful Dodger' complex. *European Journal of Criminology,* 19 (5), 1243–1259.
Kazemian, L., and Travis, J. (2015) Imperative for inclusion of long termers and lifers in research and policy. *Criminology and Public Policy,* 14 (2), 1–30.
King, S. (2014) *Desistance Transitions and the Impact of Probation.* London: Routledge.
King, S. (2013) Transformative agency and desistance from crime. *Criminology and Criminal Justice,* 13 (3), 317–335.
Klaus, W. (2023) Snares and pains, or what stands in the path to desistance from crime. In Klaud W., Rzeplińska I., and Woźniakowska-Fajst D. (Eds.), *Criminal Careers.* Oxon: Routledge, 221–278.
Kristjánsson, K. (2010) *The Self and Its Emotions.* New York, NY: Cambridge University Press.
Kuchuck, S. (2021) *The Relational Revolution in Psychoanalysis and Psychotherapy.* London: Confer Books.
Laub, J. H., and Sampson, R. J. (2001) Understanding desistance from crime. In M. Tonry (Ed.), *Crime and Justice: A Review of Research,* vol. 28. Chicago, IL: University of Chicago Press, 1–69.
Laub, J. H., and Sampson, R. J. (2003) *Shared Beginnings, Divergent Lives: Delinquent Boys to Age 70.* Cambridge, MA: Harvard University Press.
Lawler, S. (2014) *Identity: Sociological Perspectives,* 2nd edition. Cambridge: Polity Press.
LeBel, P. T., Burnett, R., Maruna, S., and Bushway, S. (2008) The 'Chicken and Egg' of subjective and social factors in desistance from crime. *European Journal of Criminology,* 5 (2), 131–195.
Lemert, E. M. (1948) Some aspects of a general theory of sociopathic behaviour. In Proceedings of the Pacific Sociological Society. Research Studies, State College of Washington, vol. 16, 23–29.
Lemert, E. M. (1967) *Human Deviance, Social Problems, and Social Control.* Englewood Cliffs, NJ: Prentice-Hal.
Leverentz, A. M. (2014) *The Ex-Prisoner's Dilemma: How Women Negotiate Competing Narratives of Reentry and Desistance.* New Brunswick: Rutgers University Press.
Liem, M. (2016) *After Life Imprisonment.* New York, NY: New York University Press.
Liem, M. (2017) Desistance after life imprisonment. In Hart L. and van Ginneken (Eds.), *New Perspectives on Desistance: Theoretical and Empirical Developments.* London: Palgrave, 85–110.
Liem, M., and Garcin, J. (2014) Post-release success among paroled lifers. *Laws,* 3 (4), 798–823.
Liem, M., and Richardson, N. J. (2014) The role of transformation narratives in desistance among released lifers. *Criminal Justice and Behavior,* 41, 692–712.
Liem, M., and Weggemans, D. (2018) Reintegration among high-profile ex-offenders. *Journal of Developmental and Life-Course Criminology,* 4 (4), 473–490.

Liu, L., and Bachman, R. (2021) Self-identity and persistent offending: A quantitative test of identity theory of desistance. *Journal of Offender Rehabilitation*, 60 (5), 341–357.

Loeber, R., Stouthamer-Loeber, M., Van Kammen, W. B., and Farrington, D. P. (1991) Initiation, escalation, and desistance in juvenile offending and their correlates. *Journal of Criminal Law and Criminology*, 82 (1), 36–82.

Lucius-Hoene, G., and Deppermann, A. (2000) Narrative identity empiricized: A dialogical and positioning approach to autobiographical research Interviews. *Narrative Inquiry*, 10 (1), 199–222.

MacIntyre, A. (1981) *After Virtue*. Notre Dame: University of Notre Dame Press.

Maruna, S. (2001) *Making Good: How Ex-convicts Reform Rebuild Their Lives*. Washington, DC: American Psychological Association.

Maruna, S., and Copes, H. (2005) What have we learned from five decades of neutralization research? *Crime and Justice*, 32, 221–320.

Maruna, S., and Farrall, S. (2004) Desistance from crime: A theoretical reformulation. *Kolner Zeitschrift fur Soziologie und Sozialpsychologie*, 43, 171–194.

Maruna, S., Lebel, T. P., Mitchell, N., and Naples, M. (2004) Pygmalion in the reintegration process: Desistance from crime through the looking glass. *Psychology, Crime & Law*, 10 (3), 271–281.

Maruna, S., LeBel, T., Naples, M., and Mitchell, N. (2009) Looking-glass identity transformation: Pygmalion and golem in the rehabilitation process. In B. Veysey, J. Christian and D.J. Martinez (Eds.), *How Offenders Transform Their Lives*. Cullompton: Willan Publishing, 30–55.

Maruna, S., and Liem, M. (2020) Where is this story going? A critical analysis of the emerging field of narrative criminology. *Annual Review of Criminology*, 4, 125–146.

Maruna, S., and Roy, K. (2007) Amputation or reconstruction? Notes on the concept of "knifing off" and desistance from crime. *Journal of Contemporary Criminal Justice*, 23 (1), 104–124.

Maruna, S, Wilson, L., and Curran, K. (2006) Why God is often found behind bars: Prison conversions and the crisis of self-narrative. *Research in Human Development*, 3 (2), 161–184.

May, H. (2000) "Murderers' relatives": Managing stigma, negotiating identity. *Journal of Contemporary Ethnography*, 29 (2), 198–221.

McAdams, D. (1985) *Power, Intimacy, and the Life Story: Personological Inquiries into Identity*. London: The Guildford Press.

McAdams, D. P. (1993) *The Stories We Live By: Personal Myth and the Making of the Self*. New York, NY: The Guildford Press.

McAdams, P. D. (2006) The problem of narrative coherence. *Journal of Constructivist Psychology*, 19, 109–125.

McCrae, R. R., and Costa, P. T. Jr. (1987) Validation of the five-factor model of personality across instruments and observers. *Journal of Personality and Social Psychology*, 52 (1), 81–90.

McNeill, F. (2010) Positive criminology, positive criminal justice? In Ronel N., and Segev D. (Eds.), *Positive Criminology*. New York, NY: Routledge, 52–63.

McNeill, F. (2006) A desistance paradigm for offender management. *Criminology and Criminal Justice*, 6 (1), 39–62.

McNeill, F. (2012) Four forms of 'offender' rehabilitation: Towards and interdisciplinary perspective. *Legal and Criminological Psychology*, 17 (1), 1–19.

Mead, G. H. (1934) *Mind, Self, and Society*. Chicago, IL: University of Chicago Press.

Mills, A. L., and Codd, H. (2008) Prisoners' families and offender management: Mobilizing social capital. *Probation Journal*, 55 (1), 9–24.

Morizot, J., and Le Blanc, M. (2007) Behavioral, self, and social control predictors of desistance from crime: A test of launch and contemporaneous effect models. *Journal of Contemporary Criminal Justice*, 23 (1), 50–71.

Nostro, A. D., Müller, V. L., Varikuti, D. P., Pläschke, R. N., Hoffstaedter, F., Langner, R., Patil, K. R., and Eickhoff, S. B. (2018) Predicting personality from network-based resting-state functional connectivity. *Brain Structure and Function*, 223, 2699–2719.

Nugent, B., and Schinkel, M. (2016) The pains of desistance. *Criminology and Criminal Justice*, 16 (5), 568–584.

Opsal, T. (2012) Livin' on the straights: Identity, desistance, and work among women post-incarceration. *Sociological Inquiry*, 82, 378–403.

Parker, I. (1992) *Discourse Dynamics: Critical Analysis for Social and Individual Psychology*. London: SAGE.

Paternoster, R., and Bushway, S. (2009) Desistence and the 'Feared Self': Toward an identity theory of criminal desistence. *The Journal of Criminal Law & Criminology*, 99 (4), 1103–1156.

Polaschek, D. L. L. (2019) The psychology of desistance. In D. L. L. Polaschek, A. Day, & C. R Hollin (Eds.), *The International Handbook of Correctional Psychology*. Hoboken, NJ: Wiley, 315–336.

Polkinghorne, D. E. (1988) *Narrative Knowing and the Human Sciences*. Albany, NY: SUNY Press.

Presser, L. (2008) *Been a Heavy Life: Stories of Violent Men*. Urbana and Chicago, IL: University of Illinois Press.

Presser, L. (2012) Getting on top through mass murder: Narrative, metaphor, and violence. *Crime Media Culture*, 8 (1), 3–21.

Presser, L., and Sandberg, S. (2015) *Narrative Criminology: Understanding Stories of Crime*. New York, NY: New York University Press.

Putnam, R. D. (2000) *Bowling Alone: The Collapse and Revival of American Community*. New York, NY: Simon and Schuster.

Redondo, S., Padrón-Goya, F., and Martín, A. M. (2022) Offenders' narratives on criminal desistance while serving a prison sentence. *Victims & Offenders*, 17 (3), 439–467.

Ricoeur, P. (1984) *Time and Narrative*, vol. 1 (K. McLaughlin & D. Pellauer, Trans.). Chicago, IL: University of Chicago Press.

Riessman, C. K. (2008) *Narrative Methods for the Human Science*. Thousand Oaks, CA: SAGE.

Roque, M. (2017) *Desistance from Crime: New Advances in Theory and Research*. New York, NY: Palgrave Macmillan.

Sampson, R., Laub, J., and Wimer, C. (2006) Does marriage reduce crime? A counterfactual approach within individual causal effects. *Criminology*, 44, 465–508.

Sampson, R. J., and Laub, J. H. (1993) *Crime in the Making: Pathways and Turning Points Through Life*. Cambridge, MA: Harvard University Press.

Sampson, R. J., and Laub, J. H. (2005) A life-course view of the development of crime. *The Annals of the American Academy of Political and Social Science*, 602 (1), 12–45.

Sampson, R. J., and Laub, J. H. (2016) Turning points and the future of life course criminology: Reflections of the 1986 criminal careers report. *Journal of Research in Crime and Delinquency*, 53 (3), 321–335.

Sapsford, R. J. (1983) *Life Sentence Prisoners: Research, Response and Change*. Milton Keynes: Open University Press.

Sapsford, R. J. (1978) Life-sentence prisoners: Psychological changes during sentence. *British Journal of Criminology*, 18 (2), 128–145.

Schur, E. M. (1971) *Labelling Deviant Behavior*. New York, NY: Harper & Row.

Scott, S. (2015) *Negotiating Identity. Symbolic Interactionist Approaches to Social Identity*. Cambridge: Polity Press.

Scully, D., and Marolla, J. (1985) "Riding the bull at Gilley's": Convicted rapists describe the rewards of rape. *Social Problems*, 32 (3), 251–263.

Serin, R. C., Chadwick, N., and Lloyd, C. D. (2016) Dynamic risk and protective factors. *Psychology, Crime & Law*, 22 (1–2), 151–170.

Shapland, J., and Bottoms, A. (2011) Reflections on social values, offending and desistance among young adult recidivists. *Punishment and Society*, 13 (3), 256–282.

Skardhamar, T., and Savolainen, J. (2014) Changes in criminal offending around the time of job entry: A study of employment and desistance. *Criminology*, 52 (2), 263–291.

Slotboom, A.-M., Rodermond, E., and Hendriks, J. (2022) Women's desistance from crime: The role of individual, relational, and socio-structural factors over time. In Langton C. M. and Worling J. R. (Eds.), *Facilitating Desistance from Aggression and Crime: Theory, Research, and Strengths-Based Practices*. Hoboken, NJ: Wiley, Blackwell, 230–250.

Smith, B. (2016) Narrative analysis. In E. Lyons & A. Coyle (Eds.), *Analysing Qualitative Data in Psychology*, 2nd edition. London: SAGE, 202–221.

Smith, B., and Sparkes, A. C. (2008) Contrasting perspectives on narrating selves and identities: An invitation to dialogue. *Qualitative Research*, 8 (5), 5–35.

Somers, R. M. (1994) The narrative constitution of identity: A relational and network approach. *Theory and Society*, 23, 605–649.

Stevens, A. (2012) 'I am the person now that I was always meant to be': Identity reconstruction and narrative reframing in therapeutic community prisons. *Criminology and Criminal Justice*, 12 (5), 527–547.

Stone, R. (2015) Pregnant women and substance use: Fear, stigma, and barriers to Care. *Health & Justice*, 3, 1–15.

Sykes, G., and Matza, D. (1957) Techniques of neutralization: A theory of delinquency. *American Sociological Review*, 22, 664–670.

Todd-Kavam, J., and Todd-Kavam, M. (2022) Talking good: Analysing narratives of desistance in Norway *The British Journal of Criminology*, 62, 914–930.

Thomas, J. J., Nguyen, H., and Jackson, E. P. (2022) Value orientations, life transitions, and desistance: Assessing competing perspectives. *Criminology*, 61, 103–131.

Tripodi, S. J., Kim, J. S., and Bender, K. (2010) Is employment associated with reduced recidivism? The complex relationship between employment and crime. *International Journal of Offender Therapy and Comparative Criminology*, 54 (5), 706–720.

Uggen, C. (2000) Work as a turning point in the life course of criminals: A duration model of age, employment and recidivism. *American Sociological Review*, 67, 529–546.

Uggen, C., Manza, J., and Behrens, A. (2004) Less than the average citizen, stigma, role transition and the civic reintegration of convicted felons. In S. Maruna, & R. Immarigeon (Eds.), *After Crime and Punishment: Pathways to Offender Reintegration*, Cullompton, Devon: Willan, 258–290.

Vaughan, B. (2007) The internal narrative of desistance. *British Journal of Criminology*, 47 (3), 390–340.

Verde, A. (2021) Whose narrative? The self as (also) an alien – For a complex concept of 'Self' in narrative criminology. *Tijdschrift Over Cultuur & Criminaliteit*, 10 (3), 35–58.

Victor, J., and Waldram, J. B. (2015) Moral habilitation and the new normal: Sexual offender narratives of posttreatment community integration. In L. Presser & S. Sandberg (Eds.), *Narrative Criminology: Understanding Stories of Crime*. New York: New York University Press, 96–124.

Villman, E. (2023) Desistance upon release from prison: Narratives of tragedy, irony, romance and comedy. *The British Journal of Criminology*, XX, 1–17.
Visher, C. A. (2013) Incarcerated fathers: Pathways from prison to home. *Criminal Justice Policy Review*, 24, 9–26.
Visher, C. A., Debus-Sherrill, S. A., and Yahner, J. (2010) Employment after prison: A longitudinal study of former prisoners. *Justice Quarterly*, 28(5), 698–718.
Visher, C. A., and Travis, J. (2003) Transitions from prison to community: Understanding individual pathways. *Annual Review of Sociology*, 29, 89–113.
Warr, J. (2019) 'Always gotta be two mans': Lifers, risk, rehabilitation, and narrative labour. *Punishment and Society*, 22 (1), 28–47.
Warr, M. (1998) Life course transitions and desistance from crime. *Criminology*, 36 (2), 183–216.
Weaver, B. (2019) Understanding desistance: A critical review of theories of desistance. *Psychology, Crime & Law*, 25 (6), 641–658.
Wright, S., Crewe, B., and Hulley, S. (2017) Suppression, denial, sublimation: Defending against the initial pains of very long sentences. *Theoretical Criminology*, 21 (2), 225–246.
Wright, J. P., Cullen, F. T., and Miller, J. T. (2001) Family social capital and delinquent involvement. *Journal of Criminal Justice*, 29 (1), 1–9.

3 Barriers to resettlement
Exploring new pathways for mandatory lifers

The previous chapter provided an outline of the concept of identity and explored its use in desistance research. It then outlined a series of definitional issues pertinent to the process of desistance and continued with an overview of the main theories and debates in the desistance literature. Despite the theoretical wrestling that was evidenced, we can draw an important preliminary consensus that *sine qua non* a fundamental, subjective identity change, long-term desistance is difficult to achieve. The problem with this pro-social internal change is that it needs maintaining despite a series of possible factors that are often outside the control of the individual (Klaus, 2023).

In this chapter, I will draw from 'pains of imprisonment' literature to suggest that homicide offenders' adaptations to long-term imprisonment may be maladaptive to their reintegration efforts post-release. In other words, it is suggested that the very coping mechanisms that protect against such pains are not suited to life outside prison walls. Adding to this point, the chapter explores a series of 'pains of release', especially focusing on stigma and the precarious nature of the post-Fordist economy. The dissolution of traditional sites of identity construction representative of the post-industrial society (Hall, 1997; Young, 2011) represents a further impediment to the identity reconstruction of the newly released mandatory lifer in pursuit of a new, successful life. Given this hypothesised deadlock, the chapter concludes rhetorically by reiterating question: "how do people who have committed murder reconstruct their lives post-release?"

Adaptations to 'imprisonment pains': The case for long term offender

Long-term imprisonment can carry irreparable damage to those who have been incarcerated; this has been succinctly described by Caird (1974: 98) in his autobiography: "Prison obviously has its effects on people's minds. If you set up a 20-foot fence around a man's (sic) body, it would be naïve to say: But I didn't mean to affect his mind". The deprivations that have been considered to accompany a prison sentence are varied. In his classical work, Sykes (1958) identified several 'pains of imprisonment' that inmates suffer while serving their sentence. These are: loss of liberty, loss of goods and services, deprivations of heterosexual relationships, loss of autonomy, and security. He famously said that "the worst thing about prison is you have to live with other prisoners" (Sykes, 1958: 77). Significantly, these dispossessions were seen as directly affecting prisoners' sense of identity. For example, considering the state of Western culture where material possessions are critical in one's construction of identities, to lose one's goods may represent an attack to the 'deepest layer of personality' (Sykes, 1958: 68). This view is closely similar to that of more recent accounts of cultural criminologists (Presdee, 2004: 280) who argue that in a consumerist society such as the one today, "to have is to exist: to have nothing is to be nothing".

The absence of heterosexual relationships represented a further attack on prisoners' identity; in the absence of any contact with the opposite sex, individuals' self-image is rendered in danger of becoming half-complete. Significantly, it was in the context of these hardships that the 'inmate society' of the prison emerged as a natural manifestation aimed at alleviating adversities. Through the loss of autonomy, the prisoner is fundamentally reduced to the "weak, helpless, dependent status of childhood" (Sykes, 1958: 75). Much of Sykes' original highlights were further developed by Goffman. In his book, *Asylums* (1961), the concept of 'mortification of the self' was used to emphasise prisoners' metamorphosis of identity which would be initiated the moment they walked through the prison gates and start to experience a series of 'degradation ceremonies' (Garfinkel, 1956). These are specifically designed to strip their sense of self. The old identity is thought to be replaced by the new identity of being a prisoner (Goffman, 1961). Therefore, the fundamental sense of existence, that of a father, husband, or worker, are partly stripped by the sentence, which is thought to ultimately lead to the construction of a new, alternative identity (Jewkes, 2002). Warr (2016) remarked that degradation ceremonies occur much earlier than Goffman suggested, typically from the time of arrest. Admittedly, the ways in which the prison system exercises its power has changed since the workings of Sykes or Goffman. Its relative anonymity, its non-corporeal nature, and pervasive reach of the late-modern prison has been related to forms of adaptation that directly affects identity deconstruction and reconstruction in institutional contexts in a Kafkaesque manner (Crewe, 2007, 2011a). The panoptic sense of supervision was described by participants in Crewe's (2011a) research via metaphors such as depth, weight, and tightness to capture what was ultimately felt as wearing an 'invisible collar' (Canton, 2022: 379).

Cohen and Taylor (1972) have also provided a sophisticated account of 'doing time'. Their long-term offenders experienced prison hardships as pertaining to ways of 'doing time', maintaining relationships with others, and engaging in the process of counteracting the insidious processes that attack personal identity. Normally, 'shattering events' affect one life domain; this essentially means that other life domains can be employed to transgress tragedy. However, the long-term prison is not allowed such 'luxuries'; Cohen and Taylor (1972: 43) stated:

> [...] he (sic) is starting a new life, one in which the routines which previously obtained in every area will be transformed. He faces two decades inside, two decades away from home, wife, children, job, social life, and friends.

This stands as evidence for the fundamentally distinct experience of imprisonment between long-term imprisonment, especially indeterminate sentences, and short-term sentenced prisoners. Furthermore, compared with those who were forced to migrate in times of war, the authors argue new prisoners are expected to assume and confront new routines, they must absorb new norms, and discover adaptive mechanisms for the new situation (Cohen and Taylor, 1972). Similarly, Irwin and Owen (2005) argued that long-term imprisonment affects personality in significant ways, including loss of agency, attacks on the self, and sexual orientation. The authors built a case around the effect of the strict schedule which prisoners must respect daily. In prison everything is planned to the minute, and this ultimately leads prisoners to lose the capacity of exercising power. The authors argue:

> Years of following repetitive, restricted routines and of being regulated by an extensive and somewhat rigidly enforced body of rules steadily erodes the skills prisoners will need to cope with life in the outside world [...].
> (Irwin and Owen, 2005: 100)

Attacks on the self are represented through a continuous lack of privacy which is paramount for the integration of feelings and ideas that impinge on their consciousness. Since the contributions of Sykes and Goffman academic research stemming from a 'pains of imprisonment' theoretical framework has expanded exponentially. Haggerty and Bucerius (2020) conducted a thematic analysis of over 50 publications on 'pains of imprisonment' published between 1960 and 2019 and managed to identify four trajectories in the penological literature: (a) additional pains to Sykes' influential study, (b) disaggregated pains (referring to the apparent uniformity in which the study treated its prisoners), (c) pains beyond the prison walls, (d) distinctly modern pains. Arguably, the appetite which has sustained over 60 years the 'pains of imprisonment' research testifies to its continuous relevance. The additional pains to Sykes' study indicate that some fundamental shifts both in the prison system's practices and prisoners' responses to such practices had taken place. Despite the age of some of these studies and their American ethnocentrism they indicate that long-term imprisonment has some long-lasting impacts upon the long-term offender. More recent research supports this claim. Klaus (2023) distinguished between pains and snares consequence of imprisonment. Snares are structural and systemic – so they have an exogenous source – such as imposition of stigma by the state and society. In turn, this leads to a series of pains such as loneliness, internalised shame, and hopelessness that extend beyond the release date of the 'offender'. Adaptations to long-term imprisonment have long-lasting effects.

Doing time and the adapting self

Positivist research (usually conducted by psychologists) have assessed a range of apparent deteriorations – mainly through psychometric testing – and were generally unsuccessful in finding cognitive deteriorations in prisoners who have served prison sentences to any significant extent (Banister et al., 1973; Dettbarn, 2012; Rasch, 1981; Sapsford, 1983; van Ginneken, 2016; Zamble, 1992; Cf. Lapornik et al., 1966; Sluga, 1977). Also, there has been little evidence for clinically sizable personality or attitudinal changes over time (Heskin et al., 1973). Nevertheless, there is some indication that imprisonment can lead to higher dependency on staff with time (Sapsford, 1978; Cf. Zamble and Porporino, 1990 on 'behavioural deep freeze').

Flanagan (1980) concluded that long-term prisoners ascribe greater importance to problems that are associated with imprisonment per se than to deprivations associated with the prison environment. In this sense, the pain of 'missing somebody', 'missing social life', and 'feeling that one's life is wasted' have been systematically found to represent the crucial elements of prison deprivations that were exemplified by prisoner as affecting their lives inside prison (Flanagan, 1980; Leigey and Ryder, 2014; Richards, 1978). Importantly, other studies found long-prison sentences to lead to self-esteem assault (Flanagan, 1981), and prisonisation (Clemmer, 1958; Porporino and Zamble, 1984; Wheeler, 1961). However, there is a controversy around the validity or the comprehensibility of such studies when considering the whole array of effects that imprisonment entails. In other words, there is a difficulty for studies using psychometric tests to fully assess the distress and changes that occur because of long-term imprisonment (Jamieson and Grounds, 2005). The 'deep freeze' that characterises life imprisonment will necessarily affect virtually all aspects of prisoners' familial and social relationships, in a world that is alien to the recently released prisoner.

Institutionalisation as well as prisonization has been conceptualised as the natural effects of long-term imprisonment. These concepts stand at the epicentre of prison sociology and of the 'deprivation model' of imprisonment. In his influential work, Clemmer (1958) has analysed changes that prisoners undertake during confinement in the United States. He described the existence of an 'inmate society' that is embodied by an inmate code, and it was thought that the existence of such prison codes represents the natural step that prisoners take in their trials to cope with long-term imprisonment and its deprivations. In the author's view, prisonisation was the "taking on, in greater or lesser degree, of the folkways, mores, customs, and general culture of the penitentiary" (Clemmer, 1958: 299). Proponents of a deprivation model of adjustment to imprisonment (Clemmer, 1958; Goffman, 1961) plead for the occurrence of prisonisation as an adaptive response against institutionalisation. A range of studies have found evidence for prisonisation to play a crucial role in prisoners' negotiation of their identity while in prison and in the protection against institutionalisation (Paterline and Petersen, 1999; Thomas, 1977; Walters, 2003).

However, those who proposed an 'importation model' (Dhami, Ayton, and Lowenstein, 2007; Irwin and Cressey, 1962; Paterline and Petersen, 1999; Porporino and Zamble, 1984) of adaptation to prison argued that individuals enter prison with a set of personal experiences, vulnerabilities, and strengths (Porporino and Zamble, 1984), that would ultimately affect their adjusting patterns. In this sense, anecdotal evidence from prisoner biographies could be fruitful in elucidating the extent to which pre-prison identities are impacting experience within prison. One notable example is Caird (1974: 100), who, as a Cambridge alumnus, argued "I imagined it would be very hard to be accepted by prisoners as 'one of them', that the barriers created by class, education and offence would be all but insurmountable". His method of choice was to embrace an intellectual attitude, where he "buried in the heavier books for which [his] education equipped [him]". This is in stark contrast with prisoners from working class backgrounds (Boyle, 1977; Cook and Wilkinson, 1998; McVicar, 1974; Weaver, 2008), who have engaged with long periods of rebellion against authority, mechanisms captured by Goffman (1961), in what he called 'secondary adjustments'. Interestingly, these 'rebellious' prisoners were found to be highly successful (compared to the 'model prisoner') by some authors (Goodstein, 1979) when released. The alternative for the hegemonic masculinity identity which would normally be suitable for working class prisoners from a middle-class background are thought by Jewkes (2005) to embrace a 'scholar' or 'student' identity to adapt to the working-class dominated culture of prison.

Irrespective of the prisoner's provenance, a range of symbolic interactionist studies (based on short term offenders) point that to 'survive', new inmates create a distinction between their 'true' identity (pre-prison identity) and a false identity (Schmid and Jones, 1991; Wheeler, 1961). The new identity, which is thought to be based on impression management skills (Goffman, 1959) – although initially designed for survival – gradually evolves into an alternative identity, especially suitable to the prison world (Schmid and Jones, 1991). Jewkes (2005) similarly said that 'wearing a mask' is the most prevalent coping strategy adopted by prisoners. The distinction between the two identities has been traditionally conceptualised as 'backstage' and 'frontstage' (Goffman, 1959). Cook and Wilkinson (1998: 32) highlights the point vividly in his autobiography:

> The terrible irony of it is that, when you have denied your true emotions for so long, it is very hard to recover them and, when you leave the prison environment, you find yourself broken, a shell of what you used to be.

Jacquelyn and Gill (2015) argued that new inmates adopt a convict identity during early imprisonment to 'stave off' the uncertainties of a threatening environment; as they become fully acculturated, later within the sentence, they begin to question the convict identity. This shift in identity, or 'the Enlightenment' (Jacquelyn and Gill, 2015), was experienced as an ambivalence that prisoners needed to negotiate throughout the sentence; on the one hand, the prison identity was seen as inauthentic, while on the other, there was a need to embrace it for 'survival'.

Research which investigated the effect of long-term imprisonment diminished significantly in the past six decades and had been predominantly conducted in North America, with much of our existing knowledge on the topic published in the 1970s and 1980s (Hulley, Crewe, and Wright, 2016). This is an important consideration given that issues that impact contemporary societies, and by extension prisons and long-term prisoners are significantly different to a few decades ago. For example, Kazemian (2019) reminded us that prisons are now more overcrowded, mental health issues more prevalent (or diagnosed more effectively), and that we now recognise that prisons are ethnically diverse places. In fact, many of these early studies betray a palpable American ethnocentrism, overlooked in British theoretisation (Young, 2011).

Further, it has been argued that the British deindustrialisation consequence of the neo-liberal policies of the 1980s alongside consumer capitalism's intrinsic driving forces had led to fundamental shifts in human subjectivity (Hall, 1997; Hall and Winlow, 2015) and the ways in which fundamental institutions function (Wieviorka, 2009). In this sense, it would be naïve to assume that ensuing cultural shifts have not creeped into the penal system and influenced the formation of subculture(s). To what extent these forces affect prison coping mechanisms and exert pressures on early released long-term offenders (homicide offenders particularly) and their identity reconstructions is unexplored.

Although much of our current knowledge on the topic of prison adaptation is outdated and focused mainly on short-term offenders, there are reasons for optimism. A range of authors from the University of Cambridge's Prisons Research Centre, led by Crewe and colleagues, have recently resuscitated interest in the area. Their research gravitates around the adaptations to imprisonment of young long-term offenders and mandatory life sentenced individuals. Their studies are limited to mandatory lifers inside prisons, but it overall serves a valuable foundation for the groundwork laid in the current book.

Mandatory lifers adapt to imprisonment and prepare for release

Recently, Crewe, Hulley, and Wright (2020) made the point that 'pains of imprisonment' as described by Sykes (1958) are intensified for people who commit murder due to the enormity of their crime and the length of their sentence. This would naturally then lead to a series of distinctive adaptive responses. In the wake of their murder conviction, mandatory lifers need to make sense of a significant disruption in their narrative coherence and integrate the enormity of having committed murder in their biographical selfhood (Crewe et al., 2020). These offenders need to answer a pressing question: "how do you survive a disaster when you are the disaster?" (Doctor, 2008: 4). The biographical rupture leads to a series of 'affective responses' such as anger, grief, and intrusive recollections of the murder, which are comparable to acute stress disorder and post-traumatic stress disorder as well as complicated grief. In addition, we need to remember that people who kill are often victims of trauma (Doctor, 2008). An index offence of homicide fragments one's identity (Adshead, Ferrito, and Bose, 2015), damage one's life story, and implicitly alters how perpetrators perceive their own selves (Ferrito, Needs, and Adshead, 2017). One participant in Parker's (1990: 111–112) journalistic account of 12 released murderers' narratives expressed the 'murderer's condition' clearly:

> My biggest difficulty, it's living with myself, trying to come to terms with myself, face what I've done. I took someone's life away [...], there's no way I can give his life back or make restitution. [...], what I'd done was final, irrevocable, and it wasn't done for any faintly acceptable reason.
> (Andi Reid, released homicide offender in Parker, 1990: 111–112)

It is not surprising that many mandatory lifers find it impossible to imagine a way to 'make good' (Maruna, 2001) after release and are often traumatised by the homicide itself (Gray et al., 2003; Liem and Kunst, 2013; Papanastassiou et al., 2004; Thomas, Adshead, and Mezey, 1994). The type of murder committed is significant in the acerbity of the symptoms (Gray et al., 2003; Papanastassiou et al., 2004) especially if the victim and perpetrator had a close relationship, for example when a family member was killed (Papanastassiou et al., 2004). Interestingly, researchers stemming from a psychodynamic tradition underlined that like in Oscar Wilde's fictional character Dorian Gray, murderous acts themselves can represent a 'projective identification' (McAlister, 2008; Motz, 2008). After a traumatic event, 'meaning-making' is challenged and the 'self' is affected (Ferrito et al., 2017).

Wright, Crewe, Hulley, and Wright (2017) remarked that the patterns of prison adjustment for homicide offenders reflect a particular 'offence-time nexus'. In other words, there is a dual psychological burden characterised by the extreme offence, combined with the time served that generate different patterns of response for murderers compared to the general prison population. The authors applied a Freudian psychoanalytic framework to explore how the mandatory lifers in the study defended against a series of specific pains such as entry shock, temporal vertigo (referring to making sense of the sentence length), and intrusive recollections (of the murder) by way of suppression, denial, and sublimation. In this sense, to defend against these pains, participants in the early stages of their sentence (within the first four years of their sentence) tended to block unwanted thoughts and minimised reality by way of suppression; some went as far as to deny the weight of the sentence and the reality of their crime. Others, in a much more positive manner, harnessed their energy into intellectual and positive endeavours. Crewe et al. (2020) added to suppression issues (which in their research had emerged as a gendered manifestation of drug abuse and self-harm in a temporal escape manifestation) pertaining to escape through self-isolation. Along with suppression and escape, prisoners reported engaging in 'jailing', a term which denotes engagement with illicit activities within the prison's informal economy. Importantly, these types of activities had a sense of nihilism as a driving force, represented by a form of 'lucid indifference' (Camus, 1954: 94 in Crewe et al., 2020: 110) but which tended to change with time. Amongst other pains, they found participants to be concerned about becoming docile, feared cognitive deterioration, and complained about their general health later in the sentence (Crewe et al., 2017).

The important point to note here is that such adaptations lead to fundamental changes in the self which may prove maladaptive on release (Hulley et al., 2016). Such results have been contextualised and situated within participants' stages of their imprisonment. The highest discrepancy in terms of deprivation was found between prisoners in the 'post-tariff' group and 'very early' and 'early group'. In this sense, 'thinking about the time they have left to serve', 'autonomy' and 'having to deal with an alien environment', were significantly more severe for the initial phase (within four years of their sentence); this could reflect coping mechanisms that prisoners engage with at the initial stages of their sentence. In this interpretation, the logical deduction then is that prisoners find the appropriate ways to cope with their new environment by redefining it but remain essentially the same. Nevertheless, this may not be an accurate representation of reality. In fact, the very coping mechanisms which are mobilised at the beginning of these sentences (and later) may be deeply transformative which means that they could potentially then affect resettlement in ways which have not been explored to any considerable extent. This is evident when considering the culture shock that indeterminate sentenced prisoners experience once they reach open prison conditions (HMIP, 2013). Imprisoned individuals often experience institutionalisation and hopelessness, as well as difficulties in socialising with other prisoners (Jarvis, Shaw, and Lovell, 2022). In fact, hopelessness often leads indeterminate sentenced prisoners to stop pursuing release altogether (Rennie and Crewe, 2023; Wright, Hulley, and Crewe, 2023).

Liem and Kunst (2013) found that once they are released, homicide offenders in America experience 'post-incarceration syndrome' (PICS). This included institutionalised personality traits such as paranoia, hampered decision-making, social sensory deprivation (especially relating to difficulties in social interactions) and a sense of societal/temporal alienation. These can ultimately account for the difference between lifers who are recalled compared to those who remain in the community (Appleton, 2010). In this sense, 'adaptive' responses to pains to imprisonment as highlighted above, once internalised work their way to construct a different type of person by the time of release (Hulley et al., 2016). This has been well captured by Cook and Wilkinson (1998: 32) when referring to coping with imprisonment and release his autobiography:

> Only afterwards, do you realize that you've destroyed your emotions in the process. This is what I found to be one of the most damaging things about prison and is the reason why many long-term inmates find it impossible to revert back to life on the outside.

Nevertheless, not all criminological research participants identified prison as an institution of intrinsic torment and human waste. In fact, a recent review by Crewe and Levins (2020) remarked that some prisoners interpret and utilise prisons as 'reinventive institutions'. Such prisoners find a silver lining in their incarceration and admit that prison had saved their lives or contributed significantly to their personal development. A range of authors argued that prison can lead to post traumatic growth (van Ginneken, 2016; Vanhooren, Leijssen, and Dezutter, 2018). Many find that their incarceration had contributed to their 'awakening' (Irwin, 2009), and that there is indeed 'lotus in the mud' (Kazemian, 2019). For example, as they progressed through their sentences, many of Crewe et al. (2017: 21) mandatory lifers started to make their sentence meaningful and constructive and ended up "swimming with the tide, rather than against it". Also, many of Crewe et al. (2020: 197) 'murderers' have been motivated by generativity in prison, where a pressing need to give back and to be 'an agent of positive change' was related to feelings of "profound remorse and self-loathing about the offence". This body of literature then evidences the panoply of prison experiences which are intrinsic and specific to people who committed homicide. It is reasonable then to suggest that the release of these men would carry equally idiosyncratic pathways to 'reintegration' which have not been explored.

The argument proposed thus far is that the very coping mechanisms that homicide offenders employ to adapt to their condition may prove maladaptive upon release. It would be naïve to assume that barriers to reintegration or desistance are purely cognitive. Adaptation to the new environment is seldom favourable due to a series of added difficulties often referred to as 'pains of probation' (Durnescu, 2011, 2019) or 'pains of desistance' (Nugent and Schinkel, 2016) and these are closely related to the ways in which stigma operates for these individuals.

Becoming an ex-murderer?

Stigma occurs through a process where one's life is dominated by their social identity. Individuals are generally assessed through this label, which is ultimately considered to be dominant and operates as a 'master status' (Becker, 1963; May, 2000). From a sociological perspective, Goffman (1963: 3) defined stigma as "an attribute that is deeply discrediting" and is representative of one's social identity (LeBel, 2008). Ultimately, stigma can affect the construction of pro-social identities post-release as the label is seen to deny certain stories, and to construct individuals as unidimensional: "In the social calculus of reality representations and tests the former identity stands as accidental; the new identity is the 'basic reality'" (Garfinkel, 1956: 422). The released lifer needs to decide whether to disclose information about themselves, to whom, and when. Goffman (1963: 126) remarked how the stigmatised can either conceal their past (to pass) or they can 'cover' (minimising it). He argued that "many of those who rarely try to pass, routinely try to cover". Analogous to these strategies, LeBel (2008) distinguished between reactive and proactive approaches to managing stigma. Nevertheless, disclosing the past is not always in the hands of ex-offenders. In England and Wales, the Rehabilitation of Offenders Act (ROA) (1974) sets out the precepts of disclosing previous convictions to employers, but no research to date has explored the ways in which mandatory lifers manage their stigmatised past post-release either in social interactions, or in finding and maintaining employment in the United Kingdom. An important modality of deflecting stigma is through the development of a new pro-social identity (Giordano, Cerkovich, and Rudolph, 2002), that usually takes the form of 'family man', 'provider' or 'good parent' (LeBel et al., 2008). In this sense, employment seems like the perfect site of pro-social identity construction, but research has found that stigma leads to social rejection including from the workplace (Canton, 2022; Durnescu, 2019; LeBel, 2012; Petersilia, 2003). The vicious circle is exacerbated if we consider how these traditional sites of identity construction have been eroded in late modernity (Young, 2011). This is the irony which Young (2011: 94) remarked, that "just as there is a greater stress on creating one's identity, the building blocks of identity become less substantial."

The job market is dramatically different to that of half a century before. Hall (2012: 115) has succinctly described this process: "deindustrialisation, unemployment, inflation and a surfeit of inactive surplus capital all rose together to threaten the social order, profitability and the value for money, all close to the heart of the dominant bourgeois class". A consumer culture emerged as an alternative or substitute to a symbolic order long left devoid of any substance after deindustrialisation (Winlow and Hall, 2016), with the accent increasingly placed on opportunity and individualism. For individuals to construct a status position is to fragment traditional communal interdependencies (Hall and Winlow, 2005).

The fact that the current service-based economy is prepared to absorb as many new employees as possible in jobs commonly described as 'McJobs' (Lloyd, 2018b) might be viewed merely as a pyrrhic victory (Rusu, 2023). Once released, mandatory lifers are thrown into the vortex of precarious, flexible, and ephemeral (Lloyd, 2018b, 2019; Winlow and Hall; 2006, 2013) 'post-modern jobs' of the leisure service economy (Bauman, 2005). This 'new' service economy, with its competitive individualist ethos, and increasingly used zero-hour contracts and part-time work, may offer a sense of false security and optimism to these 'returning citizens' as they enter unstable waters upon release. Sheppard and Ricciardelli (2020) made the point that ex-prisoners may want to refrain from rushing straight into jobs post-release, as this may expose themselves to potential exploitation. Further, the authors remarked that their sample of Canadian ex-prisoners were dissuaded from their desistance pathway by "the low waged, non-gratifying, temporary, exploitative, work for which they qualify or have the opportunity to pursue" (Sheppard and Ricciardelli, 2020: 48). The dangers of such disappointment were represented by Halsey, Armstrong, and Wright (2016: 1506) where participants engaged in 'fuck it' scenarios, where desistance is simply not worth it compared to criminal lifestyles. Then, clearly, "the current precarious job market further exacerbates the lack of employment opportunities for former prisoners" (Sheppard and Ricciardelli, 2020: 38). This is the 'capitalist realism' (Fisher, 2009) that newly released mandatory lifers will most likely encounter and navigate. Then, it may be the case that the pains of release as imagined by previous research are not comprehensive and potentially ineffective in making sense of the difficulties encountered by most homicide offenders on release.

Pains of freedom: Negotiating the 'leash of oversight'

Added to such fluid and ephemeral employment opportunities and exclusion due to stigma, there are a set of 'pains of freedom' (Crewe, 2011b; Durnescu, 2011; Liem and Kunst, 2013; McNeill, 2019; Shammas, 2014) typically related to deprivation of autonomy because of probation's hyper-supervision (Durnescu, 2011; Rennie and Crewe, 2023) or conversely, of not being seen at all (McNeill, 2018: 225). The probation officer is seen to have a direct role in either alleviating or exacerbating the existing circumstance of people released from prison. For example, Durnescu (2011) has found his participants to experience deprivation of autonomy, of time, finances, stigma, or just conceive their life as being under threat as consequences directly related to their experience of probation. They considered that their probation officers could either intensify such deprivations. Research conducted in open prisons reiterates such concerns (Shammas, 2014). For example, Shammas (2014: 110) found newly arrived prisoners to experience confusion: "you are free, but you aren't free". They are unsure of their contrasting roles within the anxious journey from closed to open prison, and finally into the community. Increasingly the onus is placed on the importance of taking ownership and responsibility; a 'submission of subjectivity' is therefore taking place with the aim of remodelling the prisoners (Foucault, 1983: 213 in Shammas, 2014: 118)

It has also been suggested that the lifer is required to navigate imprisonment with 'tact' and that there is a demand for the capacity to negotiate identities in such a way as to signal low risk to authorities, while at the same time showing signs of 'being rehabilitated' (Warr, 2019). Warr's (2019) study of young indeterminate sentenced prisoners had to engage with 'narrative labour' to navigate these contrasting expectations of the prison system. This was not without risks, as:

> If incapable performers fail to adopt these accepted linguistic tropes and have sufficient disciplinary capital, then impossible barriers are being put in their way by the very disciplinary discourses which are supposed to aid their 'rehabilitation' and release.
> (Warr, 2019: 42)

Once released, the lifer knows that

> If the responsible officer considers that the person subject to licence has failed to comply with the conditions of the licence or present a high risk of causing serious harm or further offending, the individual will be recalled to prison without going back to court.
> (HMIP, 2018: 7; HMIP, 2020)

To avoid recall to prison, the shell of soft power needs to be carried out throughout the licence period and the internalised containment of risk needs to be continuously performed (McNeill, 2018). In this context, stigma operates as an extra challenge, or a primary challenge for the returning prisoner who is trying to prove 'worthy of forgiveness' (LeBel, 2012, 2020).

McNeill (2018) found the quality of the relationship with the probation officer as crucial in ameliorating one mandatory life sentenced individual's experience of life licence. A good relationship decreases the odds of being recalled as much as 19 times for life sentenced prisoners (Appleton, 2010) while a 'bad relationship'/ supervision and imposed conditions can forestall homicide offenders' re-entry (Liem, 2017). This is relevant considering that indeterminate sentenced individuals are usually recalled due to non-compliance with licence conditions rather than due to further offending (HMIP, 2020). An important element that added to their isolation was a pervasive sense of surveillance; the eventuality of recall was seen as imminent and could be triggered for the slightest 'slip' of behaviour.

Although research on re-entry and desistance has established as one of the most fruitful areas of research in criminology (Maruna, 2001; Maruna and Immarigeon, 2011), with few notable exceptions, there is very little research focusing on the experience of life sentenced prisoners after a life imprisonment (although see Appleton, 2010; Coker and Martin, 1985 in the United Kingdom; Liem, 2016, 2017; Liem and Garcin, 2014; Liem and Kunst, 2013 in the United States).

The probation officer can assist with the development of social capital as well as human capital (Canton, 2022), but whether this is what happens in practice with mandatory lifers is unexplored. A joint inspection by HMI Probation and HMI Prisons (2013: 6) found that those subjected to a life sentence were treated the same as short-term offenders in the community. The report identified this as 'short-sighted' considering that long-term offenders may be institutionalised and therefore would present a set of idiosyncratic needs post-release. Perhaps this could partly explain breaches of licence conditions and the increasing recall rates amongst indeterminate sentenced prisoners (HMIP, 2020; Canton, 2022).

Discussion

Considering the above, resettlement for homicide offenders seems to be an impossible mission. The returning mandatory lifer needs to quickly decide on how to negotiate their spoiled identities in interaction with others and enact an internal narrative of desistance which accounts for what happened, and what should happen in the future. As traditional sites of identity construction may be unavailable, there is a pressing need for identities to be re-written and reinvented. The overly flexible and precarious character of the post-industrial service economy may not be able to provide the long-term stability that both mandatory life sentenced individuals and their case pursue.

The lifer may be further pressured to organise their identities around the consumer culture which emanates from underneath the real of such economic forces. Such a scenario may render the returning lifer disappointed and in need to innovate. Prison-based adaptive behaviours further denounce the newly released lifer as an alien and a misfit to conventional society – they need to quickly denude the vestiges of a life imprisonment. Given the above, we are left with a few pressing questions: how do mandatory lifers reconstruct their lives after release? How do mandatory lifers reconstruct their lives to live a good and useful life? What is the relevance of the type of murder committed in this process?

References

Adshead, G., Ferrito, M., and Bose, S. (2015) Recovery after homicide: Narrative shifts in therapy with homicide perpetrators. *Criminal Justice and Behaviour*, 42 (1), 70–81.
Appleton, C. (2010). *Life after Life Imprisonment*. Oxford: Oxford University Press.
Banister, P. A., Smith, F. V., Heskin, K. J., and Bolton, N. (1973) Psychological correlates of long-term imprisonment. *British Journal of Criminology*, 13 (4), 312–330.
Bauman, Z. (2005) *Work, Consumerism, and the New Poor*, 2nd edition. Milton Keynes: Open University Press.

Becker, H. S. (1963) *Outsiders: Studies in the Sociology of Deviance*. New York, NY: Free Press.
Boyle, J. (1977) *A Sense of Freedom*. London: Canongate Publishing Ltd.
Caird, R. (1974) *A good and useful life*. London: Hart-David MacGibbon.
Canton, R. (2022) After-care, resettlement, and social inclusion: The role of probation. *Probation Journal*, 69 (3), 373–390.
Clemmer, D. (1958[1940]) The Prison Community, 2nd edition. New York, NY: Holt, Rinehart & Winston.
Cohen, S. and Taylor, L. (1972) *Psychological Survival: The Experience of Long-Term Imprisonment*. London: Penguin.
Coker, J. B., and Martin, J. P. (1985) *Licensed to Live*. Oxford: Basil Blackwell.
Cook, F., and Wilkinson, M. (1998). *Hard Cell*. Liverpool: The Bluecoat Press.
Crewe, B. (2007) Power, adaptation and resistance in a late modern Men's prison. *British Journal of Criminology*, 47, 256–275.
Crewe, B. (2011a) Depth, weight, tightness: Revisiting the pains of imprisonment. *Punishment and Society*, 13 (5), 509–529.
Crewe, B. (2011b) Soft power in prison: Implications for staff-prisoner relationships, liberty and legitimacy. *European Journal of Criminology*, 8 (6), 455–468.
Crewe, B., Hulley, S., and Wright, S. (2017) Swimming with the tide: Adapting to long-term imprisonment. *Justice Quarterly*, 34 (3), 517–541.
Crewe, B., Hulley, S., and Wright, S. (2020) *Life Imprisonment from Young Adulthood Adaptation, Identity, and Time*. United Kingdom, UK: Palgrave Macmillan.
Crewe, B., and Levins, A. (2020) The prison as reinventive institution. *Theoretical Criminology*, 24 (4), 568–589.
Dettbarn, E. (2012) Effects of long-term incarceration: A statistical comparison of two expert assessment of two experts at the beginning and end of incarceration. *International Journal of Law and Psychiatry*, 35, 236–239.
Dhami, K. M., Ayton, P., and Lowenstein, G. (2007) Adaptation to imprisonment. Indigenous or imported? *Criminal Justice and Behaviour*, 34 (8), 1085–1100.
Doctor, R. (2008) Introduction. In Doctor R. (Ed.), *Murder: A Psychotherapeutic Investigation*. London: Karnac Books Ltd., 1–9.
Durnescu, I. (2011) Pains of probation: Effective practice and human rights. *International Journal of Offender Therapy and Comparative Criminology*, 55 (4), 530–545.
Durnescu, I. (2019) Pains of reentry revisited. *International Journal of Offender Therapy and Comparative Criminology*, 63 (8), 1482–1498.
Ferrito, M., Needs, A., and Adshead, G. (2017) Unveiling of shadow of meaning: Meaning making for perpetrators of homicide. *Aggression and Violent Behaviour*, 34, 263–272.
Fisher, M. (2009) *Capitalist Realism: Is There No Alternative?* Alresford: Zero Books.
Flanagan, J. T. (1981) Dealing with long-term confinement. Adaptive strategies and perspectives among long-term prisoners. *Criminal Justice and Behavior*, 8 (2), 201–222.
Flanagan, J. T. (1980) The pains of long-term imprisonment. *British Journal of Criminology*, 20 (2), 148–156.
Garfinkel, H. (1956) Conditions of successful degradation ceremonies. *American Journal of Sociology*, 61 (5), 420–424.
Giordano, P. C., Cerkovich, S. A., and Rudolph, J. L. (2002) Gender crime and desistance: Toward a theory of cognitive transformation. *American Journal of Sociology*, 107 (4), 990–1064.
Goffman, E. (1959) *The Presentation of Self in Everyday Life*. London: Penguin.
Goffman, E. (1961) *Asylums: Essays on the Social Situation of Mental Patients and Other Inmates*. London: Penguin.

Goffman, E. (1963) *Stigma Notes on the Management of Spoiled Identity*. London: Penguin.
Goodstein, L. (1979) Inmate adjustment to prison and the transition to community life. *Journal of Research in Crime and Delinquency*, 16 (2), 246–272.
Gray, S. N., Nicole, G., Carman, P. R., Malcolm, J., Hayward, P. M., and Snowden, J. R. (2003) Post-traumatic stress disorder caused in mentally disordered offenders by the committing of a serious violent or sexual offence. *The Journal of Forensic Psychiatry & Psychology*, 14 (1), 27–43.
H.M. Inspectorate of Probation (2020) A thematic review of probation recall culture and practice. Available at https://www.justiceinspectorates.gov.uk/hmiprobation/inspections/recallthematic/ [accessed 03 November 2023].
Haggerty, K. D., and Bucerius, S. (2020) The proliferating pains of imprisonment. *Incarceration*, 1 (1), 1–16.
Hall, S. (1997) Visceral cultures and criminal practices. *Theoretical Criminology*, 1 (4), 453–478.
Hall, S. (2012) *Theorizing Crime and Deviance: A New Perspective*. London: SAGE.
Hall, S., and Winlow, S. (2005) Anti-nirvana: Crime, culture, and instrumentalism in the age of insecurity. *Crime Media Culture*, 1 (1), 31–48.
Hall, S., and Winlow, S. (2015) *Revitalising Criminological Theory: Towards a New Ultra-realism*. Oxon: Routledge.
Halsey, M., Armstrong, R., and Wright, S. (2016) F*ck it! Matza and the mood of fatalism in the desistance process. *British Journal of Criminology*, 57 (5), 1041–1060.
Heskin, K. J., Smith, F. V., Banister, P. A., and Bolton, N. (1973) Psychological correlates of long-term imprisonment. *British Journal of Criminology*, 13 (4), 323–330.
Her Majesty's Inspectorate of Probation (2013) A joint inspection of life sentence prisoners. Available at: www.justiceinspectorates.gov.uk/probation/wp-content/uploads/sites/5/2014/03/life-sentence-prisoners.pdf
Her Majesty's Inspectorate of Probation (2018) Enforcement and recall: A thematic inspection by HM Inspectorate of Probation. Available at Enforcement and Recall (justiceinspectorates.gov.uk) [accessed on 15 August 2024].
Hulley, S., Crewe, B., and Wright, S. (2016) Re-examining the problems of long-term imprisonment. *British Journal of Criminology*, 56 (4), 769–792.
Irwin, J. (2009) *Lifers: Seeking Redemption in Prison*. New York, NY: Routledge.
Irwin, J., and Cressey, D. (1962) Thieves, convicts and the inmate culture. *Social Problems*, 10 (1), 142–155.
Irwin, J., and Owen, B. (2005) Harm and the contemporary prison. In Liebling A., and Maruna S. (Eds.), *The Effects of Imprisonment*. Cullompton Devon: Willan Publishing, 94–117.
Jacquelyn, B. F., and Gill, A. E. (2015) The negotiated identities of long-term inmates: Breaking the chains of problematic integration. *Western Journal of Communication*, 7 (5), 513–532.
Jamieson, R. and Grounds, B. (2005) Release and adjustment: Perspectives from studies of wrongly convicted and politically motivated prisoners. In Liebling, A. and Maruna, S. (Eds.), *The Effects of Imprisonment*. Cullompton Devon: Willan Publishing, 33–65.
Jarvis, D., Shaw, J., and Lovell, T. (2022) Service user experiences of a psychologically enhanced resettlement service [PERS] in an English open prison. *Journal of Forensic Practice*, 24 (3), 241–252.
Jewkes, Y. (2002) *Captive Audience: Media, Masculinity and Power in Prisons*. Cullompton: Willan Publishing.
Jewkes, Y. (2005) Men behind bars: Doing masculinity as an adaptation to imprisonment. *Men and Masculinities*, 8, 44–63.

Kazemian, L. (2019) *Positive Growth and Redemption in Prison: Finding Light Behind Bars and Beyond*. Abingdon, Oxon: Routledge Publishing.

Klaus, W. (2023) Snares and pains, or what stands in the path to desistance from crime. In Klaud W., Rzeplińska I., and Woźniakowska-Fajst D. (Eds.), *Criminal Careers*. Oxon: Routledge, 221–278.

Lapornik, R., Lehofer, M., Moser, M., Pump, G., Egner, S., Posch, C., Hilderbrandt, G., and Zapotoczky, H., G. (1996) Long term imprisonment leads to cognitive impairment. *Forensic Science International*, 82, 121–127.

LeBel, T. P. (2008) Perceptions of and responses to stigma. *Sociology Compass*, 2 (2), 409–432.

LeBel, T. P. (2012) Invisible stripes? Formerly incarcerated persons' perceptions of stigma. *Deviant Behavior*, 33, 89–107.

LeBel, T. P. (2020) Strengths-based re-entry and resettlement. In Ugwudike, P., Graham, H., McNeill, F., Raynor, P., Taxman, F.S., and Trotter, C. (Eds.), *The Routledge Companion to Rehabilitative Work in Criminal Justice*. London: Routledge, pp. 583–594.

LeBel, P. T., Burnett, R., Maruna, S., and Bushway, S. (2008) The 'Chicken and Egg' of subjective and social factors in desistance from crime. *European Journal of Criminology*, 5 (2), 131–195.

Leigey, E. M., and Ryder, A. M. (2014) The pains of permanent imprisonment: Examining perception of confinement among older life without parole inmates. *International Journal of Offender Therapy and Comparative Criminology*, 59(7) 1–17.

Liem, M. (2016) *After Life Imprisonment*. New York, NY: New York University Press.

Liem, M. (2017) Desistance after life imprisonment. In Hart, L. and van Ginneken, E. J. C. (Eds.), *New Perspectives on Desistance: Theoretical and Empirical Developments*. Palgrave: London, 85–110.

Liem, M., and Garcin, J. (2014) Post-release success among paroled lifers. *Laws*, 3 (4), 798–823.

Liem, M., and Kunst, M. (2013) Is there a recognizable post-incarceration syndrome among released "lifers"? *International Journal of Law and Psychiatry*, 46 (3–4), 333–337.

Lloyd, A. (2019) *The Harms of Work: An Ultra-Realist Account of the Service Economy*. Bristol: Bristol University Press.

Lloyd, A. (2018b) Serving up harm: Systemic violence, transitions to adulthood and the service economy. In Boukli, A. and Kotze, J. (Eds.), *Zemiology: Reconnecting Crime and Social Harm*. Cham, Switzerland: Palgrave MacMillan, 245–264.

Maruna, S. (2001) *Making Good: How Ex-Convicts Reform Rebuild Their Lives*. Washington, DC: American Psychological Association.

Maruna, S., and Immarigeon, R. (Eds.) (2011) *After Crime and Punishment: Pathways to Offender Reintegration*. Abingdon, Oxon: Routledge.

May, H. (2000) "Murderers' relatives": Managing stigma, negotiating identity. *Journal of Contemporary Ethnography*, 29 (2), 198–221.

McAlister, M. (2008) Killing off The shadow: The role of projective identification in murderous acts. In Doctor R. (Eds). *Murder: A Psychotherapeutic Investigation*. London: Karnak Books Ltd, 65–78.

McNeill, F. (2018) Mass supervision, misrecognition and the 'Malopticon'. *Punishment and Society*, 21 (2), 207–230.

McNeill, F. (2019) *Pervasive Punishment: Making Sense of Mass Supervision*. Bingley, UK: Emerald Publishing.

McVicar, J. (1974) *McVicar by Himself*. London: Hutchinson Publishing.

Motz, A. (2008). Women who kill: When fantasy becomes reality. In Doctor R. (Eds.), *Murder: A Psychotherapeutic Investigation*. London: Karnack Books Ltd, 51–64.

Nugent, B., and Schinkel, M. (2016) The pains of desistance. *Criminology and Criminal Justice*, 16 (5), 568–584.
Papanastassiou, M., Waldron, G., Boyle, J., and Chesterman, P. L. (2004) Post-traumatic stress disorder in mentally ill perpetrators of homicide. *The Journal of Forensic Psychiatry & Psychology*, 15, 66–75.
Parker, T. (1990) *Life After Life – Interviews with Twelve Murderers*. London: Secker and Warburg.
Paterline, A. B., and Petersen, M., D. (1999) Structural and social psychological determinants of prisonization. *Journal of Criminal Justice*, 27 (5), 427–441.
Petersilia, J. (2003) *When Prisoners Come Home: Parole and Prisoner Reentry*. London: Oxford University Press.
Porporino, J. F., and Zamble, E. (1984) Coping with imprisonment. *Canadian Journal of Criminology*, 26, 403–421.
Presdee, M. (2004) Cultural criminology: The long and winding road. *Theoretical Criminology*, 8 (3), 275–285.
Rasch, W. (1981) The effects of indeterminate detention: A study of men sentenced to life imprisonment. *International Journal of Law and Psychiatry*, 4, 417–431.
Rehabilitation of Offenders Act (1974), c. 53. Available at https://www.legislation.gov.uk/ukpga/1974/53 [accessed 15 August 2024].
Rennie, A., and Crewe, B. (2023) 'Tightness', autonomy, and release: The anticipated pains of release and life licensing. *The British Journal of Criminology*, 63, 184–200.
Richards, B. (1978) The experience of long-term imprisonment. *British Journal of Criminology*, 18 (2), 162–169.
Rusu, D.G. (2023) The Clink prison-based restaurant: Brixton, London, UK. In Lynes, A., Kelly C., Treadwell J. (Eds.), *50 Dark Destinations: Crime and Contemporary Tourism*. Bristol: Policy Press, 98–103.
Sapsford, R. J. (1983) *Life Sentence Prisoners: Research, Response and Change*. Milton Keynes: Open University Press.
Sapsford, R. J. (1978) Life-sentence prisoners: Psychological changes during sentence. *British Journal of Criminology*, 18 (2), 128–145.
Schmid, J. T., and Jones S, R. (1991) Suspended identity: Identity transformation in a maximum-security prison. *Symbolic Interaction*, 14 (4), 415–432.
Shammas, V. L. (2014) The pains of freedom: Assessing the ambiguity of Scandinavian penal exceptionalism on Norway's Prison Island. *Punishment & Society*, 16 (1), 104–123.
Sheppard, A., and Ricciardelli, R. (2020) Employment after prison: Navigating conditions of precarity and stigma. *European Journal of Probation*, 12 (1), 34–52.
Sluga, W. (1977) *Treatment of Long-Term Prisoners Considered from the Medical and Psychiatric Point of View*. Strasbourg: Council of Europe.
Sykes, G. (1958) *The Society of Captives: A Study of a Maximum-Security Prison*. Princeton, NJ: Princeton University Press.
Thomas, W. C. (1977) Theoretical perspectives on prisonization: A comparison of the importation and deprivation model. *The Journal of Criminal Law & Criminology*, 68 (1), 135–145.
Thomas, C., Adshead, G., and Mezey, G. (1994) Case report: Traumatic responses to child murder. *The Journal of Forensic Psychiatry*, 5 (1), 168–176.
van Ginneken, E. J. C. (2016) Making sense of imprisonment: Narratives of posttraumatic growth among female prisoners. *International Journal of Offender Therapy and Comparative Criminology*, 60 (2), 208–227.
Vanhooren, S., Leijssen, M., and Dezutter, J. (2018) Coping strategies and post-traumatic growth in prison. *The Prison Journal*, 98 (2), 1–20.
Walters, G. D. (2003) Changes in criminal thinking and identity in novice and experienced inmates: Prisonization revisited. *Criminal Justice and Behaviour*, 30 (4), 399–421.

Warr, J. (2016) The prisoner inside and out. In Jewkes, Y., Bennett, J., and Crewe, B. (Eds.), *Handbook on Prisons*, 2nd edition. Oxon Abingdon: Routledge, 586–604.

Warr, J. (2019) 'Always gotta be two mans': Lifers, risk, rehabilitation, and narrative labour. *Punishment and Society*, 22 (1), 28–47.

Weaver, A. (2008) *So, You Think You Know Me?*. Sheffield: Waterside Press LTD.

Wheeler, S. (1961) Socialization in correctional communities. *American Sociological Review*, 26 (5), 697–712.

Wieviorka, M. (2009) *Violence: A New Approach*. London: SAGE Publications.

Winlow, S. and Hall, S. (2006) *Violent Night*. Oxford: Berg.

Winlow, S. and Hall, S. (2013) *Rethinking Social Exclusion: The End of the Social?* London: SAGE.

Winlow, S., and Hall, S. (2016) Realist criminology and its discontents. *International Journal for Crime, Justice, and Social Democracy*, 5 (3), 80–94.

Wright, S., Crewe, B., and Hulley, S. (2017) Suppression, denial, sublimation: Defending against the initial pains of very long sentences. *Theoretical Criminology*, 21 (2), 225–246.

Wright, S., Hulley, S., and Crewe, B. (2023) Trajectories of hope/lessness among men and women in the late stage of a life sentence. *Theoretical Criminology*, 27 (1), 66–84.

Young, J. (2011) *The Criminological Imagination*. Cambridge: Polity Press.

Zamble, E. (1992) Behavior and adaptation in long-term prison inmates: Descriptive longitudinal results. *Criminal Justice and Behavior*, 19 (4), 409–425.

Zamble, E., and Porporino, F. (1990) Coping, imprisonment, and rehabilitation: Some data and their implications. *Criminal Justice and Behaviour*, 17 (1), 53–70.

4 Initial release transition
Family formation, employment

The first few years after release are crucial in redefining the identities of released ex-prisoners (Leverentz, 2014). At this critical time in their re-entry experience, mandatory lifers may have the opportunity to reflect on who they are and to contemplate on who they want to become. Leaving prison meant that the men had been given the task to resettle, socially reintegrate, and reconstruct their identities; this includes re-establishing ties, relationships, and even learning new social roles (McNeill, 2012; Western et al., 2015). As explored in Chapter 2, such resettlement-led goals may be complicated for mandatory lifers. Long-term imprisonment affects patterns of resettlement in ways explored in depth in Chapter 3. Naturally then, as Griffin and Healy (2019: 134) remarked, "life sentence prisoners are rarely in a position to demonstrate stable and prosocial family support, accommodation or employment". Homicide offenders were found to rarely resume ties with their children after such lengthy sentences (Liem, 2016; Liem and Garcin, 2014; Liem and Weggemans, 2018). Moreover, long-term offenders tend to cut ties with their families to save them from the humiliation of the visitation process – a coping strategy that has been named 'hard timing' (Kotova, 2020). Others attempt to safeguard against anxieties relating to infidelity (Crewe, Hulley, and Wright, 2020). This observed trend in specialist literature is worrying given that early release success is cumulative in predicting successful reintegration of ex-offenders (Western, 2018; Western et al., 2015).

This chapter will explore the ways in which the men had mobilised resettlement capital (Albertson and Hall, 2020; Best, Musgrove, and Hall, 2018; Best, 2019) to scaffold into normative/pro-social roles post-release. Here, the chapter draws from the men's thick description of their experiences to focus on two of the most important 'correlates of desistance' (Farrall, 2011), namely family formation and employment status, and the importance that these two social institutions played in the 'role transition' of the men from detained mandatory lifers to 'responsible citizens' (Uggen, Manza, and Behrens, 2011). In contrast to much research on homicide offenders, the chapter provides evidence that offenders' families are a crucial steppingstone to the development of capital that ultimately assists in the construction of pro-social identities post-release.

DOI: 10.4324/9781003415640-4

Timing is everything: Resuming family ties

Once released, the men felt severely disconnected from the outside world. Contrary to expectations, for most of the men family was all they had. Raul captures this sense of disconnection in our first interview, whilst recounting his initial conversation with his probation officer:

Raul: So, I was staying in a hostel in [part of London], and I was having to have my family coming out of this borough to see me, and when the parole board said to me ... oh where do you want to go next? I want to go home. What am I supposed to do? I was 17 when you put me away, I've got no life outside. This is my everything, my home, my school, everything like that so they said OK, fine, we're knocking you back for 1 year, start doing your home leaves to [redacted] and we will see how that goes. I did that for 1 year, and I came back here, and I fought with everything that I had to come back here. Sometimes I feel maybe I shouldn't have cuz ... this area is no good, you know what I mean, it's hardly people around here, yes, it is home, you love home, but I don't know, sometimes I feel suffocated here (Raul, first interview).

Raul lacked the narrative resources to perform an identity which was divorced from his 'prison self'. Prison was all he had at that stage, with one exception: he still had his family (father and sister). This fortunate story is one at odds with that of the majority of lifers in the United Kingdom (Cohen and Taylor, 1972; Flanagan, 1980), and Raul's family acted as a steppingstone to his development and construction of pro-social identities on release. Living with his father meant that he secured long-term accommodation at an 'affordable rate' and achieved a sense of security on his return. He continued to wrestle with thoughts of moving out for almost three more years but ended up accepting that his stay is founded upon a realistic analysis of financial benefits and mutual aid. In our third interview Raul had renounced any ideas of moving out:

Raul: I'm gonna stay here cuz obviously my dad's here, my family home's here, my family is around here, unless something amazing comes up ... but even that probation has to go through all of that they wouldn't let me move just like that so yah .... I try not to think about stuff like that (Raul, third interview).

Compared to Raul who maintained a good relationship with his original family throughout the sentence, Peter had resuscitated his relationship with his mother late in his life sentence. The therapy at HMP Grendon influenced his decision to 'excavate' a set of feelings he had, for a long time, repressed. Reconnected, Peter managed to reconstruct his ties with his mother and ended up living with her for well over one year before moving in with his wife. The couple's relationship with the mother has since progressively deteriorated. In our third interview, both Peter and Jasmine complained that the mother-in-law (Peter's mother) was not doing enough for her grandchild, and their relationship had completely ended by our fourth interview.

Peter: To be honest mate, it has gone downhill a bit. You know she is a ... she is not really doing anything man. We call her 'nanny Facebook' ... you know. With the kids and me and Jasmine (pseudonym) because you know, I got 3 children now, not only one, but situation also ... and (unclear) and she just doesn't engage. Last time I spoke to her I said I'll ring you as much as you ring me ... yeah? And I haven't really heard much from her since. She sent Liam a message on Facebook on his birthday and that's it ... no card in the post or fucking ... nothing for her grandson ... that's not good enough, you know, I am not having him forced to raise defence mechanisms around certain people because as I said, you know, you know why, I am weary who Liam is going to be around, who he is going to learn things from, you know .... (Peter, third interview).

What transpires in the story above is Peter's transformation from a dependent person to someone upon whom others depend on. The new home environment offered Peter the narrative resources to construct the story of a protective father who would defend his child from anyone, including from his own mother. At this point in time Peter had made an important 'leap' in developing a pro-social identity, and his mothers' initial instrumental support was paramount in the journey from a 'recently released prisoner' to a 'family man' (Laub and Sampson, 2003). By this time, around two and a half years after his release, Peter would use any potential occasion to showcase to me his little boy (the other two children are Jasmine's), his garden, and his dog over our video calls; he portrayed living in a stereotypically happy family life.

With few exceptions that focused on the re-entry experience of long-term prisoners (Boman and Mowen, 2017; Taylor, 2016) most existing research did not seriously consider participants' length of prison sentences (short term/long term) in their longitudinal analyses. Similar findings have been reported in the literature. For example, nearly all of Western's (2018) younger men interviewed in Boston lived with family members in their first few months of release. These studies have used short-term offenders as their samples and therefore has been suggested that their findings could not be possibly applied to lifer populations (Liem, 2016; Liem and Garcin, 2014) but this book provides evidence to the contrary. In some cases, family members went to the extent of introducing the men to potential romantic partners. Overall, these relationships provided the necessary social capital so that the men could practise social roles and acquire the narrative resources to reconstruct their identities and maintain desistance from crime (Albertson, 2021; Fox, 2016).

Different types of family can provide diverse types of social capital (Mills and Codd, 2008). For example, Jacob met his wife through his mother whilst he was still serving time in a high security prison. As an indeterminate sentenced prisoner, Jacob did not have a definitive date for his release, but the couple decided to marry anyway.

Jacob: My mother knew my wife and she was having a lot of difficulties she was having a lot of emotional difficulties and she was just in a mess and my mom just thought that I may be able to help her and she put her in touch with me and she came to see me and we corresponded a bit, we met and we just became friends and ah, so we considered we talked and we just had so much in common and became really good friends ah, and … then we realised that you know we were in love with each other and it seemed easy to get married in prison. She was a Muslim who converted to Christianity she wasn't a church of England uhm, member and we got permission, and we got married in a local church, we are still married 24 years later (Jacob, only interview).

In addition to the obvious instrumental benefits of providing a roof over his head once he was released, Jacob's wife represented his main pillar of emotional support for the remainder of his sentence. This was important for his desistance journey. Ex-prisoners' families are paramount in providing instrumental support (Mowen, Stansfield, and Boman, 2019; Western et al., 2015) and protection against recidivism (Boman and Mowen, 2017; Duwe and Clark, 2013). She also assisted him in developing resilience to the realities of his incarceration (Markson et al., 2015; Naser and La Vigne, 2006; Taylor, 2016).

Jacob: She (his wife) persuaded me to start participating. Gave me the presence of mind to believe that actually I could get out of prison and have a life, because I never could actually … I got to the point I accepted the fact that I'd probably wasn't going to get out of prison … and … somehow the friendship she persuaded me that I really could and so I began participating so in 1999 I was released after 20, 20 ½ years, it was quite a journey through the whole thing … there was a pointlessness, it's a little bit like some doctors, they don't look at you as a patient, they look at you as a disease and the prison system very much looks at you as a criminal, as a malformed individual (Jacob, only interview).

Not all participants met their romantic partners via their families. For example, Richard met his wife through the religious services at the

74 Life Beyond Murder

maximum-security prison where he was held. The relationship started as a friendship but soon transformed into a romantic one and culminated in their marriage once Richard was released. Their daughter was born around the same time.

Richard: I married in London Victoria, because my wife is from London, and she got to know me when I was in prison you know, and, one of the procedures with her was that my probation officer, cuz we got married quite early after I got released, had to sit there with her and tell her the full story you know, to make sure that she, she knew, so she went through that process as well, but she knew before anyway, because she got to know me when I was in [maximum security prison], just as another visitor, you know, because she is from the church, and she visited with the Church and we built a relationship there so I would say that probably the highest point after release is probably the birth of my daughter (Richard, first interview).

As evidenced, community-level social capital (Fox, 2016) characteristic of faith services (O'Connor and Bogue, 2010) turned out as critical in assisting Richard to meet new people and develop the narrative resources to construct pro-social identities (of husband and father) immediately after release. Also, as Richard remarked, one of the benefits of constructing 'resettlement capital' whilst in prison meant that he eluded the Caudine forks of stigma negotiation and family formation on release. Nathaniel met his wife during a release on temporary licence (ROTI):

Nathaniel: I was on a home leave and working out, so more or less out anyway, so I think I still was classed as a prisoner, but then obviously when I was released, we carried it on. I was on a home leave, and … obviously we just stuck up, and carried on … then obviously before, whilst I was out in the three months stage but then I was recalled obviously, uhm so I missed all the, like … the scans, the birth of my son but then obviously my re-release I had to go to the hostel, but it was still there, go home every day see my missus and the baby and I haven't missed a day since (Nathaniel, first interview).

These experiences echo Western's (2018) point that early release success is cumulative and that the first few months of release are crucial in predicting future success. In this context, the smooth transition into 'family men identities' meant that the participants had a base upon which to build and further hook pro-social identities in the future. Also, developing prison-based romantic relationships acted as an effective stigma management strategy as some of the men did not have to be concerned about disclosing or concealing their past (LeBel, 2008) to potential romantic partners after release. This finding contradicts similar research conducted in the United States. For example, Liem and Garcin (2014) found that for homicide offenders in Massachusetts social ties did not act as pro-social forces post-release; in fact, the opposite was true. Interviewees in their sample had provided several reasons for avoiding becoming involved with romantic relationships or felt that they were playing 'catch-up' when they did.

This stands in tension with the findings discussed in this chapter. This finding may be representative of fundamentally different resources available in UK prisons compared to some in the United States. A further explanation lies in the timing of building such relationships which was not considered in the American study. Had participants in this research explored the prospect of engaging in romantic partnerships or resuming ties with families strictly after their release, their experiences may well have been fundamentally different. Furthermore, the cases above contradict research which maintains a 'purist approach to prisoners' families as providers of either instrumental, interactional, or emotional support (Mowen et al., 2019). In fact, these domains of support interact in more sophisticated ways as it was evidenced above. Instrumental support through accommodation was seldom separated from emotional support in this sample of mandatory lifers. For example, Raul has been receiving support from his father and sister since he got sentenced for murder. I asked him whether he felt supported by the family on every occasion we had.

Raul: Yes, of course they did, they supported me throughout the whole thing, after release they're there for you, they do so much for you, make up for everything you missed, showing you new places, tell you about things ... and yeah ... family is everything (Raul, first interview).

Raul: It is a cultural thing, everybody kind of knows that Asian families are quite tight knit and that but then on the flipside there are other families that wouldn't have stood by me after what I did, you know what I mean? But with my family thank God, they were always supportive of me ... they didn't condone what I did, but they do know that obviously I recognise the wrong that I did, and they were willing to just get me through what I had to get through (Raul, second interview).

Whilst he was consistent in his answers, he introduced the importance of culture in family relationships in our second interview, around 2.5 years after release. Raul conceptualised his family's non-conditional support through the cultural lenses of his Asian cultural membership. Calverley (2013, 2019) highlighted that UK desisters from different ethnic and cultural backgrounds (Indian, Bangladeshi, and Black and dual heritage) vary in available social capital post-release. Although the 'family' was significant in all the men's movement away from crime, there were some observed cultural variations in the ways in which the social institution resonated in participants' lives. Both Indian and Bangladeshi families were critical in providing a strong foundation in encouraging a re-orientation towards the family as available hooks for change (Giordano, Cerkovich, and Rudolph, 2002) on release. Bangladeshi families were forgiving and supportive of their children, perhaps resembling their wider religious beliefs. Raul recounted that one of the first few things that his family offered him when he was imprisoned was a Qur'an and a praying mat. Released, and now that he was spending more time with his family meant that Raul could take the 'family role' more seriously. One year after our first interview, a pro-social identity had become evident (Giordano et al., 2002) as Raul started caring for his newly born nephew. This further cemented his family man identity:

Raul: My nephew has now been born in August, so it's my sisters' son. I spend a lot of time with him. Playing with him staying there doing a lot of things that I never thought I would do, like you know bathe him, change his nappies, feed him, that sort of thing, then I juggle that with a lot of work as well, not being as complacent as I was before, ok I am employed that's it just go to work every day that's it, now I am just trying to do as much as I can in case another lockdown comes or I lose my job again, you never know what's gonna happen nowadays, uhm, still seeing probation and that as well, and yeah that's about it really (Raul, third interview).

Evidently, Raul's family had been foundational to the development of pro-social identities post-release. He had been accepted to assume a clear role within the wider family structure despite his failed efforts to build a family of his own. This finding echoes the experiences of Bangladeshi participants in Calverley's (2013; 2019: 85) study who structured their time through "childcare and running errands for family members". Further, the finding echoes Farrall's (2019) call for research to take the role of culture in the distance process more seriously.

Participants in this sample were able to use their families as informal mechanisms of support for the construction of pro-social selves post-release. What seemed to be important was the timing of building such vital ties. The most 'successful' lifers have reconnected with their families whilst still in prison, which meant that they could use their instrumental and emotional support immediately before and after release. Nevertheless, such experiences of positive familial relationships post-release are not reflective of the general experiences of long-term offenders and indeterminate sentenced individuals in the United Kingdom (Kotova, 2020).

In some cases, families can exacerbate release stress or carry criminogenic potential (Farrington, Barnes, and Lambert, 1996). For this reason, Kay (2022) has conceptualised desistance as the reorientation of a type of capital which sustains crime (anti-social capital) to one which imbues pro-social capital.

Furthermore, developments in desistance research called for a more systematic attention paid to social capital as supporting desistance (Bottoms and Shapland, 2011; McNeill et al., 2012; Uggen, Manza, and Behrens, 2011). These authors, as Albertson (2021) summarised cite a lack of access to pro-social capital as hampering the desistance process. This analysis adds to this important conversation and highlights the ways in which mandatory lifers mobilised bonding, bridging, and resettlement capital to ensure a smooth scaffold into further pro-social post-release. Further, the chapter's findings reiterate Lord Farmer's (2017) report that the criminal justice system must prepare the necessary steps for long-term offenders' family's involvement in their resettlement planning.

Becoming working men: Employment as resettlement capital

Many studies have focused on how ex-offenders and homicide offenders particularly are denied employment based on the 'questionable nature of their moral character' and (in)existent work-experience consequence of their imprisonment (Liem, 2016, 2017; Liem and Garcin, 2014; Petersilia, 2003). As discussed in Chapter 3, experiencing stigma is one of the most significant pains of re-entry for ex-offenders, rendering reintegration a fundamentally difficult quest (LeBel, 2012). Homicide offenders and indeterminate sentenced ex-prisoners are no exception to this axion; to the contrary, these populations were found to experience exacerbated levels of stigma and stress due to unemployment history and the severity of their crime (Atherton and Buck, 2021; Liem, 2016; Liem and Garcin, 2014 for an UK review). Nevertheless, for some of the men, prison assisted with finding work outside, which in turn helped with their early re-entry experience.

Richard managed to secure a job with NACRO, a charity which is committed to the prevention of reoffending of ex-prisoners, during his imprisonment and was then offered a permanent position immediately after release. This allowed him to use his stigmatised past as an asset rather than a liability (Maruna and LeBel, 2015) when he was released. I asked Richard whether he ever feels stigmatised at work.

Richard: No, because, I suppose, it is hard for me to see, because I haven't applied for many jobs, cuz I've been in this job since 20 years this year, working for [organisation], I've been working for [broadcaster] for 15 years, but maybe if I'd apply for different jobs, probably I'd find out, aaa, so the barriers, but it hasn't been a massive barrier for me because I have been in stable jobs you know (Richard, first interview).

As evidenced above, for Richard, this initial role was a crucial steppingstone to his professional development, as it provided the social capital needed to further progress in the job market. He was then able to secure work experience and part time employment with a well-known broadcasting network and has since been working in both roles. Interestingly, Richard rated working for the broadcaster as a salient component to his new sense of identity. He was offered the job after having been observed helping someone 'who was on air' delivering a gospel programme for several years. After being offered a job, Richard felt that it was his duty to disclose his past.

Richard: Because they observed me for so long, maybe 18 months to 2 years doing work experience, they said, they could see I was a stable person now so they gave me the job; so I have had this job, part time job now, for about 15 years with the [redacted] uhm, and achievements there help me to flourish and help me sort of to look at things positively, the highlights of that particular job was that I interviewed the prime-minister, 4 years ago, David Cameron, so for me, personally, for the average person at the [redacted] is probably not much of a special thing, but for me who has served a life sentence, and been through very dark places like [maximum security prison], etc., uhm, it was kind of a big thing for me, and still is, working for the [redacted] is a privilege, and to run an organisation as well. So, I would say that is the reason I was reasonably successful after release ... you know? (Richard, first interview).

The story above contradicts Liem's (2016, 2017) and Liem and Garcin's (2014) finding that homicide offenders' employment is successful as long it provides ex-offenders with 'professional ex-criminal', generative roles. To the contrary, as Richard remarked, it is expected of individuals such as himself to land in helper roles (Brown, 1991; White, 2000) where utilising criminal pasts is a significant part of the job description. In contrast, working for a 'prestigious' media institution was seen as fundamentally at odds and in contradiction with his stigmatised identity. This role publicly validated Richard as a 'normal person', divorced from his criminal past. The quality of the individuals he has been associating with at the new role is important in validating his pro-social work identity (Wright and Cullen, 2004). Further, following King's (2014) point, Richard reminds us that it is the subjective attachment of the individual to the job rather than the job in and of itself which matters to identity commitments and ultimately, to identity desistance. It is noteworthy that Richard had disclosed his past to his employers only after he had already been observed for a long time. A similar strategy had been identified by Harding (2003) where ex-offenders disclosed information strategically, at the most opportune moment to employers. Many strategized to work as volunteers or in low-level jobs which did not necessitate thorough background checks to present themselves as worthy first and then progress into more senior roles.

Richard evidenced that contrary to the belief that family ties act as a bridge to the job market (Berg and Huebner, 2011), these two life dimensions operate in a dialectical fashion. Job stability is integral to a stable life and a stable family and both elements are important when considering entering long-term commitments with romantic partners. Employment also provides the economic resources to facilitate family formation (Lichter et al., 1991 in King, Massoglia, and MacMillan, 2007).

Richard: I suppose it works both ways really, having a job, because when I first got released uhm I started straight away, going into work, because I got employed by NACRO, and whilst I was going on day release from open prison and I was doing day release at NACRO and when I had the parole, the manager uhm, offered me a job, so I went straight into a job after that and I mean when my wife looks at me as an individual, having employment helped me: 'at least he is settled'. And also, it helped me with my licence as well because as soon as I got a job, I didn't have to see the probation service every week at that point, it was only once a month, so that was a sign of stability. Both the job and the marriage helped with stability (Richard, second interview).

Not all participants found viable work whilst still inside prison, but their prison-based contacts were relevant in finding some stability post-release. For example, Jacob used his prison-based social capital to find a few sporadic jobs immediately after being granted parole. These jobs had simply 'landed on his lap' – handed to him by some of his old prison associates. He then managed to build a successful IT company. Jacob's approach to employment represented an innovative strategy to the job market: by building his own business he managed to deflect attention from his own identity and project it onto his business.

Jacob: I've been incredibly fortunate in the, my transition, because I was able to have income and substantive income I was able to build a life which a lot of guys in the same position as me don't have these opportunities or those doors open for them or they don't have the wherewithal to start their own business and I knew that nobody would employ me, I knew that the only job I would get would be a meaningful job that that, because I would have to declare my prison history that you know, and who is going to employ somebody like me? You know? It was sadly enough to realise that if I didn't do it myself then it would I wouldn't be able to so .... that's the premise upon which I started this journey out of the prison [...], I've been fortunate because I've managed to get this far without a big sign over my head saying: 'killer', you know. There is no doubt even now I wouldn't be in the same position I am today (Jacob, only interview).

The passage above displays Jacob's self-sufficient and entrepreneurial 'character' which 'rescued' him from the potential bleak prospects of his own release. Jacob's stigma concealment strategy (LeBel, 2008) is inextricably linked to issues around exposure. Not having to apply to a multitude of jobs meant that he walked without "a big sign over [his] head saying 'killer'". He learnt early on that disclosing his past would present a set of challenges. Nevertheless, running his own business meant that he did not have to accommodate his strategy to the 'moral aspirations' of the job market.

As evidenced above, a smooth role transition into working identities was secured by either using stigmatised identities as assets as Richard has done through working with offenders, or by innovating in their approach to the job market as it was in Jacob's case. Admittedly, these results need to be considered with care and not divorced from their associated historical contexts. Jacob has been released over 25 years ago when the economic landscape in Britain was significantly different to the present. Nevertheless, the finding reinforces a criminological truism that social ties are important to prisoners who seek employment upon release (Granovetter, 2001 in Duwe and Clark, 2013; Kotova, 2020). This section evidenced that building pro-social ties in prison may act as a potential 'bridge' to the job market for long-term offenders. Nevertheless, not all five participants managed to build such useful connections during their imprisonment.

A haunting past: Raul

Raul had been released for 18 months at the time of our first interview. He had received all his gym qualifications in prison and despite his history he was given the chance to work at a local gym in East London soon after his release.

Raul: You apply for a job, when you've just been in prison for 12 years for having killed somebody, nobody's looking to hire you, I was lucky cuz I got all my gym qualifications when I was in prison and now I am a qualified personal trainer, I was doing a sports science degree at university, the guy at my local gym decided to give me a chance, he said look: you made a mistake when you were young, I don't believe that is who you are now, and he gave me a chance you know, but it's rare to find people like that (Raul, first interview).

To further understand the ways in which Raul negotiated new relationships, I then asked about his disclosure strategy. It turned out that Raul was selectively disclosing his past depending on social situations.

Dan: Do you tell people about your crime? When you meet new people?
Raul: It all comes down to the type of person you are, if you have that respect about you, that dignity about you, you don't want to sit there and lie and spit a bunch of lies, because that always comes

back to haunt you. So, I gauge the person that I'm talking to, and if I find that that's a good person, a respectful person, I've got no problem telling them, if it has any bearing on our relationship, so for example, the guy who was going to give me a job, I thought, out of the goodness of his heart, he is willing to give me a job, so, I should return that favour by being completely honest with him, rather than later down the line it comes out that I lied to him. And he's thinking, look, I gave you a chance and this is what you did. I'm not that guy you know, I'd rather be straight, upfront, this is who I am, but then, on the flipside, you don't go around advertising, you don't go about boasting, you know what I mean, kids do that, wanna be gangsters, they do that, "oh I've been in prison, I've done this I've done that", you know what I mean, it shocks people, and it worries people for a week or a month or so, and then afterwards, they start looking at me differently, do you know what I mean, so yeah (Raul, first interview).

Raul's cold analysis evidenced how mandatory lifers need to 'strike the right balance' between disclosing and concealing their past to avoid being discredited and denied opportunities after release. The leitmotif of our first interview had been represented by his sentiments of feeling 'blocked'. Raul repeatedly told me that he needed to further progress within the job market but was unable to do so due to his stigmatised past.

Raul: So I went for a job interview in Nuffield in [redacted], and uhm had the talking interview, like the face to face interview, guy loved me, then I moved to the physical interview where I had to be on the gym floor show particular exercises, and how I would react in certain situations, etc., and yeah, the guy pretty much loved me and said yeah I can't wait to see you start and that and just as I was leaving, he said yeah, uhm once the CRB (criminal record background) check is done uhm that will be it really, that shouldn't be a problem and that ... and ... yeah. The minute he said CRB check I kind of knew what was going to happen, because he didn't ask me in the end if I had anything to disclose or anything like that, so I know that you are not obliged to say unless they ask you. Yeah, once the CRB came through, he just made this story about how many others have done better than me on the physical, even though at the interview he told me that I done the best that he'd seen, so yeah, pretty much knew where he was trying to get, yeah ... I think Nuffield and these kinds of places because the level of clients they have, rich people, and stuff like that, if it is found out that they were working with an ex convicted murderer you know, people could have issues with that even though it doesn't affect them in the slightest way (Raul, first interview).

The story betrays a tension which Raul needed to navigate because of his stigma (Goffman, 1963). During situations as the one narrated, Raul has the chance to glimpse into a 'life that could have been', but which fades from reality as his 'master status' (Becker, 1963) overrides his professional qualities (Harding, 2003). Raul's experience echoes that of a multitude of participants in criminological and sociological research. Pager and Quillian (2005) found that despite initial declarative openness to hire applicants with criminal records, employers hardly ever follow through. In the United Kingdom, Atherton and Buck (2021) found that employers were especially concerned about hiring ex-prisoners who they branded as part of the 'TSM' (Terrorism, Sex Offenders and Murderers). Although murderers were more likely to be employed than the other two groups, they were still reluctant to share 'courtesy stigma' (Goffman, 1963) and to transfer image with them (Wolfensberger, 1999 in Atherton and Buck, 2021). Raul remarked that alliances with convicted murderers may not be representative of the marketing strategy of luxurious gym brands. In fact, research evidenced that employers in other jurisdictions are interested in both the severity as well as the timing of an offence when analysing potential employment (Lageson, Vuolo, and Uggen, 2015; Vuolo, Lageson, and Uggen, 2017 for an American context) and this may well have applied to Raul.

For example, a study based on surveyed businesses within 12 Texas zip-codes found that 80% of surveyed employers would not hire someone who has been to prison for a violent offense (they were more likely to employ individuals who committed 'minor' crimes, rather than violent crimes such as sexual assault and murder; also see Cerda, Stenstrom, and Curtis, 2015). Interestingly, the type of murder committed seemed significant to the employers when deciding to hire. For example, in Atherton and Bucks' (2021) study, domestic murder was constructed as a 'one-off moment of madness' and a 'crime of passion' and therefore was not perceived as abominable as other types of serious, persistent offences.

Raul was made redundant during the COVID-19 Pandemic. In our last interview, four years after we have met, Raul was happy to share that he had a few career advancements within the fitness industry, partly thanks to his increasing social capital. He was now a manager at a small gym in West London. Nevertheless, despite this progress, he was still disappointed in his romantic life which was still unfulfilling. He reminded me of one of the first conversations we had about the difficulties he encountered in finding a romantic partner willing to accept him.

Raul: It's a massive hurdle (meeting someone), you meet a girl, you tell her what you went away for, you tell her, you got to see if she is ok with it, and if she is ok with it, you got a bigger problem, is her family gonna be ok with it? Cuz she may love you and be willing to accept that, but her family are thinking, do I really want to give my daughter to a guy who killed someone; regardless of what the circumstances are, and you got to try and get over that hurdle, uhm, yes, it's just a lot of hurdles. Everything you do, what you did never leaves you, it impacts everything you know what I mean. There is no moment of everyday when you forget, you know what I mean (Raul first interview).

The passage above betrays Raul's experience of a complicated, double stigma. Not only does he need to be accepted by a potential partner, but also by her family (her father). This type of 'elimination tournament' ensures that his prospect of success is minimal. Also, Raul's fears are related to the totalising effects of the murderer's stigma which denies him any trace of humanism and human complexity. For example, the 'potential father' in the scenario above does not have to process a difficult decision: they simply need to decide whether they "want to give (sic) [their] daughters to a guy who killed someone" or not. I asked Raul whether he still felt the pressure to get married one year later:

Raul: Yeah, that's there every day because obviously I am getting older, but like I said, coming out and seeing how people are these days, girls are no different, they have changed a lot as well, do you know what I mean, they are not as worried about preserving their chastity, or their self-respect before, (unclear) they are very out there now and that's really not something that you would like to build a life with, rise kids with, so it's hard to find somebody with the same drives as yourself (Raul, third interview).

Raul's experience and conceptualisation of his own stigma seemed to have radically changed in between these two interviews. The difference is sustained by a fundamental transformation in the internalisation of his social stigma versus projecting it onto a society which he now seems to despise. His relativism observed with his initial stigma disclosing strategies had also changed drastically and became more categorical. These two radical changes in his narrative betrayed a fundamental transformation in how Raul had started to make senses of the world. I asked Raul whether he tells people about his past once more:

Raul: No, never. But I don't lie about it either, but because the life is so self-absorbed now, no one ever asks (Raul, third interview).

The 'sudden change' coincides with a fundamental change in the way that Raul had internalised a different set of values at the heart of his narrative identity. Also, it evidences Raul's rebellion and disappointment with society at large. Nevertheless, Raul's difficulties can be understood as an exception to the rule for this sample of released mandatory lifers – it serves to strengthen the point that prison-based capital can render a smoother transition into pro-social identities post-release. However, structural barriers can render the accumulation of social capital difficult, as evidenced in Raul's case. In our last interview, Raul's romantic defeatism seemed to have reached a new high:

Raul: I'm not married, uhm, I find myself socialising less and less now just because I don't see the point in it anymore, going out wasting money, acting stupid, like with people around you, it's too much responsibility having people around you that are not in as much control of themselves as I am, It's a liability, you know what I mean? Uhm, that's more about it in a nutshell. (…) You never going to be accepted and you never going to be able to make up for what you've missed. Now, I'm out in 30s I'm an ex-con, yeah, ok I drive a half decent car by the grace of God, I wear half decent clothes, by the grace of God, it's not enough for somebody to say – yeah, I'll give my daughter to you, do you understand? I'm not on the top of nobody's list, you know what I'm saying? Not that I want to be, I don't want to be, I don't give a shit, keep your daughter, it's not a problem (…) (Raul, forth interview).

Raul's defeatism evident in our latest interview raises an important criminological discussion around perceptions of agency and control in building a 'fulfilling life' post-release and the accompanying loss of hope when faced with a series of blocked opportunities (Wright, Hulley, and Crewe, 2023 for a prison-based discussion around hope). This is an important consideration given that hope has been found to represent a protective factor against suicide (Johnson and Leigey, 2020), and successful desistance (Kazemian, 2020). Raul's capacity to maintain a desisting narrative and reconstructed identity despite this conundrum was related to his accumulated narrative resources around his employment success and family man identity (King, 2013).

Discussion

This chapter explored the early resettlement transition of the mandatory lifers with a focus on the most salient experiences as narrated by the men. The chapter evidenced that two of the most-researched socio-economic 'correlates of desistance', namely family formation and gaining employment (Farrall, 2011) are crucial in the initial construction of pro-social identities for this sample of released mandatory lifers. More specifically, original families and romantic partners provided much needed 'resettlement capital' of the instrumental type (accommodation, housing, even finances) as well as emotional support, and assisted with the men's resilience to both life inside prison and outside. In turn, such support acted as a 'scaffolding' mechanism which supported the men to further develop and cement pro-social identities (family men identities) post-release. Also, the chapter drew attention to the importance of timing in accumulating social and 'resettlement capital' needed for a smooth role transition after release. In contrast to some published work, the men did not have the opportunity to simply 'inherit their families' social capital' (Farrall, 2011: 66) and end up straight into jobs. However, they managed to accumulate necessary capital during their imprisonment and skilfully mobilised their social relationships on release or secured their roles whilst they were still in prison. To avoid anticipated stigma on release, the men deflected attention from their history of unemployment and criminal past, or simply used such spoiled identities (Goffman, 1963) as assets in the community. Nevertheless, not all participants managed to accomplish this in due time and have therefore failed to achieve the 'untroubled' role transition as presented in this chapter. Prospective longitudinal accounts of the most recently released participants in this sample offered a glimpse into the experiences of stigma which were difficult to navigate, and which hampered the men's progress, as was Raul's case.

References

Albertson, K. (2021) Social capital building supporting the desistance process, Her Majesty's Inspectorate of Probation, June 2021.
Albertson, K., and Hall, L. (2020) Building social capital to encourage desistance: Lessons from a veteran-specific project. In Ugwudike P., Graham H., McNeill F., Raynor P., Taxman F.S. and Trotter C. (Eds.), *The Routledge Companion to Rehabilitative Work in Criminal Justice*. London: Routledge, 310–319.
Atherton, P., and Buck, G. (2021) Employing with conviction: The experiences of employers who actively recruit criminalised people. *Probation Journal*, 8 (2), 186–205.
Becker, H. S. (1963) *Outsiders: Studies in the Sociology of Deviance*. New York, NY: Free Press.
Berg, M., and Huebner, B. M. (2011) Reentry and the ties that bind: An examination of social ties, employment, and recidivism. *Justice Quarterly*, 28, 382–410.
Best, D. (2019) *Pathways to Recovery and Desistance: The Role of the Social Contagion and Hope*. Bristol: Policy Press.
Best, D., Musgrove, A., and Hall, L. (2018) The bridge between social identity and community capital on the path to recovery and desistance. *Probation Journal*, 65 (4), 394–406.
Boman, J. H. IV, and Mowen, T. J. (2017) Building the ties that bind, breaking the ties that don't. *Criminology & Public Policy*, 16, 753–774.
Bottoms, A. and Shapland, J. (2011) Steps towards desistance among male young adult recidivists. In Farrall, S., Hough, M., Maruna, S., and Sparks, R. (Eds.), *Escape Routes: Contemporary Perspectives on Life After Punishment*. London: Routledge, 43–80.
Brown, J. D. (1991) The professional ex-: An alternative for exiting the deviant career. *Sociological Quarterly*, 32, 219–230.
Calverley, A. (2013) *Cultures of Desistance*. London: Routledge.
Calverley, A. (2019) Exploring the processes of desistance by ethnic status: The confluence of community, familial and individual processes. In S. Farrall (Eds.), *The Architecture of Desistance*. London: Routledge, 75–95.
Cerda, J. A., Stenstrom, D. M., and Curtis, M. (2015) The role of type of offense and work qualifications on perceived employability of former offenders. *American Journal of Criminal Justice*, 40, 317–335.

Cohen, S. and Taylor, L. (1972) *Psychological Survival: The Experience of Long-Term Imprisonment*. London: Penguin.

Crewe, B., Hulley, S., and Wright, S. (2020) *Life Imprisonment from Young Adulthood Adaptation, Identity, and Time*. London: Palgrave Macmillan.

Duwe, G., and Clark, V. (2013) Blessed be the social tie that binds: The effects of prison visitation on offender recidivism. *Criminal Justice Policy Review*, 24 (3), 271–296.

Farmer, L. (2017) *The Importance of Strengthening Prisoners' Family Ties to Prevent Reoffending and Reduce Intergenerational Crime*. London: Ministry of Justice.

Farrall, S. (2011) Social capital and offender reintegration: Making probation desistance focussed. In Maruna S and Immarigeon R (Eds.), *After Crime and Punishment: Pathways to Offender Reintegration*. Cullompton: Willan, 57–82.

Farrall, S. (2019) *The Architecture of Desistance*. London: Routledge.

Farrington, D. P., Barnes, G. C., and Lambert, S. (1996) The concentration of offending in families. *Legal and Criminological Psychology*, 1, 46–63.

Flanagan, J. T. (1980) The pains of long-term imprisonment. *British Journal of Criminology*, 20 (2), 148–156.

Fox, K. J. (2016) Civic commitment: Promoting desistance through community integration. *Punishment and Society*, 18 (1), 68–94.

Giordano, P. C., Cerkovich, S. A., and Rudolph, J. L. (2002) Gender crime and desistance: Toward a theory of cognitive transformation. *American Journal of Sociology*, 107 (4), 990–1064.

Goffman, E (1963) *Stigma Notes on the Management of Spoiled Identity*. London: Penguin.

Griffin, D., and Healy, D. (2019) The pains of parole for life sentenced prisoners in Ireland: Risk, rehabilitation, and re-entry. *European Journal of Probation*, 11 (3), 124–138.

Harding, D. J. (2003) Jean Valjean's dilemma: The management of ex-convict identity in the search for employment. *Deviant Behaviour*, 24 (6), 571–595.

Johnson, R., and Leigey, M. E. (2020) The life-course of juvenile lifers: Understanding maturation and development as miller and its progeny guide juvenile life sentence release decisions. *Journal of Criminal Justice and Law*, 3 (2), 22–39.

Kay, C. (2022) Rethinking social capital in the desistance process: The 'Artful Dodger' complex. *European Journal of Criminology*, 19 (5), 1–17.

Kazemian, L (2020) *Positive Growth and Redemption in Prison: Finding Light Behind Bars and Beyond*. Oxon: Routledge.

King, S. (2014) *Desistance Transitions and the Impact of Probation*. London: Routledge.

King, S. (2013) Early desistance narratives: A qualitative analysis of probationers' transitions towards desistance. *Punishment and Society*, 15 (2), 147–165.

King, R., Massoglia, M., and MacMillan, R. (2007) The context of marriage and crime: Gender, the propensity to marry, and offending in early adulthood. *Criminology*, 45, 33–66.

Kotova, A. (2020) The role of offenders' family links in offender rehabilitation. In Ugwudike P., Graham H., McNeill F., Raynor P., Taxman F.S. and Trotter C. (Eds.), *The Routledge Companion to Rehabilitative Work in Criminal Justice*. London: Routledge, 835–843.

Lageson, S. E., Vuolo, M., and Uggen, C. (2015) Legal ambiguity and criminal records. *Law & Social Inquiry*, 40 (1), 175–204.

Laub, J. H., and Sampson, R. J. (2003) *Shared Beginnings, Divergent Lives: Delinquent Boys to Age 70*. Cambridge, MA: Harvard University Press.

LeBel, T. P. (2008) Perceptions of and responses to stigma. *Sociology Compass*, 2 (2), 409–432.

LeBel, T. P. (2012) Invisible stripes? Formerly incarcerated persons' perceptions of stigma. *Deviant Behavior*, 33, 89–107.

Leverentz, A. M. (2014) *The Ex-Prisoner's Dilemma: How Women Negotiate Competing Narratives of Reentry and Desistance*. New Brunswick: Rutgers University Press.

Liem, M. (2016) *After Life Imprisonment*. New York, NY: New York University Press.

Liem, M. (2017) Desistance after life imprisonment. In Hart L. and van Ginneken L. (Eds.), *New Perspectives on Desistance: Theoretical and Empirical Developments*. London: Palgrave, 85–110.

Liem, M., and Garcin, J. (2014) Post-release success among paroled lifers. *Laws*, 3 (4), 798–823.

Liem, M., and Weggemans, D. (2018) Reintegration among high-profile ex-offenders. *Journal of Developmental and Life-Course Criminology*, 4 (4), 473–490.

Markson, L., Lösel, F., Souza, K., and Lanskey, C. (2015) Male prisoners' family relationships and resilience in resettlement. *Criminology and Criminal Justice*, 15 (4), 1–19.

Maruna, S., and LeBel, P. T. (2015) Strengths-based restorative approaches to reentry. The evolution of creative restitution, reintegration, and destigmatisation. In Ronel N., and Segev D. (Eds.), *Positive Criminology*. New York, NY: Routledge, 65–84.

McNeill, F. (2012) Four forms of 'offender' rehabilitation: Towards and interdisciplinary perspective. *Legal and Criminological Psychology*, 17 (1), 1–19.

McNeill, F., Farrall, S., Lightowler, C., and Maruna, S. (2012) *How and Why People Stop Offending: Discovering Desistance*. Institute for Research and Innovation in Social Services. Available at: https://eprints.gla.ac.uk/79860/1/79860.pdf

Mills, A. L., and Codd, H. (2008) Prisoners' families and offender management: Mobilizing social capital. *Probation Journal*, 55 (1), 9–24.

Mowen, T. J., Stansfield, R., and Boman, J. H. (2019) Family matters: Moving beyond "If" family support matters to "Why" family support matters during reentry from prison. *Journal of Cutaneous Medicine and Surgery*, 56 (4), S12–S22.

Naser, R. L., and La Vigne, N. G. (2006) Family support in the prisoner reentry process: Expectations and realities. *Journal of Offender Rehabilitation*, 43 (1), 93–106.

O'Connor, T., and Bogue, B. (2010) Collaborating with the community, trained volunteers, and faith traditions; Building social capacity and making meaning to support desistance. In F. McNeill, P. Rayner, & C. Trotter (Eds.), *Offender Supervision: New Directions in Theory, Research and Practice*. Cullompton, UK: Willan Publishing, 301–319.

Pager, D., and Quillian, L. (2005) Walking the talk? What employers say versus what they do. *American Sociological Review*, 70 (3), 355–380.

Petersilia, J. (2003) *When Prisoners Come Home: Parole and Prisoner Reentry*. London: Oxford University Press.

Taylor, C. J. (2016) The family's role in the reintegration of formerly incarcerated individuals: The direct effects of emotional support. *The Prison Journal*, 96 (3), 331–354.

Uggen, C., Manza, J., and Behrens, A. (2011) Less than the average citizen, stigma, role transition and the civic reintegration of convicted felons. In S. Maruna, & R. Immarigeon (Eds.), *After Crime and Punishment: Pathways to Offender Reintegration*. Cullompton, Devon: Willan, 258–290.

Vuolo, M., Lageson, S., and Uggen, C. (2017) Criminal record questions in the era of 'ban the box'. *Criminology & Public Policy*, 16 (1), 139–165.

Western, B. (2018) *Homeward: Life in the Year After Prison*. New York, NY: Russel Sage Foundation.

Western, B., Braga, A. A., Davis, J., and Sirois, C. (2015) Stress and hardship after prison. *American Journal of Sociology*, 10 (5), 512–547.

White, W. L. (2000) The history of recovered people as wounded healers: II. The era of professionalization and specialization. *Alcoholism Treatment Quarterly*, 18 (2), 1–25.
Wright, J. P. and Cullen F. T. (2004) Employment, peers, and life-course transitions. *Justice Quarterly*, 21, 183–205.
Wright, S., Hulley, S., and Crewe, B. (2023) Trajectories of hope/lessness among men and women in the late stage of a life sentence. *Theoretical Criminology*, 27 (1), 66–84.

5 Negotiating the prison voice

The previous chapter evidenced the importance of family formation and employment status in offering a smooth transition into pro-social roles immediately post release. Nevertheless, as the men embraced their new 'family men' identities, they also needed to negotiate a lingering 'prisoner voice'. This internal conflict led to a series of experiences akin to the concept of Doublethink, as famously portrayed by George Orwell in his *1984* masterpiece and which was difficult to navigate. As discussed in Chapter 2, prison-based adaptive mechanisms can prove maladaptive on release and this is especially true for long-term offenders (Jamieson and Grounds, 2005) and homicide offenders particularly (Hulley, Crewe, and Wright, 2016; Liem and Kunst, 2013). The earliest stages of re-entry were identified as the most stressful by the men (Western, 2018). During these early times – especially within the first 18 months – particularly demanding was the need for shedding behaviours, as well as values which had been learned as adaptation to the ideological settings and customs of prison life (Clemmer, 1958). Goffman (1961: 13) argued that long-term prisoners are especially prone to a process he called disculturation, where an 'untraining' renders the nearly released individual "temporarily incapable of managing certain features of daily life on the outside". The re-entry narratives presented here highlight the negotiation between the cultural logics of the prison setting and life outside. This chapter presents evidence indicating that the men's adaptive strategies to prison-based violence are not suitable for life outside the prison walls. Their prolonged prison sentences have integrated such strategies deeply into the men's personalities, necessitating active negotiation and adaptation upon their release. Surprisingly, these adaptive personality traits do not necessarily disappear with the passage of time as a natural condition of readaptation. In some cases, the prisons sentence served as a necessary system of atonement and redemption, containing sentiments of guilt that stem from a murderous past which was yet to be fully metabolised. In this case, prison served an important role in emotional regulation.

Hypervigilance: Mastering the prison voice

Raul experienced a sense of hypervigilance and alertness as being representative of his early release months. He recalls being overly protective of himself and his family, to the extent of making people around him uncomfortable.

Raul: When I came out for the first at least 6 months, 9 months, I was like an owl, I was always constantly looking around, I'd be walking with my sister and my niece, and my eyes are everywhere, thinking, just trying to perceive potential threats that weren't even there, but I just wanted to make sure that if it did happen, I was there and ready to protect my family, and what I realised that was just from prison, cuz in prison that is how you are every single day, you have to make sure that you can neutralise potential threats every single day, but doing that out here, in the normal world, it took me 9 months to realise that I don't have to do that, you know, my family survived without me for 12 years, without me protecting, and now all of sudden, when somebody is walking too close, I'm having to stand in between them, or if I see someone walking that I don't like the look of, I get my family to cross the road, and there little things like that, and I realised that I don't have to do that anymore (Raul, first interview).

Raul continued to experience a heightened sense of alertness 11 months later, although this has moved away from the forefront of his mind. That is to say, the anxiety associated with the pervasive sense of threat has moved from a conscious rumination to second nature, diffusely experienced:

Raul: It's always there, it's never gonna go away if you know what I mean […], I'm never gonna switch off from that you know what I mean, and I'll be annoyed at myself if I ever did let myself fall into that false sense of security, but I have chilled out quite a bit you know, but yah, as I said it's always going to be there (Raul, second interview).

One year later (two years after we have first met), Raul reiterated the point. He had been out of prison for over 3.6 years at the time. I've asked Raul whether his heightened alertness was 'still there'.

Raul: Yeah, yeah, I'm not, it's not in the forefront of my mind as much as it was, you know. So, a few months back me and my sister, my nephew, pushing him in the pram, we were in the park, and some guys were play fight each other, it's a lady in front of us with no pram, they haven't moved out of her way, so kind of got a little bit caught up in all of that, it's all roughhousing, you know, pushing into each other and all of that stuff yah? And I don't know something just kicked in. As soon as they came near my nephew's pram I came and I physically moved them out of the way, and they were a bit surprised, taken aback by it, but at that point all I really cared about was just making sure they didn't come near my nephew you know what I mean, and they backed up after that (Raul, third interview).

Raul conditioned his heightened senses of alertness, and specifically that of fear of crime/victimisation to the area where he lives, which is constructed as a dangerous place (Hollway and Jefferson, 2000). The overprotection described in our first interview is reiterated later in the story of protecting his nephew. This could potentially explain an achieved sense of masculinity in the absence of other available resources. I've reminded him of this experience a year and a half later, in our fourth and last interview:

Dan: Tell me a bit about the hypervigilance that you were experiencing initially. You were walking in a park with your sister and niece, and you were overprotective of them. Are you the same?

Raul: I would say it has calmed down a lot from when I last saw you but it's always there. You know your eyes are always everywhere, there's no moment when you switch off. Like you asked me on my way here did I sleep on my way here (on the train) and is said: I don't sleep ever during the day ... so yeah I don't think that's ever left me uhm, it's got it's good points, it's got its bad points, bad points are you can never switch off, you can never be fully relaxed like you hear some people you know, turn it off and just forget about everything, but the good points are: you are safe, those around you are safe, it keeps you sharp, keeps you mentally always like thinking of the next step ... so yeah. I'm a lot more tolerant now, so I think spending these last few years in management positions in the gym and stuff like that you look at other ways of dealing with things that maybe I wouldn't have anticipated before, more calmer ways, more suitable ways rather than more practical ways, rather than automatically going offensive or defensive, trying to find the middle course. I think people around me have seen this as well so yeah (Raul, forth interview).

The passage above provides evidence in favour of alertness as an enduring personality trait rather than a transient defensive strategy, contrary to how it was initially presented in Raul's narrative. I then enquired about the 'prison voice' further:

Dan: The man that you developed in prison – does that man still creep in?

Raul: That man is who I am and always I will be. What you learn in prison you can't learn anywhere else: how do act, how to portray yourself, the boundaries you set the limits you set for yourself and others ... That's not something you can just brush off as soon as you come out of prison. You keep it because it keeps you safe. You can always add new skills, new personality traits to yourself like for example being in a managerial position in the gym I have to go and put a mask on everyday "hey how are you? how is your day today"? You got to deal with different questions because that's my job that's what I get paid to do whereas the real me I don't give a .... I don't care (Raul, forth interview).

Then, although moving away from his immediate awareness and perhaps decreasing in intensity over time, the prison voice is an integral part of Raul's self-perception post-release. In a very similar fashion Jacob too felt that he had an 'radar' switched on soon after he got released.

Jacob: I really struggled with sitting in a restaurant. I was talking with my wife about it the other day, ah, she is a passionate cook, so we would go out for a meal, but because of the nature of prison I could sit in a restaurant and I could hear a conversation at every table around me I was so attuned and aware of my surroundings, having to have eyes at the back of your head and ears, and knowing what was going on and what is going on around you. I used to find it really difficult to sit in and enjoy the meal in a restaurant cuz I was constantly ... my radar was operational to what was going on around me and it took me quite a long time to become comfortable doing that, and I never lost it. I am always aware of my surroundings. I see things; I observe things that no one else sees and it is in some respects a good life skill, but in other respects ... it's not paranoia, I never felt it, I've met people who had been extremely paranoid, it's just like a security system really, of, of a, actually stopping and relaxing and that was quite difficult ... The other thing I think it is as a result of the control that's exerted by the prison system even, you know, I still don't like control, I am independent, I want to do things my way, my understanding of things, uhm, you know, I analyse everything, so, you know that's good and bad, I suppose [...]. I always say to my wife 'come on let's go to Wales' ... and we would drive, come on just go, and she said why, and I said: 'well because we can' (laughs). We jump in the car and go driving and get fish and chips 100 miles away simply because we could, and I know that sounds crazy (Jacob, only interview).

Jacob is classed as a 'veteran', having been released over 20 years at the time of our interview. Nevertheless, he vividly remembered the sense of paranoia which characterised his first few years post-release. A similar effect was found in an American study on homicide offenders which showed that long-term imprisonment leads to paranoia, hampered decision-making, social sensory deprivation and temporal alienation (Liem and Kunst, 2013). Nevertheless, to make up for the lost time and his loss of autonomy (see Sykes, 1958) and the consequential deindividuation due to the neo-paternalism (Crewe, 2011) exerted by the prison system, Jacob exerted autonomy by travelling with his wife simply because they could. Similarly, Nathaniel also expressed his jubilation with the sheer amount of choice and freedom:

Dan: Do you recall how you felt when you started going out?
Nathaniel: It was just jubilation, I was proper excited, it was like Christmas, like being in a gig, just silly things like popping into a shop, going to buy different hair gel, you can't get it was just crazy, it's just the smallest things to a normal person but it was the biggest things to me, so … It was, you are always looking around and just couldn't believe how fast everything is, obviously time goes faster (Nathaniel, first interview).

I have formulated a similar question for Richard. He recalls his early release as a lot easier than he thought he was going to be, although more difficult than the upcoming re-entry phases. Specifically, Richard remembers a period of uncertainty and fear of possibly losing his licence.

Richard: The most challenging would have been the resettlement initially because I didn't know what to expect, I didn't know what it would be like, how long it would last. When I first got in, I thought probation service forever, but then I realised it was for a certain time. And not having to report to them now makes life feel normal, even though I am not officially in a normal situation because I am on a life licence … uhm, but not having to report to the probation service has brought a sense of normality, but it was a challenge at first because I had to report to them each week, and comply, and always feel that you know, will I do something that will upset them and they may revoke my licence, there's always that fear … You know, because you don't really know what to expect and I felt when I got released that they didn't explain that properly, I think that should have been explained properly from prison you know so there wouldn't be these fears, and hopefully now they do that, it's something that I look into now … so, I think uhm … that was the most difficult (Richard, first interview).

Although released more than 20 years ago, Richard's concerns echo some of more recent parolees in criminological research. For example, participants in Weaver's (2014) study complained about competing expectations from probation and which rendered the post-prison experience uncertain and ambiguous. Several of Harding, Morenoff, and Wyse (2019) previously incarcerated individuals in the United States, voiced that part of their anxiety about

94 *Life Beyond Murder*

violation stems from the fact that reincarceration can result from behaviours which normally would not have any legal consequences. The findings here echo that of these studies.

Experiencing guilt and the containing role of imprisonment

To best explain the men's sentiments of fear and ambiguity in the initial stages of their release, I return to Peter who unintentionally explains the aetiology of his early internal combat voice. He was released for over 6 months at the time:

Peter: Yes, so I was in my room the other day not long ago, my mom came in with some washing, so she washed for me, folded, and she opened the cupboard. My bells went off like mad, what the fuck and it settled in completely but at the back of my mind, because in prison no one can walk in your room like that and just open the cupboard door, that is not, that's a fight, and even though it was my mum, you know what I mean, I still had that feeling of discomfort this is not alright, and that is because of prison. And I have that a lot of the time, I have that channelling at the back of my mind, watch out, watch out for that and it's all bollocks, you know what I mean, it's all warning me of things that would be threats in prison. Even things like people can pick up a coffee you know just to have a sip of their coffee, and I am like 'wowowowow', sounds crazy … cuz it's not the big things, the big things like I said to you, job, wife baby, I knocked them down easy, you know what I mean, I bit the barrier towards these things, this is not a problem, it's the little tiny things at the back of my mind, it is exhausting, mentally drained, all the time because there's this survival mechanism from prison that is working from background all the time that I don't need anymore. Every thought that comes up it's doubled, triple by potential threat you know, is this an affront to my reputation, you know what I mean all nonsense, all from prison, all irrelevant to life outside prison, but it still has to go through the process of my mind, thinking yes, I know that is bollocks you know what I mean … does that make any sense to you Dan? (Peter, first interview).

In fact, Peter initially found life post-release significantly more traumatic than he expected. Ever since he got out of prison, he found himself caught in a 'liminal' space (van Gennep, 1960) which requires a continuous negotiation of two distinct voices.

Peter: Getting released from prison, Dan, was a way, way more traumatic event than I thought it was going to be. I realised I had lots of personality traits and alarms you know, that's a lot of subconscious that's grown up in prison, I have issues almost constantly, like you know a radio static, and it's around uhm ... everything. I can be at work standing next to a toolbox and talking to someone, you know like how people just idly pick things up and you talk to them, it means absolutely nothing, you know what I mean, you can pick up a pen up of the desk and whatever. I am at work, and a guy picks up a screwdriver and at the back of my mind, screaming, WHAT IS HE DOING? Why is he picking up a screwdriver what's going on here, but at the same time, and this is very George Orwellian, I am holding a doublethink yea, I absolutely know that it means nothing and I need to ignore all the stuff that is going on behind it, 100% I know that, but I also know that there is a potential threat and I need to be very aware of it (starts opening the windows of the car now) (Peter, first interview).

As evidenced above, the very coping mechanisms developed during his long prison sentence prove maladaptive in the outside world (Hulley et al., 2016). Some penal researchers have theorised that to survive in the prison environment, newly arrived prisoners create a distinction between their 'true' identity (pre-prison identity), and a false identity (Schmid and Jones, 1991; Wheeler, 1961). This new identity is seen as being based on impression management (Goffman, 1963) but ultimately becomes integrated within the multiplicity of the prisoners' voices. Then, as Goffman (1961: 73) has put it, "release is likely to come just when the inmate has learned the ropes on the inside". Peter's initial struggles are representative of such adaptive mechanisms, which, according to him at the time, could only disappear with the passage of time. Harding et al. (2019: 60) remarked that formerly incarcerated offenders "must quickly shed the vestige of their prison disculturation, juggle the demands of the parole supervision and requited treatment problems, and begin to put their lives together after a long period away".

These concomitant demands are stressful and can become overwhelming in periods of increased stress. Once the recorder was switched off, Peter confessed that in times of exacerbated stress, he sometimes thinks about going back to prison. Below is an entry from the research diary.

'Peter recognised that there are times he would want his prison life back. He said that "there are times when I wouldn't mind [to] go to prison, because there are two conflicting opinions in my mind, one kind of, I suppose, like a combat mode, prison mode, and the voice of everyday normality saying 'no'; and they are in balance, but when they are not in balance, maybe I would like to go back to prison, or it would be more comfortable to go to prison". Peter made this remark during a time when his girlfriend was sick in hospital. He now must go to work, sleep alone, go to hospital to visit her, all of which is 'too tiring' he said (Research Diary, 4 February 2020) (Peter, first encounter)'.

96 *Life Beyond Murder*

This passage above draws attention to the crucial timing of the first few months of release as "the most vulnerable for those who have served long-term sentences" (Shingler and Stickney, 2024: 25). In our third interview, almost two years after we have first met, Peter admitted that this sense of alertness had diminished. I asked him whether he was still experiencing 'the combat voice'.

Peter: Aaa, not so much, not so severe, I'm always on the ball, if you know what I mean, but I don't feel the threats, you know what I mean? […], I do feel a lot calmer, I don't feel so threatened. I don't like it, but sometimes everyone is sitting here and I'm holding the baby and then maybe my stepson will be here as well and the missus will come over as well and they are all in my face, I don't, I don't like, that makes me feel uncomfortable, when we are all, even when we are laughing and joking, too many heads near my head space unsettles me you know? (Peter, third interview).

In his view at the time, the panacea for this is to ridicule the inner thoughts and keep a healthy attitude where communication is key in signalling to people when he feels threatened. Nevertheless, a year and a half later, in our last interview, Peter expressed similar concerns as in our initial interviews. Here, Peter confesses once more that amid all the agitation at home he would not mind spending some time back in prison. He had been released for almost four years (3 years and 10 months).

Peter: I wouldn't want to go to a place like Bullingdon, like a starting prison with fuck all, I'd like to go back to when I settled when I was in the same cell a long time and when I was, yes stability. I sometimes feel we don't have that at home. I do occasionally think to myself that I wouldn't mind just 2 weeks or 1 week, but I know I'd miss them (his family) so much, you know just a day like today, I know I won't get home until say 9, it's going to bother me that I wasn't able to say good night to them, I may very well wake them up to tell them … you know what I mean … as far as like my prison thinking, Fight or Flight stuff it's still there but it's not as debilitating as it was and it is not as constant, it's starting to go a little bit … (Peter, forth interview).

Peter's confession contradicted my initial preconception that, given the right context, all facets of institutionalisation and prisonization in mandatory lifers would gradually diminish over time. I soon realised that this was a myopic perspective. Peter's fantasy of prison return was imbued with expressions of guilt and anxiety. His deep-felt anxiety was erupting daily, and lately, it was manifesting as Pareidolia:

Peter: Well … how it tends to manifest lately (anxiety) is with something called Pareidolia, my anxiety would start to raise, and I am not sure, some sort of chemical system in my brain starts making faces out of, you know, see this (points to the wall), two eyes and a nose, and there's two eyes, and I would get really hyped like that and I would start noticing faces all around – I know that they are not faces. It feels like it's "calm it down, calm it down, look at this look at that look at the face", it's like a distraction from the anxiety (Peter, forth interview).

Face pareidolia resembles the misconception of inanimate objects as human faces (Taubert et al., 2022). Ultimately, pareidolia it is about creating meaning where such meaning is lacking and there is evidence of an association with anxiety in certain populations (Kurumada et al., 2021). Peter remarked that the role of his pareidolia was to stave off his anxiety. It was later in the interview clarified that his anxiety was intrinsically linked to unmetabolized feelings of guilt. Interestingly, Peter's guilt was directly proportional to his happiness. He continues:

Peter: Coupled with that, like my life is alright, but sometimes I sit in my kitchen, kids are playing, I think (whispers) 'this is alright you know', and then I think I just wish it would all just fuck off, I just wish I wasn't here anymore, and it will go, that I just feel, like these kids would be better off if I were dead, if I wasn't around them, missus would be better off I was dead, you know what I mean? And it comes, I know, one of the things I've been doing is the Band of Brothers you know, and some of the work I've been doing has been around guilt you know, and so I suppose since we last spoke, I have a different understanding about the guilt that I feel, for the murder ... right? Imagine my thoughts and feeling as a cloud, or as a continuum because you can move in and out, you're not just sad or happy, it's a continuum. Like a very thin, very sharp spike of freezing, freezing ice, it goes right through the middle of all of it. Everything I do ... there is a very quiet voice "he's still dead you know", "don't fucking enjoy this too much mate" and that and that, bring to me, on one hand yeah the reminder that he is dead, that, I don't deserve any of the good things that are happening, and it makes me lean into the shitty stuff because that's what I think I do deserve, you know what I'm saying? (Peter, fourth interview).

What started to become clearer in Peter's narrative was that 'coming to terms' with the enormity of the offence is not limited to imprisonment (Crewe, Hulley, and Wright, 2020; Wright, Crewe, and Hulley, 2017). Peter's narrative around anxiety and fantasy of returning to prison indicated an important role that the prison had been performing in Peter's life: that of containing his guilt through a flagellant redemption. Peter's prison return fantasy was reflective of his need for self-flagellation as a way of coping with guilt; a similar but unrelated point was made by Nussbaum (2004: 207) who remarked that guilt is 'a type of self-punishing anger'. The happiness his family elicited, and his guilt were inextricably connected: the happier Peter felt, the more he felt was taking away from his victim. The situation ultimately represented a 'crisis of meaning' (Neimeyer and Sands, 2022: 10) around his index offence. The imminent danger of returning to prison could be explained via a need for punishment from a sense of guilt (see Freud, 1916). This is well highlighted in the following passage from my last interview with Peter:

Peter: You know we were talking about empathy, it's very difficult for me to have empathy for me, because he is dead, you know what I'm saying, and there was no real reason you know but he is dead because I wanted money for drugs. That's not all right, that's not alright mate and that's not cool, and I accept it's not cool, but I'm trying to get hold fully of the idea that this is what the abolishment of the hanging act is for innit? As luckily I was born into a country with a society where we don't kill people who kill people but we are given a second chance you know, a blank but all be it greyed page for us to go in and build another life off, and that's alright, that's what makes me think, because take morality out of the situation just for a moment if you can and the fact is I committed a crime in this country, broke the law in this country, right, went through the judicial system, was given a sentence to do as punishment for that crime and I've completed it so this life I'm having now is alright, I'm ok now …. (Peter, fourth interview).

The passage above is remarkable through its absence of neutralisations (Sykes and Matza, 1957) and excuses (Scully and Marolla, 1985) all too commonly used by people who committed crime. In fact, the passage above betrays Peter's 'crisis of meaning' around the murder and unmetabolized guilt, unleashed by the absence of visible punishment. Nevertheless, Peter's family as well as his role within the Band of Brother provided a sense of redemption and reparation which have been protective (this will be explored in more detail in Chapter 8).

Discussion

Despite the 'smooth progress' into family men identities and employment, the men's early release represented a state of liminality (Turner, 1969). These new identities needed to be negotiated alongside an identified 'prison voice' which rendered 'early resettlement' as the most difficult stage of the men's re-entry experience. The first few years coincided with their experiences of disculturation: a process where the mandatory lifers had to denude the vestiges of a life imprisonment along with its coping mechanisms. As evidenced above, the men's early re-entry narratives are characterised by a sentiment of insecurity, which indicates that they actively negotiate a multiplicity of contrasting voices. Every man reported experiencing some level of paranoia and hypervigilance after release. Initially, this state was acute, intense, and seemed transient. Nevertheless, over the course of a few years, it gradually transformed into more chronic, less intense, personality-like trait. The idea of resuming a 'pre-prison identity' (Schmid and Jones, 1991) did not seem to apply to this sample of mandatory lifers. Most of the men have referred to 'alarm systems', 'contrasting voices', and 'combat mode' to exemplify interference in accommodating to life and social encounters outside (also see Clifford, 2010). Soon after their release, the men needed to reconcile their prison voice with roles, expectations, and social situations which may require a set of interpretations at odds with the prison settings (Clemmer, 1958). This proved crucial to the extent to which Peter had almost given up life outside in periods of exacerbated stress. Luckily, his wife's pregnancy and his subsequent and imminent role of becoming a father had provided a motive for conforming (Laub and Sampson, 2003) and confronting his fears, and thus renouncing ideas of prison return. Interestingly, fantasies of prison return did not fade with time. On the contrary, Peter's case showed that these can in fact intensify when personal success excavates unmetabolized guilt perhaps stemming from a crisis of meaning. Prison, in this sense, can be conceptualised as serving an important function of containment and emotional regulation of guilt in some mandatory lifers. This raises a set of important question. What could explain Peter's experiences that were fundamentally different to the other men? Peter's case evidences the idiosyncratic ways in which mandatory lifers make sense of the enormity of their index offence and the impact this has on their lives post-release. The importance of meaning reconstruction through different forms of redemption and generativity are explored in more depth in Chapters 8 and 9.

References

Clemmer, D. (1958[1940]) *The Prison Community*, 2nd edition. New York, NY: Holt, Rinehart & Winston.

Clifford, J. L. (2010) Managing a murderous identity: How men who murder experience life imprisonment and the concept of release. PhD Thesis, University of Bath.

Crewe, B. (2011) Depth, weight, tightness: Revisiting the pains of imprisonment. *Punishment and Society*, 13 (5), 509–529.

Crewe, B., Hulley, S., and Wright, S. (2020) *Life Imprisonment from Young Adulthood Adaptation, Identity, and Time*. London, UK: Palgrave Macmillan.

Freud, S. (1916) Some character-types met with in psycho-analytic work. In Strachey, J. (Ed. & Trans.), The Standard Edition of the Complete Psychological Works of Sigmund Freud (volume XIV). London: Hogarth Press, 309–333. (Original work published 1916)

Goffman, E. (1961) *Asylums: Essays on the Social Situation of Mental Patients and Other Inmates*. London: Penguin.

Goffman, E. (1963) *Stigma Notes on the Management of Spoiled Identity*. London: Penguin.

Harding, D. J., Morenoff, J. D., and Wyse, J. B. (2019) *On the Outside: Prisoner Reentry and Reintegration*. Chicago, IL: University of Chicago Press.

Hollway, W., and Jefferson, T. (2000) *Doing Qualitative Research Differently*. London: Sage.

Hulley, S., Crewe, B., and Wright, S. (2016) Re-examining the problems of long-term imprisonment. *British Journal of Criminology*, 56 (4), 769–792.

Jamieson, R., and Grounds, B. (2005) Release and adjustment: Perspectives from studies of wrongly convicted and politically motivated prisoners. In Liebling A., and Maruna S. (Eds.), *The Effects of Imprisonment*. Cullompton, Devon: Willan Publishing, 33–65.

Kurumada, K., Gusiya, A., Hirano, S., Yamamoto, T., Yamanaka, Y., Araki, N., Yakiyama, M., Yoshitake, M., and Kuwabara, S. (2021) Pareidolia in Parkinson's disease and multiple system atrophy. *Parkinson's Disease*, 2704755, 1–6.

Laub, J. H., and Sampson, R. J. (2003) *Shared Beginnings, Divergent Lives: Delinquent Boys to Age 70*. Cambridge, MA: Harvard University Press.

Liem, M., and Kunst, M. (2013) Is there a recognizable post-incarceration syndrome among released "lifers"? *International Journal of Law and Psychiatry*, 46 (3–4), 333–337.

Neimeyer, R. A., and Sands, D. C. (2022) Meaning reconstruction in bereavement: From principles to practice. In Neimeyer R. A., Harris D. L., Winokuer H. R., Thornton G. F. (Eds.), *Grief and Bereavement in Contemporary Society: Bridging Research and Practice*, New York, NY: Routledge, 7–22.

Nussbaum, M. C. (2004) *Hiding from Humanity: Disgust, Shame, and the Law*. Princeton, NJ: Princeton University Press.

Schmid, J. T., and Jones, S. R. (1991) Suspended identity: Identity transformation in a maximum-security prison. *Symbolic Interaction*, 14 (4), 415–432.

Scully, D., and Marolla, J. (1985) "Riding the bull at Gilley's": Convicted rapists describe the rewards of rape. *Social Problems*, 32 (3), 251–263.

Shingler, J., and Stickney, J. (2024) I can see freedom, but I can't have it. In Shingler J., and Stickney J. (Eds.), *The Journey from Prison to Community*. Oxon: Routledge, 24–43.

Sykes, G. (1958) *The Society of Captives: A Study of a Maximum-Security Prison*. Princeton, NJ: Princeton University Press.

Sykes, G., and Matza, D. (1957) Techniques of neutralization: A theory of delinquency. *American Sociological Review*, 22, 664–670.

Taubert, J., Wardle, S. G., Tardiff, T. C., Koele, E. A., Kumar, S., Messinger, A., and Unglereider, L. G. (2022) The cortical and subcortical correlates of face pareidolia in the macaque brain. *Social Cognitive and Affective Neuroscience*, 17, 965–976.

Turner, V. (1969) *The Ritual Process: Structure and Anti-structure*. Chicago, IL: Aldine.

van Gennep, A. (1960) *The Rites of Passage*. Chicago, IL: The University of Chicago Press.

Weaver, B. (2014) Control or change? Developing dialogues between desistance research and public protection practices. *Probation Journal*, 61(1), 8–26.

Western, B. (2018) *Homeward: Life in the Year After Prison*. New York, NY: Russel Sage Foundation.

Wheeler, S. (1961) Socialization in correctional communities. *American Sociological Review*, 26 (5), 697–712.

Wright, S., Crewe, B., and Hulley, S. (2017) Suppression, denial, sublimation: Defending against the initial pains of very long sentences. *Theoretical Criminology*, 21 (2), 225–246.

6 Pursuing identities of success

Mandatory lifers and consumer culture

The previous chapter explored the importance of timing in accumulating social capital to ensure a smooth role transition into pro-social identities post-release. To reiterate, the men's initial aspirations and projections for their future selves were 'conventional' in following prevailing societal norms. They generally planned to construct and maintain identities around traditional family roles such as that of a husband, father, and worker. Perhaps this resembled the men's association of such ambitions with notions of traditional masculinity and masculine identities (Fletcher, 2007 in King, 2013). Generally, the men's families and employment opportunities ensured a level of narrative stability to their identities by providing social roles consistent with self-perceptions and goals (Harding et al., 2017).

In addition to such traditional aspirations, the most recently released lifers – Peter and Raul – have constructed 'early re-entry narratives' (Harding et al., 2017) which were consistent with the prevailing ideology of consumer capitalism. Notions of consumerist success interacted with the men's capacity to navigate structural obstacles in achieving traditional normative roles. As these traditional forms of identities were at times challenged due to structural impediments, the men's fragile sense of self interacted more strongly with the consumerist demands and seductions of the post-industrial, consumerist society (Bauman, 2005) which presented a set of pressures to perform successful selves through dominant consumerist symbols. The re-entry narrative sought the promises of success through the accumulation of enjoyment (Žižek, 2002) to make up for lost time as a consequence of imprisonment (in Raul's case) as well as the flexible 'work-life balance' and success promised by consumer-capitalism (in Peter's case). Early re-entry narratives of status and consumerist success were either abandoned or reframed given the structural incompatibility and biographical resources of the men.

Raul: Negotiating consumer obsolescence

We often "talk in borrowed language" (Frank, 2010: 35) which means that our identities draw from prevailing cultural building blocks and public narratives present in our society. Consequently, culture shapes individual

DOI: 10.4324/9781003415640-6

aspirations and provides narrative templates of success (Harding et al., 2017). In this sense, in addition to the men's initial aspirations which were related to building a family of their own, finding a romantic partner, and the right type of employment the men considered self-realisation through material means.

Having been released, the men were 'interpellated' (Althusser, 2001) as consumers and often felt stigmatised for their 'lack' of material wealth. The pursuit of consumerist symbols partly acted as a substitute for a fragile sense of identity that was being reconstructed in the period immediately after release. Raymen and Smith (2016: 14) succinctly made the point:

> In the relative absence of distinguishable life stages, stable relationships, work, and politics to mature into, it seems all that is left are the shops and the self as a lone competitor in the struggle for symbols that paradoxically represent both social distinction and conformity.

Apart from the stigma of having committed murder which affected both his romantic and employment prospects, as highlighted in the previous chapters, Raul experiences the stigma of not owning the right type of consumer items associated with specific moments of his life. He had become a "flawed consumer" (Bauman, 2005: 2).

Raul: I wouldn't have been in this boring normal situation that I am now if I would have had kids or had a nicer car, a nicer house, and you know … it's hard to explain … it reminds you more than anything that you have lost the normality of everything. How much better it could have been if I hadn't gone away […]. Yes, being 31 years old […]. So, people that don't know you are looking at you thinking, why is he 31 and still driving this little hatchback car, you know what I mean? Shouldn't he have a big proper car by now? And you can see that their eyebrows are raised a bit and you know, you realise that there are guys your age driving around in big Mercedes and Audis and stuff like that … you are thinking, shit that should have been me, you know what I mean? It is nothing to lose sleep over, but it is a big thing. You know …. time is frozen, or that you have lost. Lost is probably a better way of describing it, sometimes when I had a bad day you feel that you have been robbed of it. You blame everybody else you know what I mean, but yes … (Raul, first interview).

Raul characterised his life as normal and boring, but boredom has no room in consumer societies (Bauman, 2005). A boring life is ultimately an unhappy and unfulfilling life. Bauman remarked that "a happy life, as defined by consumer culture, is life insured against boredom, life in which constantly 'something happens', something new, exciting, and exciting because it is new" (Bauman, 2005: 39). Raul's normality served as a daily reminder of a life of wasted opportunities for consumption and missed enjoyments. In fact, Raul's offender stigma, which is normally classed as 'invisible', and as 'passing' in the literature (Goffman, 1963) was now experienced as conspicuous due to his (in)consumption patterns. Raul equated lost time to a period of deep freeze (Zamble and Porporino, 1990) and wasted opportunities to relish which elicited sentiments of guilt as he failed to answer the 'cultural injunction to enjoy' (Žižek, 2002) in all the time he was in prison. In our first interview, he felt that he could wait no longer. Having already achieved most of what he considered 'achievable' at that point (having been released for 18 months), he was experiencing pressure to accumulate the necessary capital to build a successful life based on the precepts of the consumerist societies.

Faced with a series of blocked opportunities and lacking in the narrative habitus (Fleetwood, 2016) to perform a set well developed identities in the period emergent of his release, Raul felt "compelled to enter the battle for consumer significance" (Hall, Winlow, and Ancrum, 2008: 65) and bought his dream car a year later – a BMW Z4 convertible. Buying the dream car meant that he recuperated lost time through imprisonment and avoided insignificance in the consumer culture of post-industrial society, or late modernity (Hayward and Yar, 2006). Raymen and Smith (2016: 18) made the point:

> Consumer objects have the ability to act as reflective mirrors of identity and distinction, temporarily staving off the anxiety of cultural obsolescence and for the individual providing a precious sliver of relational security, if only fleetingly.

Winlow and Hall (2016: 90) also remarked how traditional sources of identity, as they "recede into history", are being replaced by consumer objects of socio-symbolic significance. Raul made sure that the car he had bought was unique. He reminded me that he was the only one in the area with that colour and model, rendering him 'rare and different'. The car guaranteed Raul's golden membership to consumer culture whilst evidencing his individual qualities and characteristics (Miles, 1996). Further, the car was reinforcing Raul's internal narrative of success by reflecting it externally. In addition, it was being used as a mechanism of deflecting perceived stigma. Nevertheless, he had contemplated selling the car a year later due to financial difficulties but managed to keep it anyway. Around the same time, Raul rejected social media as a 'blind and envious world' which he does not want to engage with by any means.

Raul: To this day I haven't downloaded any social media so I am not on Facebook, I am not on Instagram, I am not on Snapchat, only because I know that in that world, is such a blind world, like people envying other people, ah look at me, he has a Lamborghini, she's got this make up and I am seeing what this is doing to people and I just don't want no part in that and that's helped me in how I am in my day to day life that I don't need to do this, that, and the other, to prove to people yeah, this is what I am, or yah this makes me a somebody because I am wearing Versace, or Louis Vuitton, or whatever, they don't mean anything to me. And that pressure that we did discuss about being our age and needing that sort of stuff, I think it only becomes a problem if you let yourself caught into that sort of world, lifestyle, and I've been lucky that I've avoided it as much as I can (Raul, second interview).

The passage above betrays an apparent rejection of consumer culture which stands in contradiction to Raul's initial narrative. Nevertheless, this was not necessarily the case once the motivations for his rejection of social media were clarified in our next interview, one year later. At that point, Raul reiterated his sense of being at a disadvantage compared to other people his age. He remarked how online public displays of luxurious lifestyles by 'rich kids' often make people envious. Given the danger of such strong emotions, he had made the decision to avoid being exposed to such content online. Nevertheless, Raul's narrative also betrays an inherent doubt about his own success, which was failing to be recognised and confirmed by others thus rendering his 'success story' unstable. In this sense, social media can be understood as providing a potential 'institutional incompatibility' (Harding et al., 2017) that challenged Raul's internal narrative of success forcing him to reconsider it altogether. I asked Raul about his social media use in our final interview, three years and six months after we have first met. He reiterated the point he made previously, but this time he was more direct about his own feelings of shame and envy that stemmed from his social status (Gilligan, 2000).

Raul: Why am I going to look at what somebody else has that I don't, and become envious and that's gonna mess up my day, just avoid it you know what I mean? Cuz everyone wants to outdo everybody, you know? Lamborghini – 'oh he's got the Lamborghini Murcielago', 'oh he's got the Lamborghini Huracan', and it just goes up and up and up it's no limit to that, I don't want none of that (Raul, forth interview).

Social media acted as the punishing cultural super-ego (Edmundson, 2023) for Raul's failure to achieve neo-liberal success and the injunction to enjoy. Rather than a rejection of consumer capitalist culture, the above signals Raul's truce with its competitive character, and his submission to its prevailing ideology. Raul recognised the narcissistic ethos of the post-political, post-industrial world of neo-liberalism which nurtures competitive individualism as its driving force (Treadwell et al., 2013). Given his 'massive disadvantage', consequence of his lengthy imprisonment, engagement with social media users' conspicuous consumption and self-promotion (Taylor, 2020) would simply serve to twist the knife in the wound created by his 'consumer insignificance'. Despite his efforts, the cracks began to show in Raul's narrative of personal distinctiveness and status given the structural and institutional constraints that were not confirming his narrative identity and ego ideal. This elicited feelings of shame and humiliation consequence of his psychological and material relative deprivation (Gilligan, 2000) and self-blame (Keen, 2023). Raul started to develop a cynical attitude towards his future; compared to our first interview, his plans were now scarce. The aspirations to accumulate material wealth seemed to have been suppressed. Raul started talking about being grateful about everything he had as opposed to portraying an insatiable need for wealth accumulation. Raul's narrative had also taken a fatalistic turn as his future was not being perceived as outside of his control, and the script of moving forward became much more ambiguous than initially portrayed. At the end of our final interview, I asked Raul about his plans.

Raul: I take each day as it comes because you are not promised anything... that doesn't mean I'm a bum who just sits around, waiting for things to happen, nah, I'm always trying to progress, always trying to get better, but I control the things I can control, that's it really man.

Dan: Who said that the stoics? Stoicism?

Raul: Yeah, I love reading about Stoicism, Marcus Aurelius...

Dan: That's influenced the way that you carry yourself. Did you read about that in prison or after release?

Raul: I became it before I knew what I was, so I started reading about it and then I realised that's exactly what I do, this is who I am, obviously I am not at the level that they are in terms of they can accept anything and everything because that is what life is, there are parts that still annoy me and that, but the premise, the fundamentals, the basics that's me all along (Raul, forth interview).

Ricoeur (1991) noted that narratives of expected future serve as maps for actions which orient individuals and provide them with a sense of motivation. I also asked what success meant to him, and he replied: "Being comfortable, taking care of your family, not having to rely on anyone, just being self-sufficient and resourceful". There were no mentions of luxurious cars and fancy houses anymore. This had been the first time I heard Raul identify as a stoic. Significantly, stoicism is built on the notion of fate and an understanding around individuals' futility to change such fate (Crawford and Helm, 2020). Once we understand the limits of our capabilities, we can then "focus on what we can control; accept whatever happens" (Salzgeber, 2019: 55). Research has found that individuals with an external locus of control – believing that life events are determined by external factors – have lower levels of optimism, especially when encountering difficult life experiences (Hand, 2004 in Peled-Laskov, Shoham, and Cojocaru, 2023). Raul's pessimism was directly proportional to his locus of control externalisation as time went on. This mechanism may also be conceptualised as a projection of his perceived consumer obsolesces onto society to defend against feelings of shame and humiliation. Importantly, Raul's transformation had not been sudden: I first observed a difference in his value and goals orientation during the COVID-19 pandemic (two years prior to our last interview), when he first started talking became 'resourceful' (just like his father) and focused on maintained a high work ethic.

From a Good Lives Model (GLM) perspective (Ward and Maruna, 2007; Ward and Stewart, 2003) Raul evidenced a fundamental change to his initial narrative identity, as performed in our first interviews. An individual's narrative identity emerges as Ward and Fortune (2013) remarked, from the value commitment and goals that individuals have and cherish to achieve their conception of a 'good life'. Raul's initial value commitment had been partly dictated by the precepts of the neo-liberal capitalist socio-economic system and its underlying consumer culture. This had occurred concomitantly but not unrelated to Raul's lack of access to sites of traditional pro-social and masculine identity constructions such as romantic relationships, or meaningful employment post-release. Initial fantasies had broken down into mere cynicism as life barriers made their way in rendering Raul's initial plans and narrative identities unattainable. Two years after we have met, his vision of a 'good life' and success was radically different: "Being comfortable, taking care of your family, not having to rely on anyone, just being self-sufficient and resourceful". Two more years later, in our last interview, Raul ascribed the course of his future to forces outside of his control. Stoicism provided the narrative framework that assisted Raul to make sense of his situation and favour an alternative identity and goals.

A return to work ethic (Bauman, 2005) as a site of identity construction meant that through hard work, Raul was becoming a resourceful and successful man despite everything that life was going to throw at him. Importantly, resourcefulness, although not perfectly aligned with his initial projected self, is a quality which has much traction in the neo-liberal world of hyper-individualisation and self-governance (Rose, 2000). It is also a resource which he associated with his father who represents a masculine role model to Raul, as well as stoicism as life philosophy. This provides evidence for Raul's capacity to make sense of projected 'future selves' and 're-entry narratives' given challenging structural and institutional obstacles.

Peter: Reframing the goal

In a similar vein to Raul, soon after his release from prison, Peter eagerly considered the promise of the globalised neo-liberal society. He lamented about getting rid of his current exploitative job and started planning to become an entrepreneur. He would then only work for his own well-being and follow his dream. A simple connection to the internet would ensure that he could make money from any corner of the globe and provide him with much-needed flexibility. He was released for six months at the time of our first interview:

Peter: It's you know, I said to you earlier, I don't want to get up in the morning and be paid not a lot of money to work my ass off towards someone else's dream, now I would say seriously that in my work, I bet within 3 days I earned that company the money that they pay me for the whole 3 months do you know what I mean… and I don't want to do that anymore, because I want to have time to spend with my children, I want to be there when he goes to bed every night and be there when he gets up in the morning, you know what I mean. I want to make myself a laptop lifestyle, you know where my work is 3-4 hours a day on my laptop and it gives me time for swimming, going for a bit of walking, going to the trampoline with the boys, to do other things. […] I said now when I go to work, I put my work in put my effort in yah, what I'm starting to do now like I said to you, I'm starting to spend a bit of time in the evenings, even when I am tired to work towards my own business (Peter, first interview).

At the time of the interview, six months after release, Peter worked for a car repairing company, and was waiting for the birth of his son. He resented his work and was prepared to move on. The neo-liberal capitalist discourse of 'self-realisation' assured Peter that he could blossom as 'his own boss'. Now that he was released, 'the sky was the limit' so he quickly started to plan for his future. The promise is that every human being 'has something entrepreneurial about them' (Dardot and Laval, 2013: 111 in Catlaw and Marshall, 2018: 10) and thus the 'entrepreneur' acted as Peter's preferred narrative identity for a future self. Peter did not provide a clear and feasible plan as to how this will be pursued and achieved.

By the time of our third interview, almost two years after we have met, the plan had evaporated. Peter was made redundant because of the COVID-19 first lockdown. We decided to talk over a video call, a few hours after Peter had taken a job interview. I was surprised to see Peter cradling his baby boy in his arms as he answered the call (which continued throughout the interview). Of course, we started by talking about this new potential job which included forklift driving among other activities. Despite his lack of the necessary qualifications to drive the machine, Peter displayed an unrealistic optimism over his future despite his narrative ambiguity around the plan to achieve financial success (Harding et al., 2017). At this point, I had asked him what he would like to do in the future:

Peter: I really want to get more into carpentry, because I like it and, I found Dan, you know, with straight lines and the angles and what have you, I, for whatever reason, I quite like that, you know, you know what I mean? (Peter, third interview).

His relaxed mannerism in discussing his (un)employment status, as well as his interest in pursuing carpentry to feed his creativity as a vocation struck me. A fundamental shift in Peter's values and orientation had taken place, and this solicited a value-laden question on my part:

Dan: What is a successful person in your view?

Peter: I don't care, I don't care man, my life is not a competition in order for success or whatever means nothing to me. The whole concept of success is just, fucking'... you know, border of this capitalist environment that we live in, you know, you got to have a bigger car and a fucking whatever, and you see people on the street, and they have a fucking Porsche truck thing, for their seven kids and their kids are dressed in fucking rags that's upside down innit? The Porsche should be gone, the kids should be well tendered. You know what I am saying? I don't, I don't believe in it as a concept, I think it's a control mechanism, and you need to be free of that, I don't say fucking go off the grid and go live in the woods and that you got to be in the system but not necessarily part of the system. We are forced to live in a machine because we are born into it. We are born into the national insurance number which is essentially your fucking employee number (kisses the baby). In any situation we can look at the model, ok right, what is going on here, you can observe the model Dan, and you can look if you are careful to find how you can be happy. Other people can't tell you when you are happy. Ralph Lauren can't teach you, that shit don't make you happy. You know, they might make some people happy but not me, there's lots of things that will give you joy in life, and they don't cost a penny, but you couldn't buy them for all the gold in the world ... and there he is! "I didn't pay a penny for you!" He then looked at the baby and said, "you are the most valuable thing that I ever seen in my life. See?" (Peter, third interview).

Compared to Raul, who constructed his identity by reference and submission to the ideological precepts of consumer capitalism, Peter repudiated ornamental consumerism, and thus constructed a resistance narrative stemming from an anti-capitalist moral position (Cherrier, 2009; Fernandez, Brittain, and Bennet, 2011). In this sense, Peter's counternarrative to the hegemonic cultural and socio-economic discourse leads to his construction of a rebel and resistant consumer identity free to reflect upon the system from objective distance. Nevertheless, Peter accepted that he cannot completely repudiate a system which 'makes us all an offer we can't refuse' (Winlow and Hall, 2016: 90) as such refusal would simply be disastrous, but highlighted those other things are important in life, such as being a good father. The function of the story depicting 'rich kids in rags' serves to organise and guide Peter's moral principles, which now stand at the heart of his narrative identity.

Since our first interview, Peter had become a father, and fatherhood equipped him with the necessary narrative resources to discard consumer culture as a mere distraction from the important things in life. This sort of clarity has become apparent only recently and stands to evidence Peter's adaptation of narrative identities to the realities of his situation and acts to stave off any consumerist pressure of capital accrual. Compared to Raul, who had struggled to accumulate the narrative resources to make sense of the structural barriers he encountered on release, Peter's adaptation had taken a fundamentally different route. Fatherhood had been crucial in this journey. Further, his ease to discuss his unemployment may be indicative of a masculinity which is achieved through his fatherhood rather than through a specific position within the neo-liberal market. Nevertheless, his resistance is illusory: Peter's commitment to traditional family as alternative to consumer capitalism only serves to position him in the front seat of one of the main drivers of capitalist economy (see Burr, 2015).

Discussion

This chapter has evidenced how the most recently released mandatory lifers in this sample, namely Raul and Peter, negotiated with master narratives of success in a consumer capitalist society which interpellated them as consumers on their release. Concomitant to initial agentic projections of taking on conventional family roles which in the end fell short due to structural barriers to resettlement, Raul had decided to enter the 'battle of consumer significance' (Hall, Winlow, and Ancrum, 2008: 65) in a race to substitute a fragile sense of identity with the consumerist symbols demanded by the post-industrial, consumerist society. Soon after his release, he experienced 'consumption melancholia', which stemmed precisely from his perceived missed opportunities to enjoy due to his lengthy imprisonment. This then pressured him to perform successful selves through dominant consumerist symbols. In fact, his inability to conspicuously consume was experienced as stigma, perhaps evidencing the need for a reconceptualisation of Goffman's theories for an application to 21st-century subjectivity.

Would-be desisters such as Raul, rather than falling onto 'habit' when encountering structural barriers as King (2012) suggested, become entangled in the ideological precepts of consumer capitalism which structure their subjectivity, and subsequent agentic movements in line with its consumerist interpellant forces. Then, it would simply be naïve to suggest that 'habit' is devoid of any ideological restraint. However, this does not render Raul as 'super dupe' (Farrall and Bowling, 1999) puppeteered by ideology. Rather, the finding is partly consistent with Farrall, Bottoms, and Shapland's (2010) adaptation of Mouzelisian sociology in that actors' own perception of their immediate surroundings and position within the social structure guide individual choices. However, not only does socialisation matter in 'dispositions' to perceive such structures, but biographical and alternative narrative resources are important in mobilising adaptive narrative identity and subsequent action. When the situation imposed it, Raul attended to available opportunities and worked extra hours to become resourceful and avoid financial difficulties. The adaptation of narrative identity to his structural position partly stemmed from his narrative habitus (Fleetwood, 2016; Frank, 2010) – an internal, biographical source, intimately linked to ideals, and stories constructed around the father figure. His value commitment to Stoicism provided the introjected philosophical framework used to reconstruct his identity and defend against feelings of shame and humiliation through acknowledging structural obstacles in shaping the self. In this sense, Raul acted as an agent who mobilised internal and external narrative resources to project an adaptive narrative self. Peter on the other hand is the example *par excellence* for the lifer who, to avoid consumer insignificance reinterpreted his social situation and lamented about having obtained the 'most expensive things in life', a new-born son and a stereotypically happy family. These narrative resources were mobilised to discard consumer capitalism as a mere distraction from what truly matters in life. Nevertheless, this resistance is illusory: from a Marxist view, the family and marriage are some of the strongest driving forces of the capitalist economy (Burr, 2015).

References

Althusser, L. (2001) *"Lenin and Philosophy" and Other Essays*, trans. Ben Brewster. New York: Monthly Review Press [1971].

Bauman, Z. (2005) *Work, Consumerism and the New Poor*, 2nd ed., Maidenhead: Open University Press

Burr, V. (2015) *Social Constructionism*, 3rd ed., New York: Routledge.

Catlaw, T. J., and Marshall, G. S. (2018) Enjoy your work! The fantasy of the neoliberal workplace and its consequences for the entrepreneurial subject. *Administrative Theory & Praxis*, 40 (2), 99–118.

Cherrier, H. (2009) Anti-consumption discourses and consumer-resistance. *Journal of Business Research*, 62 (2), 181–190.

Crawford, A. C., and Helm, B. M. (2020) How can stoic philosophy inspire psycho-social genetic counselling practice? An introduction and exploration. *Journal of Rational-Emotive*, 38, 155–172.

Edmundson, M. (2023) *The Age of Guilt: The Super-Ego in the Online World*. New Haven: Yale University Press.

Farrall, S., Bottoms, A., and Shapland, J. (2010) Social structures and desistance from crime. *British Journal of Criminology*, 7 (6), 46–70.

Farrall, S., and Bowling, B. (1999) Structuration, human development, and desistance from crime. *British Journal of Criminology*, 39, 53–268.

Fernandez, K. V., Brittain, A. J., and Bennet, S. D. (2011) "Doing the duck": Negotiating the resistance-consumer identity. *European Journal of Marketing*, 45 (11/12), 1779–1788.

Fleetwood, J. (2016) Narrative habitus: Thinking through structure/agency in the narratives of offenders. *Crime Media Culture*, 12 (2), 173–192.

Frank, W. A. (2010) *Letting Stories Breathe: A Socio-Narratology*. Chicago: University of Chicago Press.

Gilligan, J. (2000) *Violence: Reflections on Our Deadliest Epidemic*. London: Jessica Kingsley Publishers.

Goffman, E. (1963) *Stigma Notes on the Management of Spoiled Identity*. London: Penguin.

Hall, S., Winlow, S., and Ancrum, C. (2008) *Criminal Identities and Consumer Culture: Crime, Exclusion, and the New Culture of Narcissism*. Cullompton: Willan Higate.

Harding, D. J., Dobson, C., Wyse, J. J. B., and Morenoff, D. (2017) Narrative change, narrative stability, and structural constraints: the case of prisoner reentry narratives. *American Journal of Cultural Sociology*, 5 (1), 261–304.

Hayward, K., and Yar, M. (2006) The 'Chav' phenomenon: consumption, media and the construction of a new underclass. *Crime, Media, Culture*, 2 (1), 9–28.

Keen, D. (2023) *Shame: The Politics and Power of an Emotion*. Princeton: Princeton University Press.

King, S. (2012) Transformative agency and desistance from crime. *Criminology and Criminal Justice*, 13 (3), 317–335.

King, S. (2013) Transformative agency and desistance from crime. *Criminology and Criminal Justice*, 13 (3), 317–335.

Miles, S. (1996) The cultural capital of consumption: Understanding 'postmodern' identities in a cultural context. *Culture and Psychology*, 2, 139–158.

Peled-Laskov, R., Shoham, E., and Cojocaru, L. (2023) Locus of control among Arab and Jewish Israeli Parolees. *International Journal of Offender Therapy and Comparative Criminology* 0 (0), 1–16.

Raymen, T., and Smith, O. (2016) What's deviance got to do with it? Black Friday sales, violence, and hyper-conformity. *British Journal of Criminology*, 56 (2), 389–405.

Ricoeur, P. (1991) Narrative identity. *Philosophy Today*, 35 (1), 73–81.

Rose, N. (2000) Government and control. *British Journal of Criminology*, 40 (2), 321–339.

Salzgeber, J. (2019) *The Little Book of Stoicism*. Jonas Salzgeber.

Taylor, D. G. (2020) Putting the "self" in selfies: How narcissism, envy and self-promotion motivate sharing of travel photos through social media. *Journal of Travel & Tourism Marketing*, 37 (1), 64–77.

Treadwell, J., Briggs, D., Winlow, S., and Hall, S. (2013) Shopocalypse now: Consumer culture and the English Riots of 2011. *British Journal of Criminology*, 53, 1–17.

Ward, T., and Fortune, C-A. (2013) The good lives model: Aligning risk reduction with promoting offenders' personal goals. *European Journal of Probation*, 5 (2), 29–46.

Ward, T., and Maruna, S. (2007) *Rehabilitation*. Abingdon, Oxon: Routledge.

Ward, T., and Stewart, C. A. (2003) The treatment of sex offenders: Risk management and good lives. *Professional Psychology: Research and Practice*, 34, 353–360.

Winlow, S., and Hall, S. (2016) Realist criminology and its discontents. *International Journal for Crime, Justice, and Social Democracy*, 5 (3), 80–94.

Zamble, E., and Porporino, F. (1990) Coping, imprisonment, and rehabilitation: Some data and their implications. *Criminal Justice and Behaviour*, 17 (1), 53–70.

Žižek, S. (2002) *For They Know Not What They Do: Enjoyment as a Political Factor*. London: Verso.

7 Experiencing supervision

Introduction

The previous chapter offered a macro analysis of the ways in which the most recently released mandatory lifers in this sample negotiated with master narratives of consumer capitalism to construct their identities post-release, This chapter moves on to focus on the meso level of the analysis by exploring the ways in formal mechanisms of support and surveillance, especially supervision exerted by the probation system is enabling, or constraining all five mandatory lifers in constructing pro-social identities. The 'Tug of War' metaphor was used in the introduction to explain the ways in which the men negotiated with a series of forces within the liminal spaces they inhabited post release. Life on probation represents the liminal position (Turner, 1969) *par excellence* – although quasi free in the community, the probationer is subjected to the supervision and control of penal power. Thus, these men are caught in the indeterminate space between prison life and freedom.

It is argued that the mandatory lifers in this sample experienced supervision with a degree of ambivalence. The individualising discourse of neo-rehabilitation ensured that the men perceived themselves as the agents of their own-self change. Invitations to self-governance were doubled by periods of tension where the men were constructed as risky and dangerous by their case workers; the type of murder committed became relevant in this context. The most serious of the offenders were required to perform a very specific form of remorse to account for their past and to provide evidence for their redemption. Nevertheless, the men did not passively accept these positions – they drew from counter-narratives to resist probationers' constructions. At times, expressed acts of resistance almost cost the men the revocation of their life licence.

Responsible, dangerous, and risky: Mandatory lifers negotiating supervision ambivalence

Peter was content with what he called the 'length of the leash' that probation had offered him soon after release, contrary to anticipated tightness of restrictions on life post-release by imprisoned mandatory lifers (Rennie and

DOI: 10.4324/9781003415640-7

Crewe, 2023). Being left alone meant that the probation service trusted him, and this was a consequence of the great rapport he had built with his supervising officer. Nevertheless, he recognised that the length of the leash was only partly in his control. Murder, he remarked, is a political category. At the time of our first interview murderers were not in the spotlight of the mediatised public spectacle of failed rehabilitation. In fact, public attention was squarely focused on the terrorist attack at the London Bridge. This allowed mandatory lifers such as Peter space to breathe. Nevertheless, he was aware of the highly politicised nature of his own crime and his subsequent supervision which, at that time, allowed for flexibility and freedom which was built on the right context, and a good level of rapport with his probation officer.

Peter: At the moment, the people that are embarrassing probation in the media are the terrorist people aren't they. So by and large they just leave me alone, I'm not part of that group, I'm sure there will come a time when a recently released life sentenced prisoners commits a heinous crime, and they may put the spotlight back on my generation of people who've been released, you know what I mean, but at the moment, the media is firmly focused on these terrorists who done a sentence and been released early for whatever reason as I'm sure you are aware. Which means that really, I just go to the meeting, every, aa whenever, really, once about every 4-5 weeks, (says mockingly): 'how are you doing, you alright?' 'How's it going then?' They are busy, they ain't got time, and I think they have an amount of trust in me? (Peter, first interview).

Best thing they can do to help me out is to fuck off and leave me. You know what I mean, and by and large at the minute, because of the terrorist situation, that's what is happening, so I don't know, what more could they do to help me ... I don't know (Peter, first interview).

Peter's narrative was imbued with a sense of pessimism reserved for the future which, in turn, echoed *carpe diem*! The extensive 'liberty' may be short lived, so, he may as well enjoy it whilst it lasts. In fact, the probation service had been previously under scrutiny with the high-profile murders by released prisoners – for example Damien Hanson and Anthony Rice (HM Inspectorate of Probation, 2006a, 2006b). This raised the question of the safe release of those who murdered (Kemshall, 2007). Nevertheless, in a visionary fashion, the sort of invisibility that Peter referred to was indeed short-lived. A year and a half after our first conversation, Colin Pitchford, a person convicted of double murder had been recalled to prison, after approaching young women and thus breaching the conditions of his life licence. This led to a public outcry around his suitability to be released (and the role of Parole Board in the process), as well as the extent to which rehabilitation for people who committed murder is achieved in prison. Despite the attention this case has received, Peter's life had not been significantly affected perhaps because Colin Pitchford did not end up committing a further murder during his release.

Nevertheless, what makes the resettlement of 'dangerous' individuals problematic is the anxiety and fear that such crime elicits in the public (supposedly comparable with sex offending; see Kitzinger, 2004) in that 'they may do it again' (Liem and Weggemans, 2018: 474). The inquiries which followed the cases mentioned above led to what was considered a 'rebalancing of justice' between the offenders and victims (Home Office, 2006a, 2006b; Home Secretary, 2006 in Kemshall, 2007). One may justifiably ask, in this context, to what extent the fear of such a scenario repeating itself may influence probation officers' day-to-day supervision of mandatory life sentenced individuals (Phillips, Westaby, and Fowler, 2016). We now know that recall rates tend to rise in the aftermath of serious subsequent offences committed by high-profile individuals who were recently released (HMIP, 2020; Shingler and Nick, 2024). Given this, perhaps rightly, Peter though of the probation system in political terms and this meant that he recognised his supervisory style as decided elsewhere, not between him and his probation officer. Rather, it was bound to socio-political factors which were experienced as being far away.

At this initial stage of his release, Peter had been left to his own accord by the probation system; he was free to do as he pleased – he never felt 'micromanaged'. He has been caught up in a responsibilising neo-liberal discourse which works on the premise of cherished individualism and independent citizenship (Rose, 2000). Peter seemed to accept the probationer's injunction to become a willing and responsible citizen (Werth, 2011) who self-regulates and accepts governability from a distance. The following passage makes this clear; having asked him whether he believes that his probation experience can be improved, he answered:

Peter: Because of the way I live my life Dan, it's not a massive burden, I feel I am free to do whatever I want to do, because what I choose to do is the next right thing on every occasion (Peter, first interview).

Peter's strong commitment to personal responsibility is central to his life philosophy, and to the management of his own release. He conceptualises the probation system not as a provider of security, or to 'advise, assist and befriend' which used to be the original purpose of probation (Durnescu et al., 2018; Healy and Kennefick, 2023), but rather "as a partner and facilitator for active and independent citizens" (Rose, 2000: 186). Whilst this seemed to work for him at this early stage of his release, Peter later evidenced ambivalence to this supervisory style. For example, 16 months after our first interview Peter complained about not being able to get into contact with his probation officer who is never around. Interestingly, Peter's 'responsibilization' (Rose,

2000) was evident once more through his own internalisation of guilt to account for his probation officer's absence:

Peter: Mate, she won't answer the phone to me, I don't speak to her for weeks on end, supposed to speak to her every 2 weeks yeah but she is not around, I don't speak to her. You remember I had the first one who was my probation officer for all those years, they switched her with this other woman, and a... yeah man she's alright, I think she has understood that I am a changed person and you know, but it does annoy me because when I got, when I want to talk to her, I fucking ring her 2 or 3 times and it may take me 1 week of trying to ring her to actually get contact with her. [...] This is part of getting the best out of the system. Through communication, building a very quick good rapport with this new probation officer has led to her leaving me alone which gives me ... because she can be a real pain in the arse. She can have me come in every 2 days go to the probation office what have you, but she doesn't, I've committed a very fucking serious offence as you know, I've only been out of prison for a short time... (Peter, third interview).

The contradiction in the passage above is evident. Peter perceives his probationer's non-interventionist, neglectful, and distanced supervisory style as a hardly earned right. As a responsible citizen living in an advanced liberal society (Kemshall, 2002), Peter is invited to self-regulate and live independent of any serious support (Kramer, Rajah, and Sung, 2013). Kemshall (2002: 52) remarked that "as the social and its attendant notions of social justice and social processes have retreated, the space has simultaneously left has been filled by 'individualisation' with the attendant notions of the 'rational and prudential citizen' and notions of individual responsibility and blame".

For Peter, the lax and highly individualised, neo-liberalised, and 'responsibilising', self-regulatory (Perry, 2013) supervisory style was non consistent throughout his early release days and months. For example, only ten months after his release, Peter's partner, Jennifer, had given birth to their baby son. Soon after, Peter was informed that he would not be able to continue seeing the child until he had successfully completed a battery of risk assessments requested by social services. These were scheduled to take up to six weeks and were directing at assessing the risk he would carry to his own child.

Peter: I can understand that maybe one in every unspecified amount of people in my situation may cause harm to their child, but I know that I am not that one. So, me having to go through this may spare that one, but to be honest I don't fucking care, I just want to see my little boy. You know what I mean? I am quite angry about the whole situation, you know Dan. As I was saying to you earlier, I was released on parole, and a parole board is a fucking, just, it's a full risk assessment, isn't it? Do you know what I mean? And that doesn't seem to be good enough for these people, you know ... and, also, they knew that the baby boy was coming for a long time, so they should have gotten done before in my opinion. So, to vent my fucking anger at them, I instructed my solicitor that I want to legal action against them... sooner! They are terrified of a photograph of me 20 years ago, you know? They are judging me on the basis of... yeah... and that's not the way to move anything forward. They are after my offence. They are not taking any time to talk to me so far (Peter, second interview).

You know, at no point have any of the judges or the parole board ever said that you know you need to be careful, make sure you never have a child you know what I mean? It's just these other agencies that suddenly involved themselves you know... my index offence is murder yea? Not of a child, of a grown person, and I never been convicted or suspected, of otherwise, of injurious actions against any children or anything like that (Peter, second interview).

Repeated risk assessments at the hands of different agencies invited Peter to consider taking on the identity of a risky murderer who may not be trusted around his own child. Accepting this proposition would serve to deny, as well as spoil his emerging identities (especially that of fatherhood), and self-professed transformation (cf. Opsal, 2015). The story above is one of stagnation where Peter is eternally returned to his past (cf. Eliade, 1954); the risk inertia places him in a vicious circle which interferes with a pro-social construction of self. Further, the type of murder he committed, whilst important in his own subjective sense of self, was indiscernible to the assessors.

Peter was invited to accept his index offence as master status, which, in turn classifies and invites him to become a certain type of person (Werth, 2018). The 'long-leash' that he celebrated in our first interview had been exchanged for a much shorter one on account of the risk he carried once the social services got involved. In this case, social services betray a binary judgement (dangerous/not dangerous) (Werth, 2018) based on Peter's type of crime and level of multi-agency public protection arrangements (MAPPA) supervision.

Murderers such as Peter are seen to live on the precipices of serenity and where murderous impulses can return in force at any time. Social services, unlike his probation officer, pathologised Peter by '[going] after [his] offence', as opposed to talking with him, as a person. This pathologising discourse (Lacombe, 2013; Perry, 2013; Waldram, 2007) constructed Peter 'the murderer' as irrational and unpredictable. Further, there is a gendered undertone attached to the deficits cast onto him. As Perry (2013) remarked when exploring the intersecting discourses between probationers and offender identities, facilitators often draw on ideas of 'cavemen', or 'hunter gatherers' to explain the aetiology of male criminal behaviour. Of course, the image of the caveman is the image of a man who functions on impulse – and in that sense Peter is constructed as a potentially impulsive risk taker who could terminate his child's life on a whim. To reiterate, what makes the resettlement of 'dangerous' individuals problematic is the anxiety and fear that such crime elicits in the public, especially when those released kill again. Peter felt that such fear is illegitimate as his crime has no bearing on children.

Having invited him to consider and take on such a subject position, social services acted as a convergent force that hampered his progression through the liminal realm. Supervision, then, similarly to McNeill's 'Malopticon', casts its subjects as fundamentally untrustworthy and bad (McNeill, 2018). Nevertheless, as Werth (2011) remarked, individuals are not merely passive receivers of 'parole governance'. In fact, parolees can as much actively comply with the requirements as they can engage with 'small acts of striking back' (Carrabine, 2005: 906), or even overtly defy rules. In this case, Peter was not simply a passive subject of penal power. In fact, he attempted to follow rules with a degree of malleability when situations imposed it. He confessed that he had thought about ignoring the instructions and to continue visiting his child. In this situation, his imposed conditions increased his risk of recall (Shingler and Stickney, 2024). However, I have never asked whether he acted on this thought or not. Potential non-compliance for Peter was not necessarily a means of regaining autonomy as others have imagined (Opsal, 2015; Rose, 2000; Werth, 2011, 2016), although it could serve this as a secondary function. Rather, it represented an attempt at protecting his emerging fatherhood identity from being spoiled. Peter resisted social services' positioning and reconstructed the story to fit what he wants to become – a 'true father' willing to lose everything for his son. This modern, romanticised, version of fatherhood is the story that Peter prefers, and one he is willing to sacrifice everything for. He did not accept riskiness as part of his own story. In turn, he embraced a story which runs the risk of making him breach his parole conditions. The investigation ended once he managed to convince the authorities that he is not a potential risk to his son: the "initial fear of the fucking snapshot of [him] 20 years ago very quickly subsided once they got to know [him] a little bit – they were alright". As evidenced above, Peter had been experiencing supervision with a high degree of ambivalence; long periods of self-governance intersected with acute stress followed by his construction as a fundamentally dangerous and risky individual. Peter's case evidences how mandatory lifers, provided they can draw from a range of wider narrative resources, are able to resist and negotiate invitations by the probation system to take on dangerous and risky identities, and thus return them to their past. Paradoxically, these risk-related restrictions and impositions can increase the risk of recall.

Walking on eggshells: Raul

Like Peter, Raul too felt that his probation officer has been allowing him to carry on with his life without much interference. Despite the potential power that probation can exert over him, Raul is content that they have not 'not been on [his] case'. Nevertheless, such cherished freedom came with a degree of ambivalence. A pervasive sense of panoptic power (Foucault, 1975) was diffusely experienced as Raul lived in a constant fear of potentially going back if he ever makes a mistake. The sentiment of walking on eggshells is evidenced in the following passage, taken from our first interview – at the time, Raul had been out of prison for little over 18 months:

Raul: I was lucky because I always had good probation officers, since I got out, they never really nagged me, or been on my case, or breach me or anything like that, but you always know, yeah, it's always at the back of your mind, ok, if I mess up, if I do this, or that, are they gonna come on me, you know what I mean. And they do lessen the time you would have to see them, so start weekly, and then monthly, and then 6 weeks; I think I am on six weeks at the moment ... it's a little bit frustrating cuz you go there and you got to tell them everything that's going on, but when you live like a normal, mundane life, there's nothing you can say, you know, they sometimes are perceived that like you not being honest with them ... (Raul, first interview).

This passage is seemingly benign in that it projects optimism for the future, but it betrays Raul's Kafkaesque uncertainty regarding probation's expectations of him as a 'regular', 'ordinary' lifer. The sense of progression from weekly visits to presently visiting the probationer's office once every six weeks was experienced as a positive incentive that encouraged him to continue with optimism and offers sentiments of reassurance. The construction of his probation officer as 'good' is, similarly to Peter's case, strictly related to the provision of distance and liberty – both men feel they are left to their own accord. What seems to be missing from the men's narratives is a focus on how the probation service has been or could potentially be useful in their lives and future. In turn, this absence betrays a deep penetration of neo-rehabilitation (Feeley and Simon, 1992) in the men's available narrative repertoires to construct more complex expectations of their supervision. In our third interview, almost two years after we have first met, as the COVID-19 pandemic had started in earnest and the subsequent lockdown ensued, Raul experienced a setback and he felt that the probation system had begun to distrust him:

Raul: So before, they had me on my coming in every 6 weeks, sorry not even coming in, they were calling me, and you know they were trusting me and all of a sudden Covid happened and now they insist on all lifers having to come in once a month in now, so I feel like quite

	a big step back from that, they won't let me travel nowhere still even though I've been out 3.5 years, I've got an impeccable record, so that's a bit annoying, but when I go there I don't give them attitude or nothing like that, I do whatever they ask me to do, to be honest, my probation officers haven't been horrible or tried to trip me up in any ways it's just a lot of legislation and red tape that they can't get around, which I can't really hold them to account for. It's like a step back innit, I was pretty much done with all of that, what can you do, if they say jump you gotta say how high? (Raul, third interview).
Dan:	Not allowing you to move on?
Raul:	100%, if you have to still answer people to people. These little wannabe gangsters, they're all sitting there with their trousers hanging low you know giving attitudes to the reception staff, turning up like half an hour late, I've seen them every time I been in there, ahh I was meant to have an appointment at 10 it's now like 11 a clock and I'm thinking if I was to have done that, they would put me straight back in prison, you know what I mean, but this is difference between my crime and these people you know what I mean (Raul, third interview).
Dan:	Because of risk.
Raul:	Exactly.

Raul associated the pandemic and accompanying changes as a drawback in his re-entry progression, and he also decried a reduction in trust granted to lifers such as himself during lockdown. It seems to Raul that his classification as a 'lifer' and membership to the lifer category had taken primacy in how the authorities made sense of himself in such stressful moments. They are seen to simply eschew his individual progress and disregard individual differences. This is evidenced in the passage where Raul counterposed his experience of stagnation with a personal impeccable record. His crime placed Raul at the high end of the 'dangerousness'/'riskiness' scale which is felt as inappropriate given how successful and dedicated to reintegration he has been up until that moment. Compared to the life-course persistent offenders (Moffitt, 1993) that he is forced to share the waiting room with at each one of his supervisory meetings, his behaviour has been exemplary. Despite this, his classification as a mandatory lifer seems to take primacy in official analyses of Raul's behaviour. This construction is experienced with frustration and resistance and interferes with his construction of pro-social identities. Here, spatial and organisational elements of the probationer's room remind him of his criminal past as much as the 'wannabe gangsters' he referred to earlier.

Dan:	Do they remind you of authority? (the probation officers)
Raul:	Of course, they do because probation officers don't just sit there; it's like an interview at the police station. They have the alarm

along the wall, you know the thing that they have there, they sit opposite you, they got the pen and paper, and you think to yourself like, this isn't somebody who genuinely wants to know how I am feeling, and my well-being, this is somebody who has a particular box or not particular box to see if they will send you back to prison or not (Raul, third interview).

Raul's routine visit to the probationer's office is the opposite of Albertson, Philips, and Fowler's (2022) 'stigma avoiding places' which sustain desistance. In fact, Raul's space-time rhythm (May and Thrift, 2001 in Hunter and Farrall, 2015) organised around routine visits to the probationer's office gives the place (as much as his interactions with the probation officer) a meaning which in turn shapes Raul's identity (Hunter and Farrall, 2015) by way of inviting him to take the position of a dangerous ex-offender. The alarm along the wall, the interview arrangements, and pen and paper position Raul as a subject of penal power which needs to be managed and, in the end, contribute to the formalism of their interaction.

To reiterate, there seems to exist a paradox evidenced by the ambivalent mode that 'murderers' are governed in the community. Invitations to self-governance and to individual responsibility are interrupted periodically by acute panoptic (Foucault, 1975) supervisory episodes which serve to construct the men as risky and dangerous. Thus far, the men had not simply accepted these constructions, but engaged with and expressed counter-narratives to these tendencies in their negotiation of acceptable identities.

Hyper-normality: "Showing that you are not a risk, or a monster"

Nathaniel, on the other hand, is an example *par excellence* of the mandatory lifer who has internalised the 'risk paradigm' of neo-rehabilitation (Feeley and Simon, 1992). He too identified the probation service through its punitive character rather than its potential rehabilitative assistance. In our first interview, I asked Nathaniel about his relationship with the probation officer since release and whether there have been any turning points that were worth exploring in our interview:

Nathaniel: Everyone seems to think that with probation it's rapport, with probation I found it's just about longevity and maintaining good work and just being honest with them. It's not about doing a specific thing, or one specific thing, or two bad things, it's just getting the balance right, and then, just about every month they want to see that you can handle it in society, they are not there, I found that they are not there to judge whether you good or bad, it's whether you are a risk to society or a risk to breaking your conditions. There are no turning points. Because

I did nothing with probation that is special, uhm ... my reports', and have 10 minutes chats, it not like they keeping you, so... in all the time I've been out and I've reported to probation I probably still didn't have more than a week's interviews with them but it's just about the rapport you build through how long you kept your job for, uhm ... obviously that's it with probation, it's not like I am doing nothing special with them ... (Nathaniel, first interview).

As shown above, Nathaniel did not rate good rapport with his probation officer as the secret ingredient to a positive relationship, contradicting some published research (Doekhie et al., 2018; Healy, 2012). For him, consistency and honesty have been superior elements that maintained a smooth connection with the authorities. Further, Nathaniel was clear in identifying the principal role of probation officers as that of evaluators of his riskiness to society, and to his own licence conditions. The finding echoes a recent European study which explored supervision experience across jurisdictions and found probationers to associate supervision with its punitive character, rather than its rehabilitative potential (Durnescu et al., 2018). For him, "proving that [he] is not a risk or a monster" represented a mission for much of his initial time on release. Seven months after our first interview, I asked him how he has managed to achieve this:

Nathaniel: It's not about episodes or stories, it's about literally blending into society showing that you are not a risk, it's like I said, it's not like ... you don't really, not every day, like I don't come across an incident every day and I automatically like get angry over it, or... it's just about literally, just about timing, it's like watering grass, it doesn't instantly grow or instantly develop, but slowly, just water it and watch it grow, and I think that's the same with probation that it's not that you are on your case all the time, they give me enough rope and then they got the attitude well, he will hang himself ... sort of thing, so it's just literally, there's not much an incident to show that I am not a monster it's just dealing with everyday life and literally staying out of trouble, the police ain't coming to my door then obviously I am doing a good job. It's not so much about circumstance, you can only show people in time, you can't instantly change people's mind, it takes time ... (Nathaniel, second interview).

Proving that he is not a monster is Nathaniel's long-term plan with probation. This quest to prove his normality evidenced the chasm between his conceptualisation of his own personal identity, and his experiences of his social identity. The same sense of unjust perception has been experienced by all the men. Nevertheless, Nathaniel had chosen to accept probation's risk-laden discourse to negotiate identities by playing the authorities' game.

The productive power exercised by the probation system, evidenced through the 'long leash', resembles the mobilisation of technologies of the self (Foucault, 1988) – such as responsibility and empowerment – which are experienced dialectically with oppressive forms of power (Turnbull and Hannah-Moffat, 2009). Like Peter and Raul, Nathaniel too felt that he has been given sufficient space to self-govern his life on release. Nevertheless, his freedom is not entirely benign – it is experienced as a mechanism specifically designed to test his ability in managing his freedom. The 'panoptic' (Foucault, 1975) probation service is thus supervising him from a distance and is perceived as cynically waiting for him to 'slip'. Should he use his freedom, which is epitomised through the long leash, inappropriately he could eventually 'hang himself' and return to prison. As a result, Nathaniel experiences supervision as an oppressive mechanism which operates under seemingly benign means. Turnbull and Hannah-Moffat (2009: 537) have succinctly summarised a similar point:

> The paroled subject is recognized and expected to be independent, self-regulating, and willing to change, but is also constituted as requiring close monitoring and direction on how to make the necessary changes and choices. Thus, parole conditions are a technique of discipline and self-governance within an integrated exercise of penal power that is simultaneously responsibilizing and de-responsibilizing

Admittedly, Nathaniel is the only participant in this study who had been recalled to prison before for breaching his licence conditions. This may account for his acceptance of the authorities' construction of his identity, and thus his intense experience of the 'performative purgatory' (Crewe, 2011: 516). Nathaniel is concerned that leaving the 'wrong' impression may get him into trouble. Recall is known to push individuals back into 'old identities' and to communicate to individuals that they 'are risky' (Shingler and Nick, 2024). The constant threat of recall can make people dishonest about their struggles (ibid). It is difficult to ascertain truthfulness in research such as this, but perhaps the experience of a previous recall can explain the 'hyper-normality' that was being portrayed by Nathaniel and his risk-discourse as 'narrative labour' (Warr, 2019).

The metaphor of watering grass with a glass stands to portray the continuous nature of the work that he must put in to demonstrate his ordinariness. To achieve this, Nathaniel needed to construct a 'penal avatar' (Crewe, 2011: 216), which assists with the performance of his 'own containment of risk' (McNeill, 2018) in the community. Crewe (2011: 523) imagined symbiotic shell of soft power which although imposed from outside, becomes part of parolees' identity, and must be performed with much tact:

> The prisoner can jettison some of its psycho- logical weight, but he or she cannot simply detach it. The shell also represents the identity that the institution assigns to the prisoner, which has to be carried for the remainder of the sentence.

Lifers such as Nathaniel must carry such a shell of soft power whilst on a life licence – his narrative evidenced 'risk-encoded communication skill' (Lacombe, 2008: 73). In fact, 'risk reduction' is the leitmotif of Nathaniel's overall narrative and betrays an internalisation of prison-based programme parlance (Digard, 2014; Lacombe, 2008):

Nathaniel: It's only through time and doing the courses trying to enhance the way of thinking about certain scenarios. So, it's just through doing the courses that are on offer there, and that helps obviously to lower your risk and over time you have to show just the examples of your behaviour changing [...] I knew what time frame I had, I knew what sentence I had, I knew what I needed to do, what I needed to change, and I set a goal and I achieved it and that's the way I looked at it. I worked towards the goal and everything else was second... so I just focused on my goal and then I thought, what do I need to do to get to it (Nathaniel, first interview).

What Nathaniel's experience shows, as Digard (2014: 431) remarked, is the "psychological penetration that supervisory work can achieve"; he seems to 'have been coached in delivering appropriate, expected life narrative' which he attempted to achieve throughout our meetings.

In sackcloth and ashes: Showing proportional remorse

Jacob was released 20 years ago, and he expressed probation's expectation of murderers' performance vividly:

Jacob: They want to hear, their perception of someone who has taken someone's life is that you should be broken that you should be remorseful, you should have a sort of seriousness and a kind of purgatorial aah, almost like wrapping yourself in sackcloth kind of demeanour and do you know what that is absolutely meaningless because all that is self-pity (Jacob, only interview).

I demonstrated my remorse by what I doing and the person that I was not by this this, because I believe it's a lie (laughs, nervously), and I don't know whether it still goes on today and how analytical they are as individuals and so forth, but there is this sense that because of the enormity of the crime that there is this perception that people will have to be in sackcloth and ashes because they have taken somebody's life aah, and I, you know, in many respects it doesn't matter what you do wrong you demonstrate that you are sorry (Jacob, only interview).

The type of remorse demanded from mandatory lifers such as Jacob is thus exceedingly dramaturgical – it must be visible and continuous (Rossmanith, 2015, 2014). In this sense, comparable to criminological research which explored the construction of acceptable remorse in courts (Johansen, 2018; Weisman, 2009; Zhong et al., 2014) mandatory lifers, depending on the circumstances of their murder, are expected to enact an appropriate 're-morse narrative' (Rossmanith, 2014) whilst in prison as well as upon their release. Otherwise, they risk jeopardising their 'quest for freedom'. For example, Raul believed that his failure to conform to expected behavioural norms given the seriousness of his crime has resulted in decisions being taken in his detriment.

Raul: When it came to me applying to go on holiday, they knocked me back and one of the reasons was they said that the supervisors are saying cuz he's not opening up enough ...we don't know what he's thinking. That was actually a reason they used against me. (...), me sitting there telling you I'm an emotional reck, that's somebody searching for pity, for sympathy (Raul, forth interview).

Thus, some of the men felt that exhibiting behaviours seen as incompatible with remorsefulness would lead to significant setbacks. Similarly to Jacob's case, not conforming to the expected behavioural template represented possible proof for potential risk.

Jacob: The reports that they put on me, they put me down as some sort of a psychopath and, you know, very negative sort of reports even those written by Chaplains because I got to see, towards the end I got to see some of the reports, in fact I still have some of the archives, they put down very negative things about this man shows no remorse, you know but there was also this sense in which, because of the nature of the system and the way that they were, is that the pain and remorse that I feel, they are not worthy of seeing it because they don't care, and I really, really care ah, and I won't, I won't because of the ways in which I was brutalised as a child I won't show what I feel to people who aren't worthy of it, you know, I will put on a brave face and I will, they have no idea, because what I feel deeply down I only reveal to people that I care about, and that includes yourself. Because that's the problem you see... in order to get through the system you have to jump through certain hoops, you have to say certain things you have to tell them what they want to hear (Jacob, only interview).

As shown above, Jacob had not been performing an institutionally acceptable remorse, which in turn had influenced his construction as being dangerous (Weisman, 2009). Zhong et al. (2014) found that absence of visible remorse is considered by some judges to be indicative of sociopathy. Importantly, the expression of remorse proclaims the fundamental difference between the wrongdoer and the act for which they are condemned (Weisman, 2016). In this sense, the absence of 'appropriate remorse', is cast as evidence for Jacob's psychopathy, and so the crime is not separated from his identity but is essential to the subsequent construction of a dangerous identity. Griffin (2018) found that parole board members analyse the attitude that life sentenced offenders have towards their victim in order to assess their level of risk. In this sense, those who show signs of remorse and empathy were judged more favourably. Further, by not accepting the official version of his crime and identity as narrated by the authorities, Jacob ran the risk of appearing as not taking responsibility for his crime (see Weisman, 2009). The type of crime he committed may also have a bearing on the type of remorse he is demanded to enact:

Jacob: My murder was a particularly brutal one you know, we took this guy we gagged, we tied him up and we shot him three times in the back of the head that's a pretty brutal and cold, and callous and ruthless kind of murder, execution ... and that's how it was perceived, described; the reality however, of it all is very different ... aah ... and I don't know whether you want to explore that ... (Jacob, only interview).

This version of events, which is derived from the context of his murder and imposed by the criminal justice authorities stands in tension with the way Jacob interpreted what happened. Nevertheless, if expressed officially, this disagreement runs the risk of portraying Jacob as not showing responsibility for the murder and, by consequence, showing no remorse (see Gold and Weiner, 2000; Weisman, 2009). Much of his identity negotiation is related to resisting this position and constructing a narrative which reconciles an expression of deep remorse with a lack of responsibility for what happened.

The type of murder committed also emerged as significant in how the authorities and probation services dealt with Richard. To reiterate, Richard was released over 20 years ago. He had killed his girlfriend when he was 19 and has been referring to the murder as a 'crime of passion' ever since. In one of our conversations about his involvement with romantic relationships after release, his murder type emerged as significant in how the probation service dealt with him:

Richard: So, uhm, one difficult thing about that is that when I got released because of the nature of my crime, my probation officer knew that it was quite a serious relationship, so his senior said to him that he had to sit down with my prospective wife, which I think that by then was engaged and tell her all about all I did so he could be implacably sure that she knew all about, she was aware of it before she took the punch to get married to me. So that was quite a challenging thing really, but then, but my wife, I think got through that really well… considering the circumstances (Richard, second interview).

Fortunately, Richard's relationship endured, but it is easy to imagine situations where this approach can lead to 'loss of social capital', which is fundamental to pro-social identity reconstruction (Blagden, McCann, and Macmillan, 2024). I then asked Richard whether a different type of murder would have led to a different outcome:

Richard: Aaaa, probably yes, and, the reason why I think they would approach in this way, because the nature of my crime, it was a crime of passion, and so they probably felt, it was important that she knew that, cuz they would see that as a certain amount of risk to any future relationship you known, probably the risk would have been different for her, what tends to happen with gang related murders, is that it's not a risk for the person who commits the crime but a risk because the people who are after him … so she could be at risk had she been linked to him, but sometimes the gangs don't come after you, they come after the people that you love, you know, and I've seen that before as well where that's happen, with people that I had known in prison, where people have gone and done injury to their family (Richard, second interview).

Richard's risk is constructed directly in relation to his romantic partner, who fortunately had accepted him without hesitation. Nevertheless, compared to the other men, Richard discussed his crime more openly and more often. It seemed that it was easier to frame the crime as a 'one off' mistake which has been accepted by society as such – the crime seemed to be accepted as divorced from his identity. On each occasion, he has framed his relationship with probation officers in most positive terms. He remarked how officers had always been there to assist with reintegration. They were understanding of his past, like most people, although with some important exceptions. In this sense, stories depicting issues around his construction around 'risk' are scarce.

There is some limited research that assists us in making sense of this finding. Griffin (2018) remarked that members of parole boards in Ireland draw distinctions in risk level between different types of mandatory lifers based on the type of murder committed, amongst other factors (circumstances of surrounding the commission of the offence, whether it was an isolated incident, and the relationship between the offender and the victim). Nevertheless, 'crimes of passion' such as domestic murders are usually considered 'low risk'. In contrast, members considered gang-related murders, or organised crime activity as a high-risk category. Possible other explanations may revolve around intent and premeditation as well as providing men such as Richard with attenuating circumstances (victim precipitated homicide, or simply loss of control, see Brookman, 2022). Although his crime may place Richard in somewhat of a more favourable situation, he deplores the current state of the probation system.

Richard's lament refers to a probation service which had traditionally managed to find the right balance between offering freedom and support to probationers. In his view, the state of the probation service, with its managerial ethos is a direct consequence of the unfortunate 'Transforming Rehabilitation' Policy which, Richard believed, has politicised the service and led to increased caseloads to probation officers working in the National Probation Service.

Richard: It's probably got worse, and I think it is probably down to the division, bringing 'Transforming Rehabilitation', I think uhm ... there we have this private sector and national, it does not really work. I think a lot of probation officers are more interested now in how the service is going to survive rather than the good work that they need to do, and that is what has really changed as far as that is concerned. [...] If I came out now this time, I don't know how that would affect things, maybe they wouldn't have enough time for me, or maybe they are too strict, I don't know. Because I think that when I came out there was the right balance of attention and not too much freedom at the same time. Me for instance, I had to see my probation officer on a weekly basis, until I got a job, so I think the attention at that point was right, but now the caseload is so big I don't know whether the person doing a life licence get the right amount of attention and that concerns me really (Richard, first interview).

Nevertheless, on the 26th of June 2021 the probation service in England and Wales were reunified and brought back under the control of the public sphere (see Carr, 2021 for an overview). The promise was that the new 'orthodoxy of privatisation' in the criminal justice system that has fearful competition at this core (Whitehead, 2017: 220) was becoming history.

Discussion

The men's supervision emerged as significant in their identity reconstruction and negotiation post-release. The mandatory lifers in this sample did not simply accept probationers' interpellation of their identities as risky and dangerous and have constructed counter-narratives to guide their construction of identities and guide their actions. Overall, the men have been experiencing supervision with a degree of ambivalence. They were given plentiful space to function freely outside, but this was envisaged as merely a testing field, or because of a favourable political climate. The men have been constructed as risky and dangerous, and their crimes positioned them as prime suspects to 'snap' and commit a second murder – as shown in Peter's case. This is an important finding considering that we often behave in ways consistent with how we are seen by others (Blagden, McCann, and Macmillan, 2024). Peter's contemplation of breaching the conditions imposed by the social services occurred in the context of a perceived unfairness of the decision which was not reflective of his index offence and who he was as a person. This ultimately endangered his emerging fatherhood identity and invited some sort of action. Perhaps a more timely and coordinated communication between MAPPA agencies and Peter wherein he was invited to collaborate on the release plan could have circumvented this situations (Shingler and Stickney, 2024). Furter, meeting Raul in his own environment rather than the probationer's office could would have potentially cemented his 'community member' identity (ibid) rather than reinforcing this risky, murderous self. The index offence of murder emerged as significant in positioning the men as extra-ordinary compared to persistent offenders, as shown in Raul's case. Moreover, the type of murder committed (the identity of and relationship to the victim) seemed to matter too in the ways in which probationers constructed their supervisees as dangerous and risky. This was evidenced in Richard's and Jacob's case.

All the men had internalised the risk-paradigm of neo-rehabilitation (Feeley and Simon, 1992) but were able to construct their identities in negotiating with discourses projected upon them by the probation system. All men evidenced a very good understanding and skill in engaging with 'risk parlance', and a capacity to perform a 'penal avatar' to negotiate their risk in the community and manage probationers' expectations. Jacob has epitomised this in our discussion about the gravity of his murder which warranted a type of purgatorial demeanour – proportional to the brutality of his crime. This means that the men understand that the context of their own murder is important in selected the right type of performance as changed individuals on release (see Warr, 2019 for a prison-based context). For example, remorse needs to be performed visibly, and proportional to the brutality of the crime committed – this indicates that our society accepts certain types of murders as more morally blameworthy than others (see Brookman, 2022).

All the men experienced a lax and responsibilising supervision, combined with episodes of acute risk assessment, which betrayed an ideological schism in the way that the service works to construct and interpellate its subjects. One potential explanation for this dichotomic supervision is the highly politicised nature of murder. The neo-liberal probation officer, in times of structural change and stress may use recall to prison as a back-covering mechanism (Farrall, Bottoms, and Shapland, 2010). Murderers are potential liabilities who attract great attention when specific recidivism occurs, and this may warrant increased surveillance from time to time. In this equation, the type of murder committed seems to have an influence in both the intensity and balance between the two alternating discourses/approaches to supervision. Moreover, the type of murder committed seemed to warrant a very specific and public type of remorse, that would require expressions of guilt and deeply felt shame. The following chapter will introduce concepts such as 'performative remorse' and 'complicated redemption' to showcase how the men portrayed an appropriate level of remorse, proportional to the enormity of their crime throughout our interviews.

References

Albertson, K., Philips, J., and Fowler, A. (2022) Who owns desistance? A triad of agency enabling social structures in the desistance process. *Theoretical Criminology*, 26 (1), 153–172.

Althusser, L. (2001) *"Lenin and Philosophy" and Other Essays*, trans. Ben Brewster. New York: Monthly Review Press [1971].

Blagden, N., McCann, K., and Macmillan, S. (2024) "I don't have relationships anymore...": Navigating licence conditions and transition into the community for men with sexual convictions. In J. Shingler, and J. Stickney (Eds.), *The Journey from Prison to Community*. Abingdon, Oxon: Routledge, 135–151.

Brookman, F. (2022) Understanding Homicide, 2nd ed. London: Sage Publications.

Carr, N. (2021) Reunified probation. All aboard the 'justice fleet'. *Probation Journal*, 68 (3), 307–309.

Carrabine, E. (2005) Prison riots, social order, and the problem of legitimacy. *British Journal of Criminology*, 45 (6), 896–913.

Crewe, B. (2011) Depth weight, tightness: Revisiting the pains of imprisonment. *Punishment and Society*, 13 (5), 509–529.

Digard, L. (2014) Encoding risk: Probation work and sex offenders' narrative identities. *Punishment & Society*, 16 (4), 428–447.

Doekhie, J., van Ginneken, E., Dirkzwager, A., and Nieuwbeerta, P. (2018) Managing risk or supporting desistance? A longitudinal study on the nature and perceptions of parole supervision in the Netherlands. *Journal of Developmental and Life-Course Criminology*, 4, 491–515.

Durnescu, I., Kennefick, L., Sucic, I., and Glavak, T. R. (2018) Experiencing offender supervision in Europe: The Eurobarometer – lessons from the pilot study. *Probation Journal*, 65 (1), 7–26.

Eliade, M. (1954) *The Myth of the Eternal Return*. Princeton, NJ: Princeton University Press.

Farrall, S., Bottoms, A., and Shapland, J. (2010) Social structures and desistance from crime. *British Journal of Criminology*, 7 (6), 46–70.

Feeley, M. M., and Simon, J. (1992) The new penology: Notes on the emerging strategy of corrections and its implications. *Criminology*, 30 (4), 449–474.

Foucault, M. (1975) Discipline and Punish: The Birth of the Prison, trans. Alan Sheridan. London: Allen Lane 1977; New York: Random House, 1979.
Foucault, M. (1988) Technologies of the self. In L. H. Martin (Ed.), *Technologies of the Self: A Seminar with Michel Foucault*. London: Tavistock, 16–50.
Frank, W. A. (2010) *Letting Stories Breathe: A Socio-Narratology*. Chicago: University of Chicago Press.
Gold, G. J., and Weiner, B. (2000) Remorse, confession, group identity, and expectancies about repeating a transgression. *Basic and Applied Social Psychology*, 22 (4), 291–300.
Griffin, D. (2018) *Killing Time: Life Imprisonment and Parole in Ireland*. Cham: Palgrave Macmillan.
Healy, D. (2012) Advise, assist, and befriend: Can probation supervision support desistance? *Social Policy & Administration*, 46 (4), 377–394.
Healy, D., and Kennefick, L. (2023) "Advise, assist and befriend": Client Perspectives on Probation from the 1980s to Present-Day. *Working Notes*, 37 (92), 4–11.
HM Inspectorate of Probation (2006a) An Independent Review of a Serious Further Offence Case: Anthony Rice. London: Home Office.
HM Inspectorate of Probation (2006b) An Independent Review of a Serious Further Offence Case: Damien Hanson & Elliot White. London: Stationary Office.
HM Inspectorate of Probation (HMIP) (2020) A Thematic Review of Probation Recall Culture and Practice. Available at: https://www.justiceinspectorates.gov.uk/hmiprobation/inspections/recallthematic/ [accessed on 18 August 2024].
Hunter, B., and Farrall, S. (2015) Space, place and desistance from drug use. *Oñati Socio-Legal Series* [online], 5 (3), 945–968.
Johansen, L. V. (2018) 'Impressed' by feelings – How judges perceive defendants' emotional expressions in Danish courtrooms. *Social and Legal Studies*, 28 (2), 1–20.
Kemshall, H. (2002) Effective practice in probation: An example of 'advanced liberal' responsibilisation. *Howard Journal of Criminal Justice*, 41 (1), 41–58.
Kemshall, H. (2007) Dangerous offenders: Release and resettlement. In A. Hucklesby, and L. Hagley-Dickinson (Eds.), *Prisoner Resettlement: Policy and Practice*. Devon: Willan Publishing, 270–288.
Kitzinger, J. (2004). *Framing Abuse: Media Influence and Public Understanding of Sexual Violence against Children*. London: Pluto Press.
Kramer, R., Rajah, V., and Sung, H-E. (2013) Neoliberal prisons and cognitive treatment: Calibrating the subjectivity of incarcerated young men to economic inequalities. *Theoretical Criminology*, 17 (4), 535–556.
Lacombe, D. (2008) Consumed with sex: The treatment of sex offenders in risk society. *British Journal of Criminology*, 48 (1), 55–74.
Lacombe, D. (2013) "Mr. S., You do have sexual fantasies?" The parole hearing and prison treatment of a sex offender at the turn of the 21st century. *Canadian Journal of Sociology*, 38 (1), 33–63.
Liem, M., and Weggemans, D. (2018) Reintegration among high-profile ex-offenders. *Journal of Developmental and Life-Course Criminology*, 4 (4), 473–490.
McNeill, F. (2018) Mass supervision, misrecognition and the 'Malopticon'. *Punishment and Society*, 21 (2), 207–230.
Moffitt, T., E. (1993) Adolescence-limited and life-course-persistent antisocial behaviour: A developmental taxonomy. *Psychological Review*, 100 (4), 674–701.
Opsal, T. (2015) "It's Their World so You Just Gotta Get Through": Women's experience of parole governance. *Feminist Criminology*, 10 (2), 187–207.
Perry, E. (2013) 'We're not trying to turn them into middle class guardian readers': Constructing the offender in the probation 'classroom'. *British Journal of Education*, 34 (4), 525–543.
Phillips, J., Westaby, C., and Fowler, A. (2016) 'It's relentless': The impact of working primarily with high-risk offenders. *Probation Journal*, 63 (2), 182–192.

Rennie, A., and Crewe, B. (2023) 'Tightness', autonomy, and release: The anticipated pains of release and life licensing. *The British Journal of Criminology*, 63, 184–200.

Rose, N. (2000) Government and control. *British Journal of Criminology*, 40 (2), 321–339.

Rossmanith, K. (2014) Getting into the box: Risky enactments of remorse in the courtroom. *About Performance*, 12, 7–26.

Rossmanith, K. (2015) Affect and the judicial assessment of offenders: Feeling and judging remorse. *Body & Society*, 21 (2), 167–193.

Shingler, J., and Nick, W. (2024) Recall, recovery and re-release. In J. Shinger, and J. Stickney (Eds.), *The Journey from Prison to Community*. Abingdon, Oxon: Routledge, 44–59.

Shingler, J., and Stickney, J. (2024) "I can see freedom but I can't have it": Supporting people in the immediate aftermath of release. In J. Shingler, and J. Stickney (Eds.), *The Journey from Prison to Community*. Abingdon, Oxon: Routledge, pp. 21–43.

Turnbull, S., and Hannah-Moffat, K. (2009). Under these conditions: Gender, parole, and the governance of reintegration. *British Journal of Criminology*, 49 (4), 532–551.

Turner, V. (1969) *The Ritual Process: Structure and Anti-Structure*. Chicago: Aldine.

Waldram, J. B. (2007). Narrative and the construction of 'truth' in a prison-based treatment program for sexual offenders. *Ethnography*, 8 (2), 145–169.

Warr, J. (2019) 'Always gotta be two mans': Lifers, risk, rehabilitation, and narrative labour. *Punishment and Society*, 22 (1), 28–47.

Weisman, R. (2009) Being and doing: The judicial use of remorse to construct character and community. *Social and Legal Studies*, 18 (1), 47–69.

Weisman, R. (2016) *Showing Remorse: Law and the Social Control of Emotion*. Abingdon: Routledge.

Werth, R. (2011) I do what I'm told, sort of: Reformed subjects, unruly citizens, and parole. *Theoretical Criminology*, 16, 329–346.

Werth, R. (2016) Breaking the rules the right way: Resisting parole logics and asserting autonomy in the USA. In: R. Armstrong, and I. Durnescu (Eds.), *Parole and Beyond: International Experiences of Life after Prison*. Basingstoke: Palgrave, 141–170.

Werth, R. (2018) Theorizing the performative effects of penal risk technologies: (Re)producing the subject who must be dangerous. *Social & Legal Studies*, 28 (3), 327–348.

Whitehead, P. (2017) *Transforming Probation*. Bristol: Policy Press.

Zhong, R., Baranoski, M., Feigenson, N., Davidson, L., Buchanan, A., and Zonana, H. (2014) So, you're sorry? The role of remorse in criminal law. *Journal of American Academy of Psychiatry and Law*, 42 (1), 39–48.

8 Living in the shadow of guilt
Performing remorse

The previous chapters suggested that soon after release, the men had to negotiate a set of contrasting identities both internally and externally within the rich, liminal realm which they inhabited. Significantly, the types of murders committed by the men emerged as significant in their post-release trajectories and subjective experiences. This was especially relevant in relation to their emotional experiences of guilt, shame, and expectation of public displays of remorse. This chapter explores issues around guilt and remorse in more detail and shows how the men discussed about remorse in the interview context. Most men felt haunted by their past and found that 'the path to redemption' was complicated because of the irreparability and enormity of their crime. Nevertheless, some of the men managed to navigate this 'complicated redemption' through sublimating guilt and using it as a force to help others. Generativity allowed the men to solve an internal 'crisis of meaning' (Neimeyer and Sands, 2022: 10) as well as to display a public manifestation of remorse. In the end, it is shown how guilt can be "potentially creative, connected with reparation, forgiveness" as well as a possibly 'excessive self-tormenting' force (Nussbaum, 2004: 208). Nevertheless, not all the men felt a crippling sense of guilt for their past – in fact, available rationalisations of the index offence influenced the men's emotional experiences and the strategies employed to move on with life beyond murder. The movement from self-retaliatory justice to self-forgiveness and generativity allowed 'the guilty' to live with a debt that could never be fully paid back.

Four out of the five the men engaged or attempted to engage with roles which promised to deliver generative potential in giving back to the society which they have harmed. In this sense, the men perform a set of generative identities by taking on wounded healer (White, 2000) and 'professional ex-prisoner' roles (Brown, 1991) with very little difficulty. To underscore, the point being made is that the 'generative' potential of these roles assists the men to earn their 'redemption', by going 'the second mile' (Eglash, 1957, 1977) in demonstrating that they are "worthy of forgiveness" (Maruna and LeBel, 2009; Maruna and LeBel, 2015: 66). In addition, the functions of the stories were to portray an appropriate level of remorse, adequate to the enormity of their crime and avoid being 'sort

DOI: 10.4324/9781003415640-8

of remorseful' (Tudor, 2022) as well as to contain any internal stigma of an inherently malevolent self.

The guilty and the damned: Shadows of a murderous past

All men felt haunted by their past but despite this, they did not portray a crippling sense of guilt and remorse. In fact, these emotions were mediated by the meaning the men attached to the murder context, rationalisations, and blameworthiness of the victim. For Nussbaum (2004) guilt is a form of 'self-punishment anger', a reaction to the perception of having done something wrong. To feel guilty, one needs to accept the moral codes which have been transgressed as well as the authority that forbids the transgression (Taylor, 1996). Ultimately, guilt is about a rection to a given act that goes against 'the rules', moral or otherwise. This can explain the discrepancies in the emotions expressed by the men and given the meaning they attached to their murder and introjected societal discourses around appropriate violence. Remorse, on the other hand, although a moral emotion, it is distinguishable from guilt through its focus on actions and their consequences, rather than on self-assessment (Taylor, 1996). It is an outwardly concern for having done harm, often required to be publicly portrayed by the men. By showing remorse, the individual is facing the guilt and shame that emanates from their murder (Gobodo-Madikizela, 2022), it demonstrates the offenders' pain by making it visible (Hall and Rossmanith, 2022). What seemed imminently crucial to the men was to say that despite their attempts at disavowing the index offence, they could never forget what they have done.

Raul mostly tries to 'block out' the memory of the murder, except for its annual anniversary when he returns to visit the murder scene to reflect in solitude. Compared to a routine visit to the graveyard, usually to mourn and remember the deceased, Raul's presence at the murder scene reveals possibly other motives.

Dan: So, you visit the place. Why do you think you go there?
Raul: Uhm, obviously it was the biggest event of my life ever, do you know what I mean? So, you just kind sit there, you contemplate, you think about the guy himself you think about yourself, you think about past, and yeah ... it's kind of a bit of reminiscence but maybe not so much in a fond way ... do you know what I mean?
Dan: So, what kind of emotions sitting there?
Raul: I'm not a very emotional person as it is, but it's good to just run through things in your mind, it keeps you remembering the mistakes you've made, and it makes you stronger as well. Like a lot of people probably trying to block it out, or on the further end of the spectrum will go cry their eyes out. I think it's best to go right down the middle, feel whatever you need to feel, think it over, and let it go.

Dan: If I were to give certain emotions which ones would be the closest when you are there? Shame, guilt, fear, or none of them there?

Raul: It's more regret. You know what I mean? And I choose the word regret rather than remorse because I feel regret is more of a broader spectrum as opposed to remorse. Remorse is very emotive you know what I mean whereas regret is a bit more…encompasses more. Everybody throws that word around, from TV to the courts, to the probation, that's their favourite word, remorse, remorse, remorse, because apparently it holds so much weight and it's shows your emotions etc, whereas regret can be seen as a bit more pragmatic, a bit more practical, you know (Raul, fourth interview).

Unexpectedly, the yearly visits did not elicit feelings of guilt or shame, but regret. As discussed, performances around remorse as expected by the criminal justice agencies from people like Raul are particularly purgatorial and dramatic, but this seemed incompatible with his sense of self (that of a Stoic, discussed in the previous chapters). Indeed, some theorists have argued that certain emotions are incompatible with individuals' worldviews (Landman, 1996). In the absence of remorse, Raul's visit to the old murder scene may offer a sense of continuity and integrity of his identity in a world rife by a 'cacophony of voices' (Gergen, 1991).

By equating remorse with emotiveness Raul is evidencing the internalisation of probationers' expectations whilst providing a degree of resistance to it. Raul drew a sharp distinction between guilt, remorse, and regret. The latter is not based on morality, but rather it is felt in relation to something undesirable (Taylor, 1996). Regret tends to relativise agency and involvement in the undesirable situation; we can regret an action but still see it as unpreventable, thus implying some level of acceptance and justification. Raul further opened about his regret, explaining why this is different from guilt. The explanatory narrative of the index offence becomes important:

Raul: I can sleep at night knowing that I didn't go to his house to kill him, I didn't catch him when he was unaware or anything like that. He came to fight do you understand? From then on, and this may sound a bit harsh, a bit strong for your book, or whatever, but like you said live by the sword die by the sword. You signed the waiver, this is war whatever happens, happens. You were coming to hurt me; the extent of that hurt was never established, ever agreed upon (Raul, fourth interview).

Gang related murders, or confrontational homicides (Brookman, 2022) are seen by Raul as not going against something sacrosanct to the moral order, or forbidden as it is implied in guilt, but rather, as a regrettable act that needed to be done and which followed the 'code of the street' (Anderson, 1999). In this sense, Raul's violence was acceptable and externally precipitated

(Di Marco, 2023). The type of murder committed, its context, and the possible blameworthiness of the victim are crucial to Raul's internal narrative around stigma, guilt, and remorse and set the foundation of how he lives life post-release.

The guilty: Complicated redemption

For other men guilt and remorse weighted heavily as burdens on their shoulders and were crucial precursors to the newly developed identities post-release. At first, reparation seemed impossible. Murder was a debt that they could not possibly pay back. The men initially felt that they were denied ways to restore the 'equilibrium of equality' (Cavadino et al., 2020: 48) through receiving their 'just deserts' or by providing some compensation as reparation to their victims; "strictly speaking, no *lex talionis* [was] possible" (Potts, 2022: 33). The road to redemption was indeed complicated for these men. Despite this conundrum, they managed to move on with their lives in a constructive way (through generative roles in the community). At the heart of their narratives are the experiences of 'complicated redemption' – an impossibility to repair the crime alongside a need to contain the past and transform it into a constructive future. The Janus-Faced struggles that the men experienced were the driving force behind much of their generative work post-release. I asked Nathaniel whether he could ever forget what had happened.

Nathaniel: Well, I don't think you ever do, it's just, it's just, have to sort of have to look forward, you never forget, what you've done cuz it's obviously a terrible act, but you sort of, you can either self-pity in a cell, and … cuz it's not gonna get you anywhere, or you move forward and the only thing that you can do is to … you sunk to the lowest part of what you can possibly do so the only thing to do is to rise, so you gotta just keep going forward, the soon you start looking back it's gonna creep back onto you, and that's where the insecurity is and … mental health issues can rise, so I can just try focus forward, cuz … don't get me wrong, I still got days where I obviously, sad days, but I don't, they could be underlying back to my offence, but I don't want to get to that stage where I am overthinking about that and then putting them thoughts in my own head then, so … like I said, I try and keep moving forward, I got days when I am pissed off, but overall I just literally, creeping through life and try to provide for my son for a potentially good future. That's it really. Switching off, keeping busy, I don't want to dwell with the past. My past is my past, like I said. I won't forget it, but I don't want to remember it either, sort of thing. I don't want to relive that every time I open my eyes, so obviously just being a better person (Nathaniel, first interview).

136 *Life Beyond Murder*

Nathaniel's past is constructed as intrusive: it has the potential to creep in and occupy his 'mental space'. In this sense, these thoughts need to be contained, sublimated, and converted into something else. The paradoxical double negation "don't want to forget but don't want to remember" betrays the possibility for a middle position: an Orwellian 'Doublethink' (Orwell, 1961) where remembering fades from conscious thought but is enacted.

In our first interview, Peter described how the irreparability of murder was experienced by him on a day-to-day basis, and explained why redemption is complicated for those who murder.

Peter: I've committed a crime that stained my soul isn't it. Really, every bit of happiness that I ever have now is tinged with: 'don't forget what you did to that guy' you know, do you know what I mean?

Dan: When do you remember that?

Peter: All the time, all the time … I taste some nice food and I think, none for him (his victim), and that's like another channel, constant … very quiet … just like this … just every now and again… "Ohh I wouldn't mind going to the cinema and watch that"! "Yeah, you going to the cinema" … you know what I am saying? Can't wait to see my son, he can't see his son, you know what I mean?

Dan: Give it a name.

Peter: It's guilt! It's a funny one guilt, because, I just am guilty of it, do you know what I mean, so it's not about being found guilty, or I find myself guilty, or I feel guilty, or I shouldn't, the situation is I am guilty of it and I have to, what that means, me being guilty, means I have to take responsibility and ownership of it, and I have to hold a little bit of suffering for it, emotionally, and that is my biggest highs in life now are: your son will be born one day, I hope for you … and the happiness that you feel when you see him for the first time will be let's say 100 yea? Mine would be 99. Because there will be that thought he isn't going to see his son, you know what I mean … That's the way it is. I don't argue about that thought in any way because the fact is, I am guilty, there is no case to answer, there's no … there's no getting away from it, I did it, so therefore I am responsible for it, you know where I am coming from? In the nicest possible way Dan, dead is dead, dead is dead. I can take that from you and say, right, I'm not gonna give it back to you, and then you say come on … alright there you go. And I replace it, and then you could say … alright Dan, have mine because I took yours, that's nice, I am sorry … and I mean that as I say that. I can't look him in the eyes because he is dead. I can't look at his family in the eye and say do you know I am seriously sorry this is happened, and I would like to show you how sorry I am by replacing the item I have taken, you know what I mean ... it's not possible to do when a murder has happened, is it? You can't put it back, you can't restore it, you know, they have restorative justice, how can I put that back? How can I? If there was a button for me and him to swap places, I would press it (Peter, first interview).

The passage above shows Peter's experience of complicated redemption – it is complicated due to the irreparability and enormity of the act which casts him as 'eternally stained'. This has been causing Peter significant stress and psychological auto-flagellation throughout the years of his release. Four years after his release, Peter was still at times crippled by guilt:

Peter: Everything I do ... there is a very quiet voice "he's still dead you know", "don't fucking enjoy this too much mate" and that bring to me, on one hand yeah the reminder that he is dead, that I don't deserve any of the good things that are happening, and it makes me lean into the shitty stuff because that's what I think I do deserve, you know what I'm saying? It's very difficult for me to have empathy for me because he is dead, you know what I'm saying, and there was no real reason, you know, but he is dead because I wanted money for drugs. That's not all right, that's not alright mate and that's not cool, and I accept it's not cool, but, I'm trying to get hold fully of the idea that this is what the abolishment of the hanging act is for innit? Luckily, I was born into a country with a society where we don't kill people who kill people, but we are given a second chance you know. A blank but all be it greyed page for us to go in and build another live off, and that's alright, that's what makes me think, because take morality out of the situation just for a moment if you can and the fact is I committed a crime in this country, broke the law in this country, right, went through the judicial system, was given a sentence to do as punishment for that crime and I've completed it so this life I'm having now is alright (Peter, fourth interview).

Peter's retaliatory logic betrays an attachment to a 'just-desert' narrative that had not been achieved. Despite having 'paid' for his crime from a legal perspective, Peter still believed he did not morally pay for his crime. The abolishment of the capital punishment meant that he was given a second chance by the state whilst removing the possibility for a moral reparation via just deserts. Moreover, reparation which would assist with his guilt management seemed impossible. The 'crisis of meaning' (Neimeyer and Sands, 2022: 9–10), around his own motivation to kill denies neutralisations of guilt and offers very little scope for personal forgiveness. Compared to Raul, who considered that his victim 'signed a life waver' when entered a gangster lifestyle,

Peter had a much more difficult time to extract appropriate meaning from his crime. As an elderly man, his victim was seen as vulnerable, and stealing for drugs casts Peter's motive as questionable and selfish. Peter experienced 'complicated redemption' – it is complicated due to the irreparability and enormity of the act which casts him as 'eternally stained', causing significant stress and psychological auto-flagellation. For Peter the phantasy of self-flagellation was intended to repair the harm done by 'paying back'. A similar point was raised by Jacob whom I asked whether he ever forgets what he has done:

Jacob: Oh God … ah, trying it's been very difficult. Most of the time I am a workaholic, so If I engage in lots of activity then, that is a cover, but it's only a cover for it, I don't really know, I know I need to forgive myself and I do periodically (laughs), ah … but it's something that I have to keep working at really, to all intents and purposes as far as the system is concerned I paid the price I've done the time, and never missed a supervision for 15 years or so it's just down to me and how I feel about it, I really, I struggle with it … ah, I try to … mitigate that as I've said I, leading a meaningful life and caring for other people, but I think I am caring anyway, I think I would be the same person, ah, if even, I just think I would uhm, I think the fundamental nature is with you from birth somehow so I struggle with it, I really do. There are particular times of the year when it is difficult for me and uhm … uhm … I don't think it will ever go away, I … uhm … (evidence signs of distress) and it's just something that I have to live with really, I don't know if that is answering your question really … I suppose in spite of how I beat myself up, or punish myself, for what happened, I made this decision to live the best life that I could (Jacob, only interview).

The tension between personal forgiveness and moral justice is evident in Jacob's narrative. Forgiveness is about finding a "manner of living rather than magically fixing a broken past" (Potts, 2022), it is forward facing. Nevertheless, these individuals cannot simply forget their past in favour of a bright future, as this would simply portray a lack of remorse – the past needs to be continuously contained and enacted in a sublimated form as generativity. All the men mentioned that rumination can be destructive, but they could not afford becoming 'remorseful but forgetful offenders' by burying their past. Remembering is intrinsic to any type of redemption (Tudor, 2001; Tudor, 2022: 99–100) and is something that is seen as expected of them. Ultimately, the men have contained intrinsic anxieties and guilt by sublimating the past (Freud, 1930), and transforming it into a force for good. They realised that guilt can be contained by giving back to society, and remorse can be displayed visibly through such roles.

Crafting the redemptive arc: Generative pathways to reparation

The men progressively understood that there is a solution towards redemption and more efficient ways to manage their guilt and display remorse outside prison. Some engaged with a range of generative roles which offered the appearance of reparation. In other words, some of the men felt they could save lives, and in turn, go some way in 'repairing' the harm they once caused. For example, four years after his release, Peter started to do work for an organisation called 'A band of Brothers' (BOB). The organisation works with young men who get involved in the criminal justice system and offers them a sense of purpose, connection, and belonging. One of their aims is to assist these young men to stay away from crime. I've asked Peter how his involvement with the organisation helped with his pressing guilt:

Peter: I love working with the Band of Brothers. I can see a kind of perhaps a redemptive arc for me through the band of brothers, I've seen and helped a little bit not much a young fellow, David. When I first saw him, he was a little kind of empty, very rarely look you in the eye, you know a lot of people when, you kind of look at them and shake hands, he wouldn't do that, he was awkward because he had shit going on. I wasn't his mentor, but the circles that we attend, and he was there, I saw the change in him over 6 months, like, he like, rather than sort of scope into the room, he'd almost peacocking into the room. He now comes into the room, "wow, what's happening, you alright Peter"? it was different, and I felt proud of him you know, you know I felt proper paternally proud of himself and he thanked me because it has been things that I've said that had helped him you know, that was a wonderful feeling, this is different man, this is saving lives now, and ever since then, I've been taking the band of brothers extremely seriously, because it is, look, murder, knife crime, it's always on the rise, all the time, band of brothers stops some of them, doing shit like that or being victims of it even, and I know that I can do that, I can be decisive, I can be the father figure, I can hold the frame, I can help them make better choices, I can pass band of brothers knowledge onto them, to help them to flourish, yeah? (Peter, fourth interview).

In our conversation, Peter disclosed that his engagement with the BOB was much more valuable than trying to deal with his guilt via counselling. The latter would be a selfish way out of his situation. He continued:

Peter: If I'm just sitting in grief counselling, there's nothing in that is there? It's just a selfish thing for me, that's why I can't do it. With the BOB you give something back, so then I am allowed to take something, in some fucking twisted up mind (Peter, fourth interview).

140 *Life Beyond Murder*

To save himself, Peter felt that he needed to help others. Further, his involvement in the organisation, apart from offering belonging and a sense of identity it opened new possibilities for reparation as well as a public way to display his remorse. Peter has also been a devoted member of Alcoholic Anonymous and Narcotic Anonymous ever since he was in prison and was still attending the weekly meetings. Befriending and helping others are integral components of 12 step groups through their member-sponsor relationship (Zemore, Kaskutas, and Ammon, 2004). As a sponsor, Peter accumulates the narrative resources to perform an introspective, generative identity post-release. Continuous membership to AA group and his role of being an active sponsor (mentoring role) have been identified as salient in providing the narrative resources needed to sustain this prosocial self throughout the years.

Peter: Sometimes, sometimes, this is the beautiful thing about Alcoholic Anonymous and Narcotic Anonymous, Dan, because that's where I can go and see somebody who is essentially a carbon copy of myself from 25 years ago and they can come and say I am in pain in trouble I don't know what is going on and I can say to them 'you know what mate, it's like this'. I can be open and honest to share my experience of which problems I have personally and how I manage to overcome them and sharing that experience is in a sense an estimable thing, innit? Makes me feel good because I can see that I am helping that person get better because I don't believe that drug addicts are bad people. Addicts are not bad, some of them are, because there's arseholes in every fucking cult, or call it, addicts are sick people who need to get better and I know that it's exactly how I'm saying, it's this fucking spiritual disorder, breaking the link between subconscious and your conscious sets off a fucking mental obsession about things you know what I mean all the time, about everything and then you try and take drugs to fucking just to shut it out for a minute. And that's why a lot of people, a lot of proper junkies, their aim is to go to the edge properly as close to death as possible without going over what they want to. They are seeking oblivion. And I know that's true Dan, not because of any book that I have read, but because I have done it, I have lived in that way where I feel disappointed that I've woken up the next morning (Peter, third interview).

Peter finds that the practical and experiential nature of the help he provides is saturated with a type of credibility (see Matthews, 2021) which is lacking in 'theoreticians of addiction' and their supporting literature. As a recovered counsellor (White, 2000), the emphasise is clearly placed on his own "woundedness" (Nixon, 2020: 54) – *sine qua non* – 'true' knowledge of physiology, psychology, or culture (Maruna and Lebel, 2009; White, 2000) of addiction cannot be acquired. Thus, "having been there too"

(Humphreys, 2004: 15), renders Peter's stories accurate articulations of the type of pains of recovery experienced by his peers and have the potential to change the lives of those whom listen to them (see White, 2000).

Evidently, the narrative resources portrayed indicate that Peter had adopted the narrative framework dictated by the group to interpret human behaviour (Denzin, 1986; Frings and Albery, 2015; Gubrium and Holstein, 2008; Loseke, 2007). Gubrium and Holstein (2008: 179) have argued that "the selves that emerge under AA's auspices draw upon a shared stock of interpretative resources from which selves may be crafted". Peter engages in what he perceives as an 'estimable act', which, in the end, means doing the right thing. Riessman (1965, 1976) suggested through the 'helper therapy principle' that 'those who help are helped the most' (Gartner and Riessman, 1984: 19). Helping others provides Peter with status and increases his commitment to therapy (Zemore, Kaskutas, and Ammon, 2004), in the end making him feel good about himself (Aresti, Eatough, and Brooks-Gordon, 2010). Much of Peter's release narrative identity represents a mobilisation of institutionally and organisationally (see Loseke, 2007) derived narrative resources which aimed at sustaining the performance of therapeutic self and of a helper in the community (Best, Musgrove, and Hall, 2018). This type of self-construction was initially projected from within the cultural horizons of AA discourse, thus having an 'organizationally embedded' (Gubrium and Holstein, 2008: 165) dimension and has expanded to include his role in 'A Band of Brothers' a few years later. Attendance to both AA meetings and the BOB provides the resources and the credibility in performing a generative, remorseful self which assists him in giving back, and save the live he has once taken.

Similarly, Richard's re-entry narrative is presented as a 'smooth transition' into the natural role of the 'helper'. Released for 20 years, Richard dedicates his whole life to helping others.

Richard: I think ... If someone would ask me what my purpose in life was, I would say it's about help and support. On my WhatsApp profile you'll see: 'I'm here to help' (his WhatsApp status). It's help people, and solve problems, I see myself as a problem solver, solution finder to issues, people come to me all the time, so... so, I suppose me wanting to be that problem solver uhm, is realising that people do come to me to help all the time, even this morning, they will ring me or they will text me or send a message, I've got this problem you know, I need you to help me and what's helped me to do that is my massive network (Richard, first interview).

Richard's redemptive narrative started in prison. He is consistent throughout interviews in referring to the value that he attaches to his professional life, evidencing the helper role as foundation to who he is now. Richard had started his role at National Association for the Care and Resettlement of Offenders (NACRO) during his imprisonment as well as for a well-known broadcaster network. Twenty years later Richard runs an organisation which raises awareness around penal issues and is concerned with the re-entry of ex-offenders. During our first interview, I asked Richard what these jobs mean to him. His response resembles the traditional 'Marunian' 'redemptive narrative'. Richard told me that his jobs represent a continuous act of asking for forgiveness.

Richard: I think unconsciously a lot of my activity, a lot of the things that I do is because of guilt. I think, my driving force, in many ways aaa, to whom I am, people often see me doing lots of different things as well as the [redacted], I do a lot of community work too, with different organisations, and I don't really think about it, but then I stop and think and each new thing is me trying to pay back, be trying to make up for what I've done, which I will never do, so I think guilt is a massive part in my life really. It's an underlying, current of guilt that keeps me, that drives me to do what I do, because I like to see things positively. I've turned the guilt into something, as an energy if that makes sense (Richard, first interview).

These roles provide Richard with mechanisms of reconciliation with society and his own past; they are a viable way to redeem himself for past mistakes, and to continuously ask for forgiveness (Heidemann et al., 2016). Fraley (2001) remarked that offenders can seldom make amends directly with victims. In this sense, reconciliation can target other aspects of offenders' lives and even other people. Naturally, for mandatory lifers, direct reconciliation with the victim is virtually impossible (Liem and Richardson, 2014). Richard's guilt, as he remarked, had been transformed into a positive energy dedicated to helping others. This finding reiterates LeBel's (2007) point those feelings of remorse are a strong predictor of the helper orientation in ex-offenders. Further, the job continues to offer the narrative resource necessary for the development of generative stories that guide who Richard is, and who he can become (Frank, 2010). An abundance of research has found voluntary peer-mentoring to offer a 'hook for change' (Giordano, Cerkovich, and Rudolph, 2002: 312), and a 'renewed sense of self' as the ex-offenders gives back (see Bazemore and Karp, 2004; Buck, 2020; Irwin, 2005; Lebel, 2007; LeBel, Richie, and Maruna, 2015; Nixon, 2019; Nixon, 2020: 54; White, 2000) and subsequently feels accepted in the community (Kavanagh and Borrill, 2013).

Maruna (2011: 13) said that "successful reintegration is a two-way process". As such, it requires an effort on the part of the ex-offender as well as that of some wider society which should forgive and accept those who have harmed. It is not sufficient for the returning prisoner to simply 'ask for forgiveness', especially if their call is left unanswered. This may even place the ex-offender in a state of 'liminality' (Maruna, 2011; van Gennep, 1960). In Richard's case, the professional ex-prisoner/lifer role had placed him in an ideal situation to receive the public recognition necessary to reconcile with his past and society. For a 'returning citizen' status, elevation ceremonies such as the one described below provide his life with meaning and imbue his reconstructed self with credibility for continuous performance upon release. Richard had received an award by the [redacted] police force for his exemplary work and contribution in the field of criminal justice.

Dan: What did you feel when you got that award?
Richard: I felt, really shocked and elated, really, looking at the paradox of all those years ago the police has arrested me, bringing me to the prison cells, and now they are awarding me, uhm, but, I felt slightly uncomfortable as well, what would happen if her family would hear of this, you know, the victim's family, because you have to think about that as well you know, it's always about the victim, but it was very pleasing for me of course, and good for my children as well, because one thing that I have to do is to get them into the idea that yes dad has been into prison, committed this terrible offence, which they know about now, but so when I receive things like this it helps me to sort of manage that process, my kids knowing that dad is a murderer, you know, that that is the stark truth, you know, so it certainly helped with that you know, any positive thing like that it help so it is a good feel (Richard, first interview).

The story above allows Richard to view and present himself as a 'returning citizen', reconciled with his past and with the society that he has harmed. Importantly, Richard explicitly remarks that he is now able to manage his stigma, especially as experienced through the eyes of his children. In this sense, the stigmatising identity of being 'a murderer' had been acutely experienced in the context of an emerging 'fatherhood' identity, perceived to be spoiled (Neale, Nettleton, and Pickering, 2011). LeBel, Richie, and Maruna (2015) too remarked that professional ex-criminals and wounded healers perceive less personal stigma and increased psychological well-being because of their roles (Maruna and LeBel, 2009). As McNeill and Maruna (2010) have argued, an offender must pay back before they can trade up to a restored social position as a 'citizen of good character' (McNeill and Maruna, 2010 in McNeill, 2012: 13). Status elevation ceremonies are the 'mirrored parallel processes' of Garfinkel's (1956) status degradation ceremonies (Rouse, 1996: 21), typically experienced by prisoners and ex-prisoners. They can facilitate the manufacturing of an identity (Rouse, 1996), or, as in this case, offer a credible performance of a reconstructed identity post-release. An evaluation takes place "when an actor's old self is typed by the self and others as untrue" (Rouse, 1996: 38).

144 *Life Beyond Murder*

As discussed, Richard presents a life dedicated to helping others and redemption is constructed as a positive, ongoing process. His professional ex-prisoner role makes him feel good and offers a clear purpose in life as well as meaning to the murder. Further, as shown above, these roles offer Richard a degree of public recognition to his reformed self and the necessary narrative resource to perform a pious, generative identity post-release. The official and public nature of the role renders the 'helper orientation' as the pinnacle of who he is now, post-release. Status elevation ceremonies further cement the public nature of harm recognition and appeals for forgiveness and assist in stigma management.

Beyond the obvious pecuniary advantages of owning a successful business, for Jacob, true value lies in the humanistic, generative, and altruistic potential that leading a successful business can offer. Jacob explicitly remarked on the generative motivation that lies behind his business: he wants to 'give back' to future generations. He employs individuals with no skills, some of whom suffer from disability.

Jacob: Ah, it's a very niche and unique business, and the guys I have working for me are all clever. They have all got different skills and abilities, and it's been wonderful for me working with them, where they come in and join with no skills and they acquire them and it's always a revelation to me so you know … and I mean I've got one young guy who is 20 now, he is with us 2 years, he knew nothing about writing code when he joined us, he is autistic, and he is absolutely brilliant, and he is writing better code than I am, and it's amazing. They are building something and something for which other people benefit and is a huge amount of satisfaction and fortunately through this Covid thing, we haven't had to let anyone go, you know, it's a big worry of mine that you know, a lot of businesses had to, you know furlough hasn't been an option for us, you know, if they don't work there is no money, so, but fortunately we are doing well you know, ah, the way I see it these guys committed themselves to the business and are dependent they got children, the responsibility is huge uhm, and I care, I really care about, yes I am in business with my business partner to make money ultimately, but we are also trying to build a business that has a future for development for these guys too so, I am getting a lot of satisfaction … uhm, seeing them grow, their careers take off (Jacob, first interview).

Dan: So, is there a sense of giving back here?

Jacob: Oh yah, I mean, argh, and that's what I believe in, life is about sharing, uhm, ah, and being in a position to do that is great … but having said that at the time these guys give back a lot too, they put a lot, you only get out of life what you put into it, you

> know ... and they put a lot of effort in and, I don't have an ego when it comes to being a boss or being the holder of all knowledge. The fact that you know Kristopher is barely 20. He is writing better code than I am, doesn't make me feel envious, it makes me feel happy. I just think wow, you know, this is cool (laughs) you know ... seeing other people [unclear] is like gardening isn't it. You plant something you get a beautiful flower; it gives you know, just a huge satisfaction (Jacob, first interview).

In comparison to Peter and Richard, Jacob's generativity is not delivered in official capacity, or as part of a peer-mentoring programme and he does not seem to seek public recognition for his benevolence. When considered in isolation to the rest of the narrative, the passage above seems to represent the natural resolution to Erikson's (1958, 1963) psychosocial stage of 'Generativity versus Stagnation', typically found in mature men (between the ages of 45 and 60; Jacob was 60 at the time of this interview). Erikson argued that during this 'conflicting stage' the mature individual orients their energy towards giving something of value to the next generation (McAdams, 2007). Also, Jacob was the only participant that discussed self-forgiveness, thus opening an important conversation about the distinction between restoration, reparation, and loss (Potts, 2022) in the lives of mandatory lifers.

Nevertheless, with one exception (Raul) participants in this sample have all expressed their interest in 'giving back', albeit in a myriad of different forms, irrespective of their age. We know from desistance research that 'generative activities' translate into successful reformation of identity (Maruna, 2001; Maruna and LeBel, 2009; Vaughan, 2007). The most recently released men, who did not have opportunities to engage with generative behaviours have expressed their desire to do so in the future. They would like to make a difference through 'giving back' and this made up their imagined future selves. For Nathaniel, as an example, participating in this piece of research represented his 'foot in the door', hoping that his involvement will lead to other opportunities to get engaged in the future.

Discussion

The findings discussed above partly reinforce that "one of the consistent findings emerging out of the research on the lives of successfully desisting ex-prisoners is that successful reintegration often appears to involve an explicit investment in what developmental psychologists call 'generativity'" (McAdams, Hart, and Maruna, 1998 in Maruna and LeBel, 2015: 66). However, it was not clear as to whether this was possible for people who committed murder and the mechanisms by which generativity becomes indispensable to desistance in this population remained unclear. Importantly, not all the men actively sought redemption. In fact, generativity was particularly salient for the men who discussed about experiencing guilt.

The men had initially perceived themselves their crime as 'irredeemable' but reconsidered this position later. Generativity offered Peter somewhat of a resolution to guilt through the possibility of reparation of the past in the present. Stein (2007) saw murder as possession and identity merger – by 'taking a life' the murderer merges their identity with that of the victim. In this sense, generative work can represent a form of reconciliation and reparation of this deformed self by possibly saving other people's lives and by providing meaning to life beyond murder. It represents the sublimated energy that fuels the helper role. Raul, on the other hand, did not show a desire for such reparations post-release, as he did not feel he transgressed the forbidden – his opponent 'lived by the sword and died by the sword' and the consequences of such lives were difficult to prevent. For him, it was regrettable that this reality ended up destroying two lives. Despite this, Raul acknowledged that he is expected to perform remorse in a visible way, evidencing that he 'long haul of remorse' extends beyond the parole board well into the community (Hall and Rossmanith, 2022). Raul's explanatory narration of 'either him or me' (Di Marco, 2023) ensured that blame for murder was relativised to the extent that he may not have had another choice but to commit the index offence. In turn, this rationalisation, specific to the details of his index offence influenced the emotional repertoire that Raul experienced post-release and the stigma negotiation strategies employed at discursive level. Rationalisations and justifications will be explored in more depth in the next chapters.

Peter, Richard, and Jocob performed a set of generative identities by taking on wounded healer (White, 2000) and 'professional ex-prisoner' roles (Brown, 1991) with little difficulty. These ultimately represented their sublimated and enacted guilt as reparatory mechanisms.. The men did not discard previous identities in favour of pro-social ones (Herbert, 2018; Liem, 2016; Liem and Richardson, 2014; Maruna, 2001). This would represent not taking responsibility for the index offence and betray a lack of remorse. The complicated redemption narrative is evidence for their continuation. The past was not repudiated but rather sublimated and capitalised upon (Brown, 1991: 221) – these old identities 'lingered on' albeit latently. An important function of the helper stories shared with me by the men was to portray an appropriate level of remorse, adequate to the enormity of their crime, and avoid being 'sort of remorseful' (Tudor, 2022) as well as to contain any internal stigma of an inherently malevolent self. Importantly, the men's strategies in dealing with their past moved from initial disavowal to sublimation and enactment via generative activities. In this way, the men managed to contain the stigma of their past, whilst performing an appropriate level of remorse through enactment. The chapter also opens a set of questions about a possible stage transition from self-flagellation representing the 'just-desert' logic of debt re-payment to fantasies of reparation, and lastly to self-forgiveness in the lives of mandatory lifers who committed murder. Further, it explored the importance of the type of murder committed in this process, as not all the men expressed remorse and guilt for their index offence. In fact, Raul utilised a set of 'ready-made excuses' (Gadd and Jefferson, 2007: 44) to justify his crime which ultimately influenced his emotional response to murder.

References

Anderson, E. (1999) *Code of the Street: Decency, Violence, and the Moral Life of the Inner City*. New York: Norton.
Aresti, A., Eatough, V., and Brooks-Gordon, B. (2010) Doing time after time: An interpretative phenomenological analysis of reformed ex-prisoners' experience of self-change, identity and career opportunities. *Psychology Crime and Law*, 16 (3), 168–190.
Bazemore, G., and Karp, D. R. (2004) A civic justice corps: Community service as a means of reintegration. *Justice Policy Journal*, 1 (3), 1–37.
Brookman, F. (2022) *Understanding Homicide*. 2nd ed. London: Sage Publications.
Brown, J. D. (1991) The professional ex-: An alternative for exiting the deviant career. *Sociological Quarterly*, 32, 219–230.
Buck, G. (2020) *Peer Mentoring in Criminal Justice*. New York, NY: Routledge. Carson.
Cavadino, M., Dignan, J., Mair, G., and Bennett, J. (2020) *The Penal System: An Introduction*, 6th ed. London: SAGE.
Denzin, N. K. (1986) *Treating Alcoholism*. Newbury Park, CA: Sage.
Di Marco, M. H. (2023) Why? How perpetrators of male-male homicide explain the crime. *Journal of Interpersonal Violence*, 38 (1–2), 366–390.
Eglash, A. (1957) Creative restitution – A broader meaning for an old term. *Journal of Criminal Law and Criminology*, 48, 619–626.
Eglash, A. (1977) Beyond restitution: Creative restitution. In J. Hudson, and B. Galaway (Eds.), *Restitution in Criminal Justice*. Lexington, MA: D.C. Heath, 91–129.
Erikson, E. H. (1958) *Young Man Luther: A Study in Psychoanalysis and History*. New York: Norton.
Erikson, E. H. (1963) *Childhood and Society*. 2nd ed. New York: Norton.
Fraley, S. (2001) The meaning of reconciliation for prisoners serving long sentences. *Contemporary Justice Review*, 4, 59–74.
Frank, W. A. (2010) *Letting Stories Breathe: A Socio-narratology*. Chicago: University of Chicago Press.
Freud, S. (1930) *Civilisation and Its Discontents*. Harmondsworth: Penguin.
Frings, D., and Albery, I. (2015) The social identity model of cessation maintenance: Formulation and initial evidence. *Addictive Behaviors*, 44, 35–42.
Garfinkel, H. (1956) Conditions of successful degradation ceremonies. *American Journal of Sociology*, 61 (5), 420–424.
Gartner, A., and Riessman, F. (1984) *The Self-Help Revolution*. New York: Human Sciences Press.
Gergen, K. J. (1991) *The Saturated Self: Dilemmas of Identity in Contemporary Life*. New York: Basic Books.
Giordano, P. C., Cerkovich, S. A., and Rudolph, J. L. (2002) Gender crime and desistance: Toward a theory of cognitive transformation. *American Journal of Sociology*, 107 (4), 990–1064.
Gobodo-Madikizela, P. (2022) Remorse as ethical encounter and the impossibility of repair. In S. Tudor, R. Weisman, M. Proeve, and K. Rossmanith (Eds.), *Remorse and the Criminal Justice: Multidisciplinary Perspectives*. New York: Routledge, 243–264.

Gubrium, F. J., and Holstein, A. J. (2008) *Analyzing Narrative Reality*. London: Sage.
Hall, M., and Rossmanith, K. (2022) Long haul remorse: The continuous performance of repentance throughout the prison sentences. In S. Tudor, R. Weisman, M. Proeve, and K. Rossmanith (Eds.), *Remorse and Criminal Justice: Multi-Disciplinary Perspectives*. Abingdon, Oxon: Routledge, 156–174.
Heidemann, G., Cederbaum, J. A., Martinez, S., and LeBel, T. P. (2016) Wounded healers: How formerly incarcerated women help themselves by helping others. *Punishment & Society*, 18 (1), 3–26.
Herbert, S. K. (2018) Inside or outside? Expanding the narratives about life-sentenced prisoners. *Punishment and Society*, 20 (5), 628–645.
Humphreys, K. (2004) *Circles of Recovery: Self-help Organizations for Addictions*. Cambridge, UK: Cambridge University Press.
Irwin, J. (2005) *The Warehouse Prison: Disposal of the New Dangerous Class*. Los Angeles: Roxbury Publishing Company.
Kavanagh, L., and Borrill, J. (2013) Exploring the experiences of ex-offender mentors. *Probation Journal*, 60 (4), 400–414.
Landman, J. (1996) Social control of 'Negative' emotions: The case of regret. In R. Hare, and W. Parrott (Eds.), *The Emotions: Social, Cultural and Biological Dimensions*. London: Sage Publications, 89–116.
Lebel, T. P. (2007) An examination of the impact of formerly incarcerated persons helping others. *Journal of Offender Rehabilitation*, 46 (1–2), 1–24.
LeBel, T. P., Richie, M., and Maruna, S. (2015) Helping others as a response to reconcile a criminal past: The role of the wounded healer in prisoner reentry programs. *Criminal Justice and Behavior*, 42 (1), 108–120.
Liem, M. (2016) *After Life Imprisonment*. New York: New York University Press.
Liem, M. and Richardson, N. J. (2014) The role of transformation narratives in desistance among released lifers. *Criminal Justice and Behavior*, 41, 692–712.
Loseke, D. R. (2007) The study of identity as cultural, institutional, organizational, and personal narrative: Theoretical and empirical integrations. *Sociological Quarterly*, 48, 661–688.
Maruna, S. (2001) *Making Good: How Ex-Convicts Reform Rebuild Their Lives*. Washington, DC: American Psychological Association.
Maruna, S. (2011) Reentry as a rite of passage. *Punishment and Society*, 13 (1), 3–28.
Maruna, S., and LeBel, T., P. (2009) Strengths-based approaches to reentry: Extra mileage toward reintegration and destigmatization. *Japanese Journal of Sociological Criminology*, 34, 59–80.
Maruna, S., and LeBel, P., T. (2015) Strengths-based restorative approaches to reentry. The evolution of creative restitution, reintegration, and destigmatisation. In Ronel N., and Segev D. (Eds.), *Positive Criminology*. New York: Routledge, 65–84.
Matthews, E. (2021) Peer-focused prison reentry programs: Which peer characteristic matters most? *Incarceration*, 2(2), 1–19.
McAdams, D. P. (2007) *The Redemptive Self: Stories Americans Live By*. Oxford and New York: Oxford University Press.
McNeill, F. (2012) Four forms of 'offender' rehabilitation: Towards and interdisciplinary perspective. *Legal and Criminological Psychology*, 17 (1), 1–19.
Neale, J., Nettleton, S., and Pickering, L. (2011) Recovery from problem drug use: What can we learn from the sociologist Erving Goffman? *Drugs: Education, Prevention & Policy*, 18, 3–9.
Neimeyer, R. A., and Sands, D. C. (2022) Meaning reconstruction in bereavement: From principles to practice. In R. A. Neimeyer, D. L. Harris, H. R. Winokuer, and G. F. Thornton (Eds.), *Grief and Bereavement in Contemporary Society: Bridging Research and Practice*. New York: Routledge, 7–22.
Nixon, S. (2019) 'I Just Want to Give Something Back': Peer work in prison. *Prison Service Journal*, 245, 44–53.

Nixon, S. (2020) 'Giving back and getting on with my life': Peer mentoring, desistance and recovery of ex-offenders. *Probation Journal*, 67 (1), 47–64.

Nussbaum, M. C. (2004) *Hiding from Humanity: Disgust, Shame, and the Law*. New Jersey: Princeton University Press.

Orwell, G. (1961) *Nineteen eighty-four*. New York, NY: Signet Classics (original work published 1949).

Potts, M., I. (2022) *Forgiveness: An Alternative Account*. USA: Yale University Press.

Riessman, F. (1965) The 'helper therapy' principle. *Social Work*, 10, 27–32.

Riessman, F. (1976) How does self-help work? *Social Policy*, 7, 41–45.

Rouse, T. P. (1996) Conditions for a successful status elevation ceremony. *Deviant Behavior*, 17 (1), 21–42.

Stein, A. (2007) *Prologue to Violence: Child Abuse, Dissociation, and Crime*. Mahwah: The Analytic Press.

Taylor, G. (1996) Guilt and remorse. In R. Hare, and W. Parrott (Eds.), *The Emotions: Social, Cultural and Biological Dimensions*. London: Sage Publications, 57–73.

Tudor, S. (2001) *Compassion and Remorse: Acknowledging the Suffering Other*. Leuven: Peeters.

Tudor, S. (2022) Reflections on the grey zone: "Sort of remorseful" offenders. In S. Tudor, R. Weisman, M. Proeve, and K. Rossmanith (Eds.), *Remorse and the Criminal Justice: Multi-Disciplinary Perspectives*. Abingdon, Oxon: Routledge, 97–113.

van Gennep, A. (1960) *The Rites of Passage*. Chicago: The University of Chicago Press.

Vaughan, B. (2007) The internal narrative of desistance. *British Journal of Criminology*, 47 (3), 390–404.

White, W. L. (2000) The history of recovered people as wounded healers: II. The era of professionalization and specialization. *Alcoholism Treatment Quarterly*, 18 (2), 1–25.

Zemore, E. S., Kaskutas, L. A., and Ammon, L. N. (2004) In 12-step groups, helping helps the helper. *Addiction*, 99, 1015–1023.

9 Life beyond murder
The splitting narrative

Introduction

The performance of 'an appropriate level of remorse', evidenced in the previous chapter was paradoxically reconciled with the men's relativisation of their own involvement in the index offence and capacity for agency at the time of the murder. However, the men did not project the blame externally, explicitly onto their victims (with some exceptions explored in the previous chapter) but drew from a range of cultural and institutional discourses to develop explanatory narratives around an ontologically insecure (Laing, 1960), and murderous previous self. Stories of the past (especially childhood) are reconstructed to provide coherency to these explanatory narratives. The paradoxical and contradictory presence of remorse alongside such relativisations created the premise for a splitting narrative: to perform remorse for a crime which was de facto outside of their control. The context of their own murder (typology, motivation, victim) played a pivotal role in shaping this narrative, as it hinged upon the prevailing discourses surrounding specific forms of homicide. The men moved on an 'agency continuum' (O'Connor, 1995, 2000: 38) 'deflecting', 'problematizing', or claiming complete agency in their murder stories. The men's conflicting statements on their actual and symbolic involvement in the murder – beyond evidencing the men's reflective stance (O'Connor, 1995, 2000) – is representative of more complex identity work.

For Stein (2007: 96) murder is typically dissociated enactment of violence, which explains why perpetrators project blame onto a 'not me' persona, a parallel self that is accountable for the crime. It is unsurprising, then, that so many people who commit murder are shocked by their own violence and ruminate in disbelief well into their sentences (Crewe, Hulley, and Wright, 2020). Blame is projected outwards, onto the victim as "what one cannot live with one has to get rid of" (Taylor, 1996: 64). In this way many homicide offenders deny any level of personal responsibility and guilt for the murder (Gobodo-Madikizela, 2022). Nevertheless, these primitive projections of guilt would be considered justifications and excuses (Scully and Marolla, 1985) of the homicide by most criminal justice professionals, which in turn would indicate a lack of remorse and jeopardise their release. The men did not invoke a parallel self to account for the murder, neither did they outwardly project blame on their victims (with the exception explored in the previous chapter). Through a highly skilled 'narrative labour' (Warr, 2019), most men managed to show remorse whilst relativising their capacity for agency by employing a 'Splitting Narrative'. The make sense of this narrative the secret is to look beyond the content of the men's stories (although these are crucial) to their structure, that is the 'secret of this form itself' (Žižek, 2008: 3).

The splitting narrative

The overall goal of the 'Splitting Narrative' is to provide narrative coherence and to portray the men as good and moral people in the present who had struggled to rise from an unfortunate event. The main discursive device used is an 'agentic split' which creates a sense of responsibility for a crime which was outside of their control. There is typically a biographical turning point which accounts for their transformation (unlike the identity stability observed in the narrative of Raul who projected the blame onto his victim). Negotiating a sense of responsibility is crucial given that the men are on a life licence for murder: it is reflective of their 'narrative labour' (Warr, 2019), and institutional as well as public narrative templates (Harding et al., 2017) to take responsibility for the crime, and thus signal low risk to authorities (Fox, 1999 McKendy, 2006). A specific temporal order is used: childhoods are recreated to provide justifications for the specific index offence as either traumatic (employing medical and psychotherapeutic discourse), or banal (to justify murder as accidental through a 'crime of passion discourse', see Monckton-Smith, 2020). The murder is constructed as taking place under the influence of the 'Other' (represented by passionate love, early abuse, lack of identity, the family, or drugs and alcohol). These justifications provide a glimpse into to the web of discourses internalised and utilised by the men to account for their past and index offence. The prison sentence is presented as a place of crossroads and revelatory identity reconstruction. Despite their subtle rationalisations, the men decry a deep sense of guilt which seems contradictory.

The men also relativised their involvement in the murder at a socio-linguistic level, through the language they employed. Analysing utterances on specific stories of violence and/or murder was revealing of the ways in which the men made sense of their murders, as well as the ways in which they employed discourse to negotiate/distance themselves from the murder scene. O'Connor (2000: 58) presented situations where her participants at times deflect agency, whilst other times take full responsibility for their crimes, in the active voice. In her view, this is to achieve narrative coherence. In addition to this role, these constructions may also provide evidence for specific identity work, and 'narrative labour' (Warr, 2019) aimed at reconciling contrasting expectations of the men. Taken together, "the formal aspects of structure express the identities, moral dilemmas, perceptions, and values of the storyteller" (Phoenix and Smith, 2011: 631), and thus assists with painting a complete picture of the identity work and the stories that the men live by. In this sense, these murder scene stories serve to problematise agency, and evidence some deflection of responsibility (O'Connor, 1995), for a past self, whilst demonstrating an agentive self in the 'interview-present'. Further, there is an internalisation of institutional discourses coming to light (Fox, 1999; McKendy, 2006; Wright, Crewe, and Hulley, 2017).

The childhood – murder nexus: Explanatory narratives

Most of the men's stories of early childhood are imbued with a sense of isolation, passivity, and inadequacy. These stories are causally linked (Gergen and Gergen, 1988) with the 'murder stories' which follow strictly after. The exception is Richard's story which starts with the murder scene, and which constructs childhood as loving and banal. As it will be shown, this is relevant to setting up rationalisations around index offence motivation.

A loving childhood and the accident: Richard's crime of passion

Richard described his childhood with a degree of ambivalence. Born of 'rich Caribbean heritage', he enjoyed a loving childhood. Despite his family's intrinsic love for each other, he felt that they were dysfunctional and disorganised due to their socio-economic position as immigrants:

Richard: Just like all rest of African-Caribbeans they (the parents) came to make some money and then get back home, and things like the poverty in England for black people, the lack of work in certain areas, the discrimination, uhm, made our families a bit dysfunctional really, plus we had kids, siblings that were in Jamaica, that were older than us, and there was no bonding between us you see, so for me it was making sense of all that really, the migration from Jamaica, and [...]. My position as a black Briton, I don't really I think I understood really, we were taught everything about our culture and, for me I was kind of lost when it came to culture, when it came to identity, the only thing that kind of helped to a certain extent, was in the late 70s when the Rastafarian – a lot of records were about culture in Africa, and the process of slavery and then the police started to drop us, people in my age group (not clear), and that's why things the way they were. But I think my childhood was reasonably happy, my parents loved me, it was very poor though, you know, we didn't have much (laughs), so it is good to be able to give our kids a bit more, aaaa, and there was a spiritual upbringing as well that helped, that helped bring the moral compass, in a sense, really, doing things right, of course until that big, big mistake you know, it was quite a happy childhood.

Richard identifies his early sense of self with his family's immigration from the Caribbean's to the United Kingdom, and with the hardships which ensued. He could not grasp his position as a young Briton; he felt lost when it came to identity; his confusion was one which was shared by many at the time as the term 'black' was emerging as a political category (Sarup, 1996). Nevertheless, the story also serves to evidence the banality of his childhood in the sense that it was commonplace to go through such experiences at the time. He started the story with the syntagm "just like all rest of African Caribbeans", thus evidencing the banality and commonality of his own childhood. Further, his relationship with the family, despite difficulties, was a loving one. This works to produce a contrast at the end between the usualness of his upbringing and the unusual turn of events: only an accident could possibly explain his index offence.

Richard manages to label his murder as a 'crime of passion' within the first few minutes of our first interview, thus priming (Bargh, 2006; Chartrand and Bargh, 1996) a specific interpretation of what follows. Further, the murder scene serves to portray himself as being acted upon by forces outside of his control (Sykes and Matza, 1957). By providing so little information about his upbringing, one could argue that Richard constructs his past as inconsequential to the story (Spector-Mersel, 2011).

Richard: Well, I suppose, what happened to me, very sad really, I suppose you can call it a crime of passion, it involved my fiancé, and it all started when were quite young when we got together, we were at school, and we first met because two schools joined together to form a comprehensive school, and we found that we played the same instrument, the brass band, so that was kind of a romantic beginning I suppose, really, and our relationship developed quite intensely from a young age. At the age of 13 we met, and by the age of 14 we were having sexual intercourse together you know; we were young, and we got involved very quickly [...]. Looking back, we thought that we will be together for the rest of our lives, because our love was so intense, and we would do things like sneak out at night-time of the house at night, and meet in the park, it was really intense.

Richard started seeing other girls which culminated with him 'getting someone pregnant' and which led to his fiancé 'deciding to leave him'.

Richard: Then she decided to leave me, so I begged her to come back to me, and in all that chaos, I couldn't cope basically, you know, because it was like, I was a young male probably 19 years old at the time, didn't know how to cope with my emotions, and so I thought probably the best way to deal with this may be to experiment with drugs to see whether I can escape the trauma because I never took drugs in my life before, so I started to take cannabis, I was mad a few days, I didn't sleep, so, in the end, it was like a psychotic experience really I just felt everything was chaotic, and I became very emotional and I ... everything intensified, I went to her and begged her to come back to me, so I met her in the park one day, I decided that if I couldn't, if she didn't come back to me, nobody could, so I strangled her, you know that was something that I decided before, in all the chaos, that that's what I will do. So, uhm, when I realised what I'd done, after I strangled her, I ran off, uhm, trying to suicide myself, I went into a train station, got into the train, and bought bottles of whiskey, and tablets and stuff like that, took them on the train, and I expected to die that day.

He was saved by the ticket inspector who called an ambulance; he then woke up in hospital the next morning. Richard uses utterances such as 'happened to me' to evidence the passive nature of his involvement in the murder (Ferrito, 2020). The episode was fatidic, and thus his involvement is minimal. The plot intensifies towards the culmination point – the murder scene, and then ends abruptly. By the end of the story, Richard is demonstrating a stronger commitment to what he has done by saying that he decided to commit the murder, albeit in a moment of chaos (emotional and drug related) – thus problematising his unmitigated involvement in the murder. Nevertheless, he is showing 'strong evaluation' (O'Connor, 1995) of what happened back then, through his interview positioning. This is an important element which signals Richard as a moral agent capable of reflection, and of moral reasoning – and therefore an agentic person in the present. His story culminates with his passage on 'decision making' – he later deflects agency again, when considering what has happened, reflexively:

Richard: This was something that happened to me that was totally out of character, uhm, and I wasn't, I sort of wasn't involved with criminal culture you know, so it's all been developmental.

In bringing his confession forward (below) he is declaratively showing responsibility for the crime, and signals his charitable, pious side – by confessing his crime – he protected the victim's family from further emotional turmoil. Nevertheless, Richard negotiated a stable moral self (Presser, 2009) by presenting the murder as forced onto him by the Other – that of unbearable love, and thus excusing (Scully and Marolla, 1985) the crime as out of character.

Richard: You know, it was obvious that I committed the crime, so I confessed, and it was quite straightforward really, there was no trial, and even though some people said that at that time, I should've pleaded diminished responsibilities. I wasn't really bothered about that and the reason why I didn't, because I was told that if I did, there would be a trial, and that would mean getting their family involved getting them in court and all sort of these things and I didn't want to bring them into that, aa so, I just pleaded guilty in court and in 1982 I got set down for life in court and that was the start of my licence really.

Richard drew from a 'crime of passion discourse' (Monckton-Smith, 2020) to construct a justification narrative which paints the index offence as uncontrollable and motivated by his fiancé's decision to leave. Importantly, he does not explicitly blame his victim. Richard's childhood story offers a poignant contrast to the stereotypical abusive history of a violent individual, to further strengthen the accidental nature of the crime. He is a skilled storyteller that manages to move on the agency continuum to present himself as a morally ethical individual. The crime of passion discourse has intimate ties with dominant domestic violence discourses and romantic heterosexual relationships (Monckton-Smith, 2020) that Richard draws from.

Peter's psycho-medical insight: The primal wound

Peter narrates the early life of an isolated child, incapable of expressing and understanding emotions. He identified an early emotional inarticulation and feeling guilty as the leitmotifs of his childhood:

Peter: I Think the guilt has been a theme along through my life, right? I think I have also, the primal wound you know, being left by my mother to my grandparents, but then growing up with my biological dad there, aged 17, living with his mom and dad who were rising me, telling me "you need be grateful for what they do for you", putting guilt on me straight away, we talked about that before, I think that's been a big thing in my life.

After his mother's abandonment, Peter was legally adopted by his grandparents at the age of eight. The syntagm 'putting guilt on me' evidences the internalisation of guilt for his mother's abandonment. His early life is represented by his difficulties to construct an identity of his own. According to Verrier (2009: 30) early abandonment by the mother leads to a compromised sense of self in children, which was coined the 'primal wound'. It refers to the feeling that part of oneself has disappeared leaving the child incomplete. In such situations, many children end up developing a 'false self', a defence mechanism developed to adjust to their environment. Peter was existing, but unable to become a person. He provided a clear example of his 'ontological insecurity' (Laing, 1960: 42–43) in the following 'reflection narrative'

(Brookman, 2015). Peter explained that much of his early life he felt he did not have an identity of his own:

Peter: As I was growing up my identity was defined by the facts that my father told me, there were external influences that defined myself, you know what I say, or my identity […] that's how I was, I'd be with someone and 'I'd start to become like them, I had no real identity of myself, you know what I mean.

Peter: Now we are talking about many years of being clear minded, drug free, clarity, conscious, and introspective. I know my own thoughts and feelings, you know. So really, no other thing or a person can really have an effect on who I am, because whatever is said to me, whatever argument is put to me, I am free, to give my own opinion, I am able to think what my opinion is to construct my opinion, you know what I mean?

He found comfort in reading books, and then soon engaged with a prolonged period of hedonism by using drugs. Peter's quick transition from an avid reader to an avid drug user provided a viable way of escaping the present and assisted in forging relationships with others (Chatterton and Hollands, 2002; Hall and Winlow, 2005). Peter referred to his drug story as a common one. His decline eventually culminated with the index offence. This is sequenced in two distinct parts. Peter initially shifted the focus from the act of having killed someone to his position as being acted upon (O'Connor, 2000: 50) by saying that he was 'put in prison for murder'. The sentence serves to highlight something that happened to Peter rather than placing the emphasis on what Peter has done. Further, he constructs the imagery of speed – a stereotypical story of drug abuse provides an 'acceleration of the narrative slope' up until the murder scene which occurs one year later in the story (Gergen and Gergen, 1988: 27).

Peter: What I think the next thing that is important is Halloween 2001, I went to see a band called the Fear Factory, played at Brixton academy, and for the first time, someone offered me some crack to smoke, and I thought yea, because of my mindset, so I said yea, and I smoked it (makes that smoking sound again), and boy I didn't stop smoking it since … I literally did not stop smoking it from the 31 October 2001 until 20 June 2002 when I got put in prison for murder, I smoked crack and heroin every day, and ketamine, and the first time I smoked it … it took me away I loved it loved it loved it, I wanted more, more, more all the time, and I spent everything I had and more.

Peter then explored the murder story in more detail:

Peter: I got into some trouble in [City], you know, basically, I hit someone and the person I hit was someone you shouldn't hit, you know, and uhm ... I got a message come through to my family: 'he needs to get outside of town and sort himself out because he is in danger', so I left town, and ended up near over [place] and then, on a gypsy site, living in a caravan yeah? And then I met this guy there, he was a smoker as well, so I was smoking with him, and we basically ended up going and doing a robbery together where there was somebody in the house. A burglary initially, but it turned out there was an elderly gentleman in the house and through whatever means I am responsible for his death you know, and I got put in prison for that I was arrested within 3 weeks and put in prison straight away (Peter).

Here, Peter explained that he is 'responsible for his death' through 'whatever means' – thus claiming some responsibility for his victim's death, and evidences a reflective stance: whatever the means, he has reflected upon that night, and drew the necessary conclusions. Interestingly, Peter does not use the word murder once in this murder story. In fact, he tacitly problematises his unmitigated involvement in the index offence. Had he not been an abandoned as a child he could have exerted control over his actions and the murder could have been avoided. I asked Peter whether the above sequence was correct:

Dan: It's a story around guilt growing up, taking a path of drugs, leading to index offence, prison – becoming lucid, get released and continue with the new life story and become a family man. Is this a true representation of your story?
Peter: Yes, absolutely.

For Peter, murder is inextricably linked to a profound sense of loss associated with his early childhood. Given his early development of a 'false self', the murder can be considered to have been committed by an 'Other'. The use of psychological concepts such as 'primal wound', established in psychological and psychotherapeutic circles provides a glimpse into the institutional discourses used by Peter to account and possibly rationalise his crime. Peter's expert insight showcases the 'digging and delving' into his past and the index offence specific to group-work therapy and narrative reframing at His Majesty's Prisons (HMP) Grendon (Stevens, 2012: 537), where Peter has spent a few years. His problematisation of agency around the index offence was implied rather than explicitly which could be read in the context of his therapeutic journey in places such as HMP Grendon which taught Peter to take responsibility for his crime.

Jacob's family feud – identifying with the abuser

Jacob's stories paint an isolated, alienated child who could never fit in, and was not capable of decision-making, or agency. His parents moved houses many times which had always rendered him as an outsider in endless new environments. Jacob recollects having had a very difficult relationship with his father who used to brutalise him and his brother, with whom he shared the index offence:

Jacob: I had a very I had a very difficult relationship with my father uhm, who was very unemotional, he was very clever, and he was very handy with his hands, things, and I used to love doing things, with him ... but he never he never any affirmation, he never got to school, he never got involved with anything, he was very distant, so you know, you know, often you know, open days have uhm ... parents would come, but my parents, you know, my mother was too busy, my father was just ... they were never there, they were never part of those years, and obviously I reflected deeply on this over the years.

I didn't realise at the time but I realise it now, they were very brutal and abusive, you know, if we did something wrong uhm we wouldn't just be given a slap or something, we would be beaten, you know my father used a riding crop on us regularly, in terms of sort of discipline, to us... it was normal, we didn't, I didn't realise until years later, I mean these days they would be put in prison probably for the way we were treated.

The brutality of his father made Jacob more and more insular. He could never fit in anywhere and could never reach his father's expectations. In addition to blaming the brother, Jacob made sense of the murder scene unwittingly through conceptualising it as a form of transference/countertransference (Polnay et al., 2023) and projective identification (Klein, 1946 in McAlister, 2008) with the victim. Transference refers to the act of bringing in the 'here and now' of previous relationships (Polnay et al., 2023). By killing the victim, the two brothers were in fact killing their father upon whom they projected unbearable parts of their own selves.

Jacob: I do have a theory about the whole thing. Ah, and ... I've never discussed this with anybody, but my brother was very insistent to the point of threatening me. He pointed his gun at me and the point of saying, we have to kill this guy and he was very insistent that it was something that we did together. I did not realise it then but it was drawing me into something that he wanted to do and it was very, very clear to me that he really wanted to kill this guy and on reflection, uhm, this guy looked very much like my father, it was a likeness in age in looks even, the amount of hair that the guy had, it was a similarity, and I really believe that in some way my brother was killing my father uhm because my father really brutalised us and my elder brother in particular, aah, they were, he was cruel and he wasn't a good man, and my eldest brother more than any of us was I think once my parents realised the effects of the brutality did to him they started to be a little less brutal with us, you know, aah, and I really feel that was the case.

The brother is described as the true mastermind who 'really wanted' to commit the murder:

Jacob: One day my eldest brother came back we went out we had some drinks with some girls you know, the 3 of us, he said come on let's just go somewhere so, we started going around the country and we did some armed robberies and getting money and so on, and uhm, it was a very short period of time and one day we found a chat sitting in a layby in a car we hijacked the car and we took him to some woodland and my eldest brother said he got to see my face and we had to kill him and because otherwise he would recognize us and it was very you know … uhm … threatening situation I was in and … so I agreed with my brother and we shot this guy and killed him and took his car and did some more robberies at which time we had the police looking for us. We escaped the country, we were captured we were extradited, and we were tried for the murder and obviously found guilty and uhm, we … we went, we were sent to prison. Whilst I take full responsibility for what happened, ah, I didn't do it willingly, I was, you know, a brother, I didn't tell this to the prison authorities or anybody, because ironically, I thought that was a betrayal of him, even though he always blamed me for everything, [unclear] it's not something that I wanted to do (Jacob).

As evidenced in the first extract, Jacob problematises agency by introducing the influence of his brother, who really wanted to commit the murder, to the extent to which, Jacob was forced, at gunpoint to get involved. There is a sense of shared responsibility being portrayed initially, but he subsequently declaratively takes 'full responsibility' for what happened, although somewhat partially: 'to take responsibility for something you did not do willingly'. Throughout, Jacob evidences an exceptional capacity to evaluate what has happened and to position himself as a moral agent capable of reflecting upon his life. Paradoxically, Jacob talked at length about his struggle to forgive himself for the murder, which contradicts the externalisation of blame onto the brother.

The stories presented here are animated by a visible sense of contradiction and neutralisations. This is not necessarily new in criminological literature (Brookman, 2015; Sandberg, 2009). Presser (2013), for example, made the point that "an actor might both deny responsibility for a harmful action and deny that it causes injury: 'I can't help it. Anyway, it won't hurt anyone'". The men in this sample are characterised by such paradoxes. After their apprehension and trial, the men received their life sentences and were put in prison. Here, the men have made sense of what happened and radically refashioned their personal myth (McAdams, 1993).

The prison experience: Crossroads for becoming

All the men (who employed the splitting narrative) have described their prison journeys as a profoundly transformative experience (F-Dufour and Brassard, 2014; Schinkel, 2014), especially in gaining some control over their lives through reconstructing themselves. For the first few years of their imprisonment the men had ruminated over what had happened (Richard, Jacob, Peter), and struggled to navigate the realities of their new environment (Richard, Jacob) (Crewe, Hulley, and Wright, 2017; Crewe, Hulley, and Wright, 2020). Initial hardship and trauma (including that which was offence related) has ultimately given way to positive outcomes (F-Dufour and Brassard, 2014; van Ginneken, 2016; Vanhooren, Leijssen, and Dezutter 2018) and opportunities to refashion the men's personal myths (McAdams, 1993) in the later stages of the sentence (Crewe, Hulley, and Wright, 2020). The men's movement from 'reactive' to 'productive agency' (Crewe, Hulley, and Wright, 2017: 538; Jarman, 2020) followed a clear sequence of events.

The men had to first make sense of the murder (Adshead, 2014; Crewe, Hulley, and Wright, 2020; Ferrito et al., 2020; Honeywell, 2015), and refashion their life myth (McAdams, 1993). In this sense, the men underwent revelatory experiences (spiritual and religious, see Schroeder and Frana, 2009) which had equipped them with a set of new 'meaning systems' (Maruna, Wilson, and Curran, 2006) to interpret their own condition, and to reconstruct their narrative identities. The revelatory stories are like that of Irwin's (2009) lifers' stories of 'awakening' – the men have unshackled from the influence of the Other and were able to reinvent their narrative identities. An agentic split had been constructed between a murderous self, and the person in the interview present (see James, 1958 for an overview of the 'divided self'). Other research has identified similar moments which they named 'cognitive shifts' and 'epiphanies', in prisoners' lives (Liem, 2016), although with the assistance of vehicles for change (such as prison rehabilitation programmes). Herbert (2019: 28) referred to this process as simply 'maturation' and 'recognition of interdependency'. In this sense, the men's life stories followed similar structures, but the meaning attached to their prison time is sharply distinct.

Trauma and early prison adaptation

In contrast to much penological research (Crewe, Hulley, and Wright, 2020; Goffman, 1961; Richardson, 2012; Sykes, 1958) the men in the sample did not refer to the weight of their prison sentence (Crewe, 2011; Crewe,

Liebling, and Hulley, 2014), or to difficulties in managing and coping with the passage of time whilst on a life sentence (Cohen and Taylor, 1972; Crawley and Sparks, 2006) perhaps because they were released. Alternatively, the men told stories of physical abuse, emotional numbness, and trauma as representative of their early prison years.

Two of the men have presented symptoms associated with perpetration induced posttraumatic stress disorder (PTSD) (Badenes-Ribera et al., 2021; MacNair, 2005) after they had committed the murder. For the first few years, for example, Peter had been 'emotionally numb'. Time had just passed by; he continued to abuse drugs; and was surprised at how time evaporated:

Peter: The first few years just passed by [...], all those years of drug abuse distilled my emotions down to: I was stoned, I was bored, or I was angry.

Peter has never been given a diagnosis of PTSD, although emotional numbness is associated with the disorder (Duek et al., 2023). A comprehensive body of literature suggests that homicide perpetrators can develop PTSD because of their killing (see Di, Chung, and Wan, 2018; Fraser, 1988 Harry and Resnick, 1986; Pollock, 1999; Ternes, Cooper, and Griesel, 2020; Papanastassiou et al., 2004). Soon after he completed a detox course at his own request, Peter started to experience 'night terrors'.

Peter: My sleep was disturbed by these things called 'night terrors', have you ever heard of night terrors? It's like a real lucid nightmare, where... some examples of my own personal I can give you, you know the offence, the murder is happening again, in my sleep in my dream, but it feels real, but my family is there, and they are saying: What are you doing? Why are you doing this? And I am trying to stop this from happening, but it is still happening anyway, and I can't stop it from stopping, and it would be different family members, sometimes it would be children, from my family, and they're saying what are you doing? Stop, stop, stop and I am trying to stop, but it happening anyway in my dream, and I thought I can't fucking handle this what am I supposed to fucking do? I'm fucking going crazy, I'm cracking up, and aa, a I had some sort of serendipity, somebody told me about Grendon, you know, you need to start talking about your shit, man that's what you need to do, yeah right, just a bunch of nonces, and I went to the doctor, and I said look, cuz I thought that tablets might be the answer and I said look, I have these fucking things in my sleep and aaa, he said, aa, yeah I know what they are they are called night terrors, he said, next week, come and see me on Friday and I will bring you some literature you can read about the night terror and it might help you out ... ah yeah, thanks a

> fucking lot mate. (whispers), I wanted tablets to stop it from happening, and then you give me some fucking book, right? I went to see him anyway and the literature he gave me, on the top of the pile, 'night terrors', and there is a little drawing and it says night terrors, there's a little girl holding a teddy bear, crying, cuz she's got night terrors, and I thought to myself that's me, and all this gangster number 1, that's me I am now, I am a crying little child, and I thought, I need to go to Grendon and see what the fuck is going on.[…], that night I had one, my hand up to my elbow was in blood, literally.

Peter's 'night terrors' were vivid recollections of the murder scene – the intrusive images were demonstrating his struggle for agency and revealed some of Peter's emotional rumination over what he had done. Richard too, describes the murder as a traumatic event. Soon after he had killed his girlfriend, he attempted suicide and started to present with symptoms associated with PTSD (Harry and Resnick, 1986) and this continued for a few more years after his imprisonment.

Richard: In those first few years, 1 or 2 years, I still wanted to die because I thought I can't live with this thing, you know it is terrible. After a few years I was sent to Gartree which was at the time a top security prison and that was the first prison where I was able to analyse what I've been through and who I was really you know to find out what was going through my head still, and to get psychiatric reports, just to see how I responded in that environment.

Previous case studies suggest that emotional attachment to the victim exacerbates the experience of PTSD in homicide offenders (Harry and Resnick, 1986; Rynearson, 1984). The type of guilt expressed by Richard reminds of Fraser's (1988: 128) 'complicated mourning', usually found in those who kill someone who they loved. This is strikingly different to the other two men in this sample, both of whom killed strangers. The finding also echoes that of Sapsford (1983), who found that domestic murderers have a difficult time integrating the murder into their picture of themselves, and who expressed more remorse, compared to other types of killers (although this last point is debatable in the given case). Richard ruminated (Evans et al., 2007) over what happened for the first couple of years of the prison sentence before 'it all made sense' and became a 'new kind of person' (Crewe, Hulley, and Wright, 2020; Vaughan, 2007).

Jacob's initial prison struggles are different to Peter's and Richard's, who 'enthusiastically' (Crewe, 2006) complied with prison authority (Richard), or retreated into drugs (Peter). He seemed to be 'swimming against the tide' (see Crewe, Hulley, and Wright, 2017). Jacob's prison stories are initially constructed under the auspices of a pervasive sentiment of injustice. After his co-defendant (his brother) "concocted an elaborated story" portraying him as an informer to other inmates, he was bound to experience a particularly brutal prison experience:

Jacob: I mean I was 18, 19, at the time, I mean ... ah we were treated in maximum security prisons and we were put in London, maximum security terrorist wing, so there I was a 19 year old kid surrounded by IRA terrorists, Libyan terrorists, uhm hitmen, you know, the crème de la crème of armed robbers and so on ... and my brother sort of fitted in with these guys and because of what was happening in the newspapers and so on ... he told this story that I was informing on him and these guys bullied me, they pressured me to uhm ... they treated me terribly, so I had a really hard time there I was at a top security prison, convicted, and ... uhm ... I was send to Hull prison and once again the news followed I had a difficult time, I was beaten up, assaulted, uhm, I ended up in the segregation unit, punishment block, under protection and spent 9 months in total isolation really, and I sort of lost it really, in that I was, I was being punished for something above and beyond, I was beating myself up, for what we done, the sort of responsibility that I felt for the whole thing.

Jacob's early abuse was attributed to his brother who 'fitted in with these guys'. The fact that he did not fit in with *the crème de la crème* of British criminal underworld marks Jacob's importation of a different set of norms within the prison system (Dhami, Ayton, and Lowenstein, 2007; Irwin and Cressey, 1962; Paterline and Petersen, 1999; Porporino and Zamble, 1984), fundamentally at odds with that environment. He soon established himself as a 'player' (Crewe, 2009) initially outwardly repudiating prison culture and disregarding authority, but in the end became compliant, and controlled; a prisoner 'easy to keep' (Herbert, 2019).

Jacob: My rebellion against that culture on both sides of the authority point of view and from the prison culture point of view I just, it wasn't for me, and I wasn't going to be part of it. I had to live in it, but I always excluded myself from that, because I just couldn't participate.

As it has been shown, initial prison years were representative of the men's emotional struggle to make sense of the enormity of their crime, as well as to navigate their new environments (Crewe, Hulley, and Wright, 2020). None of the men had been given an official diagnosis for PTSD. Nevertheless, a meta-analysis (Badenes-Ribera et al., 2021) found that 46.2% of incarcerated adult killers meet the criteria for a full PTSD diagnosis after committing homicide. The men had started to come to terms with what they had done, after eventually having reached 'rock bottom' (Paternoster and Bushway, 2009). This was followed by a spiritual 'awakening' (Irwin, 2009), which assisted the men to reconstruct their personal myth (McAdams, 1993).

Reconstructing identities

Most of the men eventually reached some form of 'rock bottom' (Paternoster and Bushway, 2009) during their prison time which heralded an acute need for radical change. The men underwent transformative experiences (often religious, Schroeder and Frana, 2009) which equipped them with a set of new 'meaning systems' (Maruna, Wilson, and Curran, 2006) to interpret their own condition, make sense of their crime, and to reconstruct their narrative identities. When a person gives up a specific view over the world for another, the process is referred to as a 'conversion' (Lofland and Stark, 1965). The conversion narratives explored below are spiritual and religious, and assisted the men in coping with the enormity and irreparability of their crime and helped to achieve forgiveness. Further, the new meaning systems provided the men with purpose in life and allowed the emergence of 'redemptive selves' (Blagden, Winder, and Livesley, 2020; Maruna, 2001).

Peter provided an example of spiritual awakening (Irwin, 2009) from a process of ontological insecurity to one of existence in the world. As mentioned previously, the journey started in prison. Peter told me about a cell mate who he spent much time within detention due to their drug use, but whom he loathed but saw himself 'becoming just like him':

Peter: One day someone said to me, you (whispers) you getting like him, you know the way he talks to people and that, I say (whispers and in contempt): 'fuck off', but it went in ... and then I started to watch, because that's what you do isn't it, introspect, you just watch, and I found myself talking like him on a few occasions, and I thought fuck! I don't like this guy, I am becoming him and also, we both had attained the same tariff but I did 3 years and a bit, he done like 12, and we were both in the same prison, and I thought ok, so if I carry on like this, this is what's gonna happen to me, you know what I mean, and I got myself, a few other things happened around that time, and I got myself so hyped one afternoon I thought fuck it, I went to the office, I knocked on the door, and a screw opened the door, it was the worst one, was an asshole, you know there is always an arsehole, so I'll tell you his name, it was it was [redacted] and he says (whispers again) "what do you fucking want?". I said look, you know I got a drug problem, I've had enough, how do I sort it out?

The above passage shows Peter's 'crystallization of discontent' by imagining his imminent engulfment (Laing, 1960) into a 'Feared Self' (Paternoster and Bushway, 2009) represented by the cellmate. This, in turn, opened a set of possible new selves to Peter who developed an initial motivation to change (Giordano, Cerkovich, and Rudolph, 2002; Vaughan, 2007). Vaughan (2007: 391) found that "very often, it is through seeing the self through the eyes of others that raises questions about the worthiness of past and present choices". It is precisely this type of emotional empathy that ignites the process of identity reconstruction (Vaughan, 2007). Peter's self-appraisal initiated a journey into reconnecting with his emotional self in HMP Grendon, and to ultimately discover his identity by navigating the Alcoholic Anonymous' 12 step recovery process during his time at HMP Kingston.

Peter: So, I started going to AA when I was at Kingston, and I found a few connections there, you know, like I found a kinship, a family, these are my family, my people you know? And now ... I started to realise there was a lot of people with a similar mindset with me, you know, so I went to (not clear) and almost straight away put myself to the program. I did that for 6 months and that really have me a good opportunity to work my way through the steps you know the 12 steps, I worked my way through it slowly and through steps, you know, are you familiar with... through my step four I really discovered my identity you know what I mean, and I realised that out there were points in my life where my identity did not belong to me... you know what I mean, as I was growing up my identity was defined by the facts that my father told me, there was external influences that defined myself, you know what I say ... and when I was in prison I said that I was becoming that guy, because that's how I was, I'd be with someone and id start to become like them, I had no real identity of myself, you know what I mean, writing down my step four (is uhm... basically, your life story, essentially) ... writing it down, going through and going back to it and going back to it really gave me a sense of my own identity ... you know what I mean ... and from then on that felt precious to me and that something I was not willing to give up again, you know what I mean?

In addition, Peter's recovery through Alcoholic Anonymous is founded upon a complex set of spiritual principles (McInerney and Cross, 2021; Segal, 2020). The main premise, well represented by step three, is that one needs to "make a decision to turn our lives over to the care of God as we understand him" (Segal, 2020: 3), and to accept that a major change of character is needed (ibid). Peter's time in prison was now transformed into a positive experience (F-Dufour and Brassard, 2014; Schinkel, 2014).

Religious conversion narratives

In contrast to Paul's secular spiritual transformation, Richard and Jacob had started to make sense of their murder through religious conversion narratives (Kerley and Copes, 2009; Maruna, Wilson, and Curran, 2006). Irwin (2009: 68) suggests that "religion has a great appeal to lifers", because it offers meaning and purpose to an unsatisfying past which needs reconciliation

166 *Life Beyond Murder*

and expiation. Both men referred to pervasive sentiments of guilt which stemmed from the irreparable nature of their crime (as explored in the previous chapter). Jacob embarked on a long journey of spiritual search before the truth revealed to him under the Christian credence. His quest for spiritual transformation began after a brief conversation with a priest who refused to assure Jacob of ultimate salvation. During his time at HMP Parkhurst, Jacob embarked onto a 'quest for meaning', trying to come to terms with the guilt of what he had done. His awakening is narrated alike an initiation rite; having initially flirted with Buddhism and meditation, he then moved on to study Islam. Finally, Jacob experienced a revelatory experience after reading the 51st Psalm in the Bible.

Jacob: It's a long story with King David [...], but he wrote a song which started to created me [...] and reading that song I realised, I don't know what happened but I realised that there was a presence and I realised that I could be forgiven and it was a complete revelation to me and I read that song, on my knees weeping and somehow from that moment there was clarity in my mind in the circumstances that I was in. It was like somebody in the environment around me had switched on a fluorescent light; everything in the prison was just cleaner, brighter, and it was different and I felt different and I didn't really understand what had happened and I continued going to church and it was kind of meaningless to me, and I continued to read the words of Jesus in the Bible and I knew that somehow it all made sense and from the moment through my prison journey I met with other people like [...] and so on who also had some sort of religious experience of God and it was meaningful where they found forgiveness and faith and an empowerment and that faith got me through a lot.

The reference to Psalm 51 holds significant meaning. It represents king David's prayer of penitence for his involvement in the murder of Uriah the Hittie. Jacob referred the Psalm as the 'sinner's prayer', employed by those who murdered in asking for repentance. Ultimately, Psalm 51 is a plea for forgiveness, mercy, and contrition. Richard, too, found that Christianity provided the "language and framework for forgiveness" (Maruna, Wilson, and Curran, 2006: 175).

Richard: I think, the way I was looking at the whole panorama, of people offending, and looking what I was going through spiritually as well, and forgiveness, because the whole thing about Christianity is about forgiveness really, and try to get to a situation where I can almost forgive myself, and, uhm, it came to me that if god forgives people and has forgiven me then maybe I should have an attempt at forgiving myself as well, and trying to make good, and also, the support of my family and friends, and the support of the chaplaincy, was good, and that made me think you know, I can't let them down, why should I still want to kill myself, and that people still want to invest in me, people in [university], still wanted to support me, so I thought having all that support I need, made me want to respond to that support and it was that that started to change my thinking as far as my life is concerned. Because I never really had a criminal mentality but, the problem, when I was at Gartree, I was very suicidal at first, cuz I thought this is such a terrible thing that I'd never get over it, and even at those dark days at Gartree sometimes I thought I'd never get released and even if I would get released how could I live a normal life? So, it was quite a transition for me really.

As with baptism, which serves the symbolic effect of erasing original sin, religious conversion offers an opportunity to the men to start anew. Both Richard and Jacob had made specific comments about forgiveness in the Christian religion which, as Maruna, Wilson, and Curran (2006: 177) argues: "provides a stronger foundation for forgiveness than nearly any other meta-narrative available in modern Western society". For these two men forgiveness "responds to wrongs that cannot be overcome" and assists with accepting their irrevocable pasts (Potts, 2022: 50).

Richard: There is this concept in Christianity, of the original sin, that all men are guilty, are naturally simple, there is a proclivity to commit sin, whether its stealing or doing something as drastic as murder. And what Christianity said is that all sins are just as bad as the other, even though the sin of the word, without confession of that, will bring you to hell. So, I suppose that concept has helped although the reality is that you are still aware that you committed something really bad. So, Christianity helped me to manage that process in a spiritual sense.

As shown above, spirituality and religion had provided the men with a set of resources to alleviate some of the hardships associated with their crime, and to cope with their new environment (Crewe, Hulley, and Wright, 2017; Schroeder and Frana, 2009). Further, available religious discourses (Warr, 2019) offered the men a "hook for moral transformation and identity change" (Crewe, Hulley, and Wright, 2017: 19), and a readily available formal redemptive narrative (Warr, 2019: 39) which has been performed continuously ever since. Maruna, Wilson, and Curran (2006: 168) also remarked that incarceration can be a catalyst for identity reconstruction as "prisoners [...] face a crisis of self-narrative". James (1902/1958:177) observed that with religious conversion a "complete division is established in the twinkling of an eye between the old life and the new". He goes on to add that this involves a dissolution of the past and the construction of a new identity. A sort of a positive subjective religious 'knifing off' (Maruna and Roy, 2007) which may explain why "religion has a great appeal to lifers" (Irwin, 2009: 68). Kerley and

168 *Life Beyond Murder*

Copes (2009) observed that religious epiphanies are particularly important in reconciling past and current selves. The men have henceforth constructed a split between a murderous self and newly found, generative, and agentic self. This narrative split emerged due to the traumatic and irreparable nature of committing murder – which renders it difficult to reconcile with a 'good core self' (Maruna, 2001), or stable moral self (Presser, 2008).

Despite the divide created between an old self and the new, guilt is present as it operates as a 'narrative binding agent' in the men's narrative, linking a reinterpreted version of the 'murderous self' (see Snow and Machalek, 1983) with a present, agentic, and generative self (Ferrito et al., 2020). Guilt assists the men to achieve coherence in the context of the creating agentic split. In the absence of guilt, the men's dissociation from their previous, murderous self, would become pathological, and perhaps would be flagged by authorities as not taking responsibility for their crime.

Discussion

To reiterate, the most skilled and discursively remorseful participants (Jacob, Peter, and Richard) employed a specific temporal order which provided a platform to their problematisation of agency. These men did not project blame outwards, onto the victim, and neither did they invoke a 'parallel self' to account for the crime (Stein, 2007). Their explanatory narratives drew from a range of public narratives (Harding et al., 2017), cultural (for example crime of passion discourse), as well as organisational discourses (psycho-medical) to account for their specific murder. Childhood stories were reconstructed to provide coherence to these narratives (for example as banal or violent) and structurally set up the murder stories. Not all men constructed a splitting narrative trying to reconciliate guilt alongside index offence rationalisations. For example, Raul's story (presented in the previous chapter) followed a stable plot where blame was simply projected onto his victim who 'knew what he was getting himself into'. Raul did not dwell on issues of morality, guilty, or remorse, such as the men in this chapter.

The men envisioned their prison sentences as a transformative experience (Schinkel, 2014); much of early trauma was conceptualised through positive lenses, later in the sentence. Had it not been for the lengthy time behind bars, Peter would have never regained his emotional self and write a life story as a natural process of AA therapy, and God may have never revealed itself to Richard and Jacob. Religion and religious narratives offered both Richard and Jacob the 'language and framework for forgiveness' (Maruna, Wilson, and Curran, 2006: 175) and the resources values needed to reconstruct their identities (although these were not necessarily used as tools to make sense of the murder motivation).

Personal narratives, as Riessman (2004: 35) said, are simply 'meaning-making units of discourse'; narrators "interpret the past in their stories rather than reproduce it as it was". Given Riessman's words, the structure presented here offers a glimpse into the way the men have made sense of their lives and have organised these coherently in narrative form. It evidences the natural progression of events leading up to the murder and thereafter. The men managed to show remorse at discursive level whilst justifying their unmitigated involvement in the murder scenes. This was evident in the form of the story as much as in the content. Potentially, the growth out of trauma displayed by the men may also be a form of accounting for much of the early suffering, as effort justification (Aronson and Mills, 1959; Harmon-Jones and Mills, 1999).

The men in this sample are put in the paradoxical situation of showing guilt for a crime which was 'inevitable' or an 'accident' (Hulley, Crewe, and Wright, 2019). In sum, the 'Murder's Identity Paradox' is solved through a series of competing/conflicting stories which serve to construct a dichotomy between the murderous past persona, often characterised by ontological insecurity (Laing, 1960) subjected to the Other's influence and a new self, distanced, and alien to the 'murderous self'. Stories of guilt are used binding agent to the story arc, linking the past identity to the present one (and thus solving any possibilities for pathologies of dissociation). Further, the men use stories of guilt in anticipation of perceived expectations, as "many practitioners believe that offenders in denial present a high risk of offending in the future, since they are seen to be making themselves unaccountable for their past action" (Vaughan, 2007: 400).

The men are skilled users of narrative as an identity management (Laws, 2020; Warr, 2019) who are displeased with the continuous request of penitence and self-flagellation (Warr, 2019) requested by the authorities. These shifts may be considered strategic (Brookman, 2015), presenting of cognitive dissonance (Festinger, 1957), and aimed at reconciling their paradoxical situation. The splitting narrative provides coherency between a murderous past and an ethical, moral self-present in a way which is not pathologically dissociative, functions as an internal narrative of change which reconciliates the past with the present and the future (acting as an internal and external stigma management mechanism), and presents/performs acceptable identities and reform to authorities to minimise their risk and to solve a paradox that stands at the centre of the narratives.

References

Adshead, G. (2014) Safety in numbers: Group therapy-based index offence work in secure psychiatric care. *Psychoanalytic Psychotherapy*, 29 (3), 295–310.

Aronson, E., and Mills, J. (1959) The effect of severity of initiation on liking for a group. *Journal of Abnormal and Social Psychology*, 59, 177–181.

Badenes-Ribera, L., Molla-Esparza, C., Longobardi, C., Sánchez-Meca, J., and Fabris, A. M. (2021) Homicide as a source of post-traumatic stress? A meta-analysis of the prevalence of posttraumatic stress disorder after committing homicide. *Journal of Traumatic Stress*, 34, 345–356.

Bargh, J. A. (2006) What have we been priming all these years? On the development, mechanisms, and ecology of nonconscious social behaviour. *European Journal of Social Psychology*, 36 (2), 147–168.

Blagden, N., Winder, B., and Livesley, R. (2020) The resurrection after the old has gone and the new has come': Understanding narratives of forgiveness, redemption and resurrection in Christian individuals serving time in custody for a sexual offence. *Psychology, Crime, and Law*, 20 (1), 1–42.

Brookman, F. (2015) Researching homicide offenders, offenses, and detectives using qualitative methods. In H. Copes and M. J. Miller (Eds.), *The Routledge Handbook of Qualitative Criminology*. Oxon: Routledge, 236–252.

Chartrand, T. L., and Bargh, J. A. (1996) Automatic activation of impression formation and memorization goals: Nonconscious goal priming reproduces effects of explicit task instructions. *Journal of Personality and Social Psychology*, 71 (3), 464–478.

Chatterton, P., and Hollands, R. (2002) Theorising urban playscapes: Producing, regulating and consuming youthful nightlife city spaces. *Urban Studies*, 39 (1), 95–116.

Cohen, S., and Taylor, L. (1972) *Psychological Survival: The Experience of Long-Term Imprisonment*. London: Penguin.

Crewe, B. (2006) Power, adaptation and resistance in a late modern Men's prison. *British Journal of Criminology*, 47, 256–275.

Crewe, B. (2009) *The Prisoner Society: Power, Adaptation and Social Life in an English Prison*. Oxford: Oxford University Press.

Crewe, B. (2011) Depth, weight, tightness: Revisiting the pains of imprisonment. *Punishment and Society*, 13 (5), 509–529.

Crewe, B., Hulley, S., and Wright, S. (2017) Swimming with the tide: Adapting to long-term imprisonment. *Justice Quarterly*, 34 (3), 517–541.

Crewe, B., Hulley, S., and Wright, S. (2020) *Life Imprisonment from Young Adulthood Adaptation, Identity, and Time*. United Kingdom, UK: Palgrave Macmillan.

Crewe, B., Liebling, A., and Hulley, S. (2014) Heavy-absent, absent-present: Rethinking the 'weight' of imprisonment. *The British Journal of Sociology*, 65 (1), 387–410.

Crawley, E., and Sparks, R. (2006) Is there life after imprisonment? How elderly men talk about imprisonment after release. *Criminology and Criminal Justice*, 6 (1), 63–82.

Dhami, K., M., Ayton, P., and Lowenstein, G. (2007) Adaptation to imprisonment. Indigenous or imported? *Criminal Justice and Behaviour*, 34 (8), 1085–1100.

Di, X., Chung, M. C., and Wan, K. H. (2018) Investigating the impact of past trauma and defense styles on posttraumatic stress following homicide and psychiatric comorbidity. *Psychiatric Quarterly*, 89 (2), 439–444.

Duek, O., Seidemann, R., Pietrzak, R., H., and Harpaz-Rotem, I. (2023) Distinguishing emotional numbing symptoms of posttraumatic stress disorder from major depressive disorder. *Journal of Affective Disorders*, 324, 294–299.

Evans, C., Ehlers, A., Mezey, G., and Clark, D. M. (2007) Intrusive memories and ruminations related to violent crime among young offenders: Phenomenological characteristics. *Journal of Traumatic Stress*, 20 (2), 183–196.

F-Dufour, I., and Brassard, R. (2014) The convert, the remorseful, and the rescued: Three different processes of desistance from crime. *Australian and New Zealand Journal of Criminology*, 47, 313–335.

Ferrito, G. (2020) Life after taking a life: The process of meaning reconstruction and identity for men who committed homicide, Unpublished Doctoral Dissertation. University of Portsmouth.

Ferrito, M., Needs, A., Jingree, T., and Pearson, D. (2020) Making sense of the dark: A study on the identity of men who committed homicide. *Journal of Forensic Psychology Research and Practice*, 20 (2), 163–184.

Festinger, L. (1957) *A Theory of Cognitive Dissonance*. Evanston, IL: Row, Peterson [Database]

Fox, K. J. (1999) Changing violent minds: Discursive correction and resistance in the cognitive treatment of violent offenders in prison. *Social Problems*, 46 (1), 88–103.

Fraser, K. A. (1988) Bereavement in those who have killed. *Medical Sociological Law*, 28 (2), 127–130.

Gergen, K. K., and Gergen, M. M. (1988) Narrative and the self as relationship. *Advances in Experimental Social Psychology*, 21, 17–56.

Giordano, P. C., Cerkovich, S. A., and Rudolph, J. L. (2002) Gender crime and desistance: Toward a theory of cognitive transformation. *American Journal of Sociology*, 107 (4), 990–1064.

Gobodo-Madikizela, P. (2022) Remorse as ethical encounter and the impossibility of repair. In S. Tudor, R. Weisman, M. Proeve, and K. Rossmanith (Eds.), *Remorse and the Criminal Justice: Multidisciplinary Perspectives*. New York: Routledge, 243–264.

Goffman, E. (1961) *Asylums: Essays on the Social Situation of Mental Patients and Other Inmates*. London: Penguin.

Hall, S. and Winlow, S. (2005) Anti-Nirvana: Crime, culture, and instrumentalism in the age of insecurity. *Crime Media Culture*, 1 (1), 31–48.

Harding, D. J., Dobson, C., Wyse, J. J. B., and Morenoff, D. (2017) Narrative change, narrative stability, and structural constraints: The case of prisoner reentry narratives. *American Journal of Cultural Sociology*, 5 (1), 261–304.

Harmon-Jones, E., and Mills, J. (1999) *Cognitive Dissonance: Progress on a Pivotal Theory in Social Psychology*. Washington, DC: American Psychological Association.

Harry, B. and Resnick, P. J. (1986) Posttraumatic stress disorder in murderers. *Journal of Forensic Science*, 31 (2), 609–613.

Herbert, S. K. (2019) *Too Easy to Keep: Life-Sentenced Prisoners and the Future of Mass Incarceration*. Oakland, CA: University of California Press.

Honeywell, D. (2015) Doing time with lifers: A reflective study of life sentence prisoners. *British Journal of Community Justice*, 13 (1), 93–104.

Hulley, S., Crewe, B., and Wright, S. (2019) Making sense of "Joint Enterprise" for murder: Legal legitimacy or instrumental acquiescence? *The British Journal of Criminology*, 59, 1328–1346.

Irwin, J. (2009) *Lifers: Seeking Redemption in Prison*. New York: Routledge.

Irwin, J., and Cressey, D. (1962) Thieves, convicts and the inmate culture. *Social Problems*, 10 (1), 142–155.

James, W. (1902/1958) *The Varieties of Religious Experience*. New York: New American Library.

Jarman, B. (2020) Only one way to swim? The offence and the life course in accounts of adaptation to life imprisonment. *The British Journal of Criminology*, 60 (6), 1460–1479.

Kerley, K. R., and Copes, H. (2009) "Keepin' my Mind Right": Identity maintenance and religious social support in the prison context. *International Journal of Offender Therapy and Comparative Criminology*, 53 (2), 228–244.

Laing, R., D. (1960) *The Divided Self: An Existential Study in Sanity and Madness*. Middlesex, England: Penguin Books.

Laws, B. (2020) Reimaging 'the Self' in criminology: Transcendence, unconscious states and the limits of narrative criminology. *Theoretical Criminology*, 26 (3), 475–493.

Liem, M. (2016) *After Life Imprisonment*. New York: New York University Press.

Lofland, J., and Stark, R. (1965) Becoming a world-saver: A theory of conversion to a deviant perspective. *American Sociological Review*, 30 (6), 862–875.

MacNair, R. M. (2005) *Perpetration-Induced Traumatic Stress: The Psychological Consequences of Killing*. Lincoln: Praeger/Greenwood Publishing.

Maruna, S. (2001) *Making Good: How Ex-Convicts Reform Rebuild Their Lives*. Washington, DC: American Psychological Association. [Database]

Maruna, S., and Roy, K. (2007) Amputation or reconstruction? Notes on the concept of "knifing off" and desistance from crime. *Journal of Contemporary Criminal Justice*, 23 (1), 104–124.

Maruna, S, Wilson, L., and Curran, K. (2006) Why God is often found behind bars: Prison conversions and the crisis of self-narrative. *Research in Human Development*, 3 (2), 161–184.

McAdams, D. P. (1993) *The Stories We Live By: Personal Myth and the Making of the Self*. The Guildford Press: New York.

McAlister, M. (2008) Killing off the shadow: The role of projective identification in murderous acts. In R. Doctor (Ed.), *Murder: A Psychotherapeutic Investigation*. London: Karnak Books Ltd, 65–78.

McInerney, K., and Cross, A. (2021) A phenomenological study: Exploring the meaning of spirituality in long-term recovery in alcoholic anonymous. *Alcohol Treatment Quarterly*, 39 (2), 282–300.

McKendy, J. P. (2006) 'I'm very careful about that': Narrative and agency of men in prison. *Discourse & Society*, 17 (4), 473–502.

Monckton-Smith, J. (2020) Intimate partner femicide: Using Foucauldian analysis to track and eight stage progression to homicide. *Violence Against Women*, 8, 476–494.

O'Connor, P. (1995) Speaking of crime: I don't know what made me do it. *Discourse and Society*, 6 (3), 429–456.

O'Connor, P. (2000) *Speaking of Crime: Narratives of Prisoners*. Lincoln: University of Nebraska Press.

Papanastassiou, M., Waldron, G., Boyle, J., and Chesterman, P. L. (2004) Post-traumatic stress disorder in mentally ill perpetrators of homicide. *The Journal of Forensic Psychiatry & Psychology*, 15, 66–75.

Paterline, A. B., and Petersen, M. D. (1999) Structural and social psychological determinants of prisonization. *Journal of Criminal Justice*, 27 (5), 427–441.

Paternoster, R., and Bushway, S. (2009) Desistence and the 'Feared Self': Toward an identity theory of criminal desistence. *The Journal of Criminal Law & Criminology*, 99 (4), 1103–1156.

Phoenix, C., and Smith, B. (2011) Telling a (good?) Counterstory of aging: Natural bodybuilding meets the narrative of decline *The Journals of Gerontology, Psychological Sciences and Social Sciences*, 66 (5), 628–639.

Pollock, P. H. (1999) When the killer suffers: Post-traumatic stress reactions following homicide. *Legal and Criminological Psychology*, 4, 185–202.

Polnay, A., Pugh, R., Barker, V., Bell, D., Beveridge, A., Burley, A., Lumsden, A., Mizeb, C. M., and Wilson, L. (2023) *Cambridge Guide to Psychodynamic Psychotherapy*. Cambridge: Cambridge University Press.

Porporino, J. F., and Zamble, E. (1984) Coping with imprisonment. *Canadian Journal of Criminology*, 26, 403–421.

Potts, M. I. (2022) *Forgiveness: An Alternative Account*. USA: Yale University Press.

Presser, L. (2008) *Been a Heavy Life: Stories of Violent Men*. Urbana and Chicago: University of Illinois Press.

Presser, L. (2009) The narratives of offenders. *Theoretical Criminology*, 13 (2), 177–200.

Presser, L. (2013) *Why We Harm*. New Brunswick, NJ: Rutgers University Press.

Richardson, M. (2012) Lifers: An exploration of coping among male life sentence prisoners. Rehabilitation, research, and reform: prison policy in Ireland. *Irish Probation Journal*, 9, 142–162.

Riessman, C. (2004) Accidental cases: Extending the concept of positioning in narrative studies. In M. Bamberg, and M. Andrews (Eds.), *Considering Counter-Narratives: Narrating, Resisting, Making Sense*. Amsterdam/Philadelphia: Benjamins Publishing, 33–38.

Rynearson, E. K. (1984) Bereavement after homicide: A descriptive study. *The American Journal of Psychiatry*, 141 (11), 1452–1454.
Sandberg, S. (2009) Gangster, victim, or both? The interdiscursive construction of sameness and difference in self-presentations. *British Journal of Sociology*, 60 (3), 523–542.
Sapsford, R. J. (1983) *Life Sentence Prisoners: Research, Response and Change*. Milton Keynes: Open University Press.
Sarup, M. (1996) *Identity, Culture, and the Postmodern World*. Edinburgh: Edinburgh University Press.
Schinkel, M. (2014) *Being Imprisoned: Punishment, Adaptation, and Desistance*. Hampshire: Palgrave.
Schroeder, R. D., and Frana, J. F. (2009) Spirituality and religion, emotional coping, and criminal desistance: A qualitative study of men undergoing change. *Sociological Spectrum*, 29, 718–741.
Scully, D., and Marolla, J. (1985) "Riding the bull at Gilley's": Convicted rapists describe the rewards of rape. *Social Problems*, 32 (3), 251–263.
Segal, G. (2020) Alcoholic anonymous "Spirituality" and long-term sobriety maintenance as a topic for interdisciplinary study. *Behavioural Brain Research*, 389, 1–9.
Snow, D. A., and Machalek, R. (1983) The convert as a social type. *Sociological Theory*, 1 (1), 259–289.
Spector-Mersel, G. (2011) Mechanisms of selection in claiming narrative identities: A model for interpreting narratives. *Qualitative Inquiry*, 17 (2), 172–185.
Stein, A. (2007) *Prologue to Violence: Child Abuse, Dissociation, and Crime*. Mahwah: The Analytic Press.
Stevens, A. (2012) 'I am the person now that I was always meant to be': Identity reconstruction and narrative reframing in therapeutic community prisons. *Criminology and Criminal Justice*, 12 (5), 527–547.
Sykes, G. (1958) *The Society of Captives: A Study of a Maximum-Security Prison*. Princeton, NJ: Princeton University Press.
Sykes, G., & Matza, D. (1957) Techniques of neutralization: A theory of delinquency. *American Sociological Review*, 22, 664–670.
Taylor, G. (1996) Guilt and remorse. In R. Hare, and W. Parrott (Eds.), *The Emotions: Social, Cultural and Biological Dimensions*. London: Sage Publications, 57–73.
Ternes, M., Cooper, B. S., and Griesel, D. (2020) The perpetration of violence and the experience of trauma: Exploring predictors of PTSD symptoms in male violent offenders. *International Journal of Forensic Mental Health*, 19 (1), 68–83.
van Ginneken, E. J. C. (2016) Making sense of imprisonment: Narratives of posttraumatic growth among female prisoners. *International Journal of Offender Therapy and Comparative Criminology*, 60 (2), 208–227.
Vanhooren, S., Leijssen, M., and Dezutter, J. (2018) Coping strategies and posttraumatic growth in prison. *The Prison Journal*, 98 (2), 123–142.
Vaughan, B. (2007) The internal narrative of desistance. *British Journal of Criminology*, 47 (3), 390–404.
Verrier, N. N. (2009) *The Primal Wound: Understanding the Adopted Child*. Baltimore: Gateway Press.
Warr, J. (2019) Always gotta be two mans': Lifers, risk, rehabilitation, and narrative labour. *Punishment and Society*, 22 (1), 28–47.
Wright, S., Crewe, B., and Hulley, S. (2017) Suppression, denial, sublimation: Defending against the initial pains of very long sentences. *Theoretical Criminology*, 21 (2), 225–246.
Žižek, S. (2008) *The Sublime Object of Ideology*. London: Verso.

10 Managing shame
Hierarchies of moral abomination

Starting from the premise that "the experience of stigma for perpetrators of homicide cannot be separated from their social context" (Ferrito et al., 2020: 15), I will turn to discuss the theme of reconstructing identities in the interview context. Specifically, I focus on the ways in which the men constructed ethical selves by othering different types of murderers as the truly reprehensible type. In this sense, the type of murder committed turned out to be significant, in that it allowed a set of narratives to emerge in response to the men's experience of stigmatised identities post-release (Goffman, 1959). Importantly, the management of stigma is a crucial precursor to the construction and performance of identities (Copes, Hochstetler, and Williams, 2008; Hochstetler, Copes, and Williams, 2010: 494), and the interview context provided the ideal environment for ethical identities to be negotiated (Ugelvik, 2012). The men resisted stigmatising identities and shame by creating hierarchies of moral abomination. The research environment emerged as an ideal place where ethical identities could be reconstructed (Ugelvik, 2012). The context of the murder and its type are placed on a hierarchy of moral abomination where victims' identities take central importance.

All the stories presented here are constructed with specific audiences in mind; they draw from master narratives (Hammack, 2008; McLean and Syed, 2015; Plummer, 2019; Sandberg and Fondevila, 2020), and stereotypes around masculinities, love, patriarchy, as well as specific local cultural relevancies as narrative resources (Loseke, 2007). Master narratives are dominant stories (Sandberg and Fondevila, 2020) which hold power in our societies. This is because they are considered truthful, or 'the truth' (Sandberg and Colvin, 2020), and such master narratives are "directed from and ultimately constructed and reproduced as social reality by dominant institutions, agents, and systems" (Snajdr, 2013: 234). Lilgendahl (2015: 490) has suggested that "master narratives are critical for identity development because they can shape how individuals engage in meaning-making in response to their own life experiences". Master narratives were indeed critical for identity construction, and negotiation by providing a backdrop against which stigma was managed by the men. In negotiating with master

DOI: 10.4324/9781003415640-10

narratives (Plummer, 2019), the type of murder committed emerged as significant in the men's attempt to deflect shame and negotiate some level of acceptability.

Hierarchies of murder acceptability: 'Inauthentic Murderers'

Having killed his partner out of 'passion', Richard found that his intimate partner homicide (Brookman, 2022) renders him as 'worthy of forgiveness' (LeBel, Richie, and Maruna, 2015: 117).

Dan: Is the type of murder committed important in experiencing stigma?
Richard: Yes, because mine was a crime of passion, I felt that people were much more forgiving. Obviously, the act of murder, but they had sympathy, because they kind of knew that I wasn't a violent person in the first place and they knew I was young at the time, so I was 19 at the time, so, it was that type of murder, crime of passion murder, uhm there wasn't much condemnation from people that knew about it. Uhm, people who live in the area saw that as a crime of passion, I imagine if for instance I killed an old person, or I killed a child then people would be, when it is a crime of passion, in my experience, people are a lot more compassionate (**Intimate Partner Femicide**)

Richard outwardly seems to appeal to mainstream society's acceptance of him, and constructs himself through 'othering' (Plummer, 2019; Sarup, 1996) those who kill children, or the elderly as contemptible murderers. This murder hierarchy allowed the creation of distance, through establishing difference between those who have engaged in the righteous type of murder, or 'acceptable' murder in contrast to the abominable, unacceptable 'killer' (Jenkins, 2004). Acceptability showed up as dependent on whom the victim was and constructed children, and the elderly, as 'undeserving victims' (Maruna and Copes, 2005; Sykes and Matza, 1957). Richard characterises himself 'not a violent person in the first place' – thus constructing an image of someone authentically non-violent (Hochstetler, Copes, and Williams, 2010; Scully and Marolla, 1985), a characteristic incompatible with 'true murderers'. Frank (2010: 35) made the important point that 'we talk in borrowed language' – a point which is central in considering how Richard drew from gender normative, master narratives around uncontrollable love and passion (Mullen, 1993), as well as stereotypes surrounding 'true murderers' to make sense of his killing and to manage stigma. As Monckton-Smith (2020) reminds us, a crime of passion discourse is characterised by 'unpredictable' violence which is mistakenly seen as triggered by something that the victim has done. In this case, Richard was rejected by the victim. The label feeds into a specific view held within the public imagination of patriarchal societies, where men are lacking in control over their needs and urges

(Ryan, 2011, 2019). Having his version of the events accepted, or rejected by mainstream society is a necessary precursor to maintaining his reconstructed identity and to creating a sense of belonging upon re-entry (Fox, 2016):

Richard: Uhm, I think, I am trying to think of the lowest point really, probably, because, a lot of people in the town that I offended, [redacted] uhm, perceive it to be a crime of passion, they were quite fine with me and kind of understood the history, but of course some people haven't you know, so, probably, the lowest point was when I went to a funeral in [redacted], and I went to shake the hands of one of my cousins, and they said I don't want to talk with you but that sort of reactions have been very few, so that was why it was so upsetting really, uhm, but I understand, because not everyone sees is the way that everybody sees it, most people see it as a crime of passion, most people can't deal with it you know, and so that was kind of a low point. And that made me realise that if he felt that way maybe other people felt the same way you know, so that was a low point (**Intimate Partner Femicide**)

As previously discussed, identity is a relational enterprise and 'degradation ceremonies' (Garfinkel, 1956) such as exemplified above, serve to remind Richard of his spoiled identity (Goffman, 1963), and so run the risk of rendering his personal myth (McAdams, 1993) implausible. Such situations are presented as upsetting and in tension with his hard-earned 'redemption' (Bazemore, 1999: 768), but too limited to warrant a reinterpretation of his life through some sort of 'looking glass self' (Maruna et al., 2004). So, framing his murder as stemming from pure, uncontrollable passion opened a set of possible identity management strategies, and ways to negotiate stigma on the outside. The internalisation of the 'crime of passion discourse' (Monckton-Smith, 2020: 1272) allowed him to solve a potential cognitive dissonance (Festinger, 1957) in his own personal myth (McAdams, 1993) as well as to negotiate acceptability after release.

To reiterate, Raul killed his opponent during an arranged street fight. For him, the type of murder committed resembles a 'lifestyle choice', which is suggestive of a life once lived, and which sets the parameters of identity management on release. Having been released into a small part of de- industrialised London, he feels that the murder is not shameful. He negotiates an acceptable identity by othering 'petty' murderers, and thus separates himself from those murderers having a lower status (Copes, Hochstetler, and Williams, 2008):

Raul: The type of offence you committed reflects the lifestyle that you have led. You know what I mean. Uhm, so it's not as if I come out and I have to be as extremely as ashamed as some who's on a sex offenders register, or … offenders, or burglar, or you know something like that, petty stuff like that. What I did I am not proud

	of, it's not something to be proud of, but at the end of the day I can still walk around with my own self dignity you know what I mean... like no one can look down on me or tell me that you know, what you did that was a scumbag thing to do, you know what I mean, circumstances of what happened, there was a fight, you know what I mean, something that was kind of normal to us, yeah ok, he got stabbed, yah ok, he died, it's ruined his life, it's ruined my life, his family's life, at the end of the day he knew what he was walking into, and I knew what I was walking into, as best as you can accept. So, yea, depending on the type of crime you did it does judge how you are when you come out. (**Confrontational/ Revenge murder**)
Dan:	Because of the stigma?
Raul:	Yes. If I walked around the streets and people knew ah that's the guy who killed a woman, or killed an elderly person or a child, you're a scumbag you know, you are on the same level as rapists or paedophiles, but, at least when I walk around people that do remember what happened now and they say: ah ok, it was a fight, and these things happen, men will be men and boys will be boys, you know what I mean so yeah [...] So, if I went to somewhere else, obviously no one will know and I wouldn't find any need to say it, you know what I mean ... if I was going for a job nothing was said, but like I said, it's not something you brag around or you wear a t-shirt, yeah, this is what I did, blah blah blah. I would talk about it here because people remember, some people remember what happened then you know what I mean, and they know the circumstances of it and they know it was a terrible accident, it wasn't, he wasn't meant to die, and people understand that in some ways (**confrontational/revenge murder**).

He went on to further explore the hierarchy of shame based on the dichotomy of the deserving and undeserving victim:

Raul:	Nobody has ever come up to me and say you killed an innocent person, and I never had to sit there and think to myself oh, I went out of my way to kill this person who had nothing to do with anything, do you know what I mean? (**Confrontational/Revenge murder**)

Raul's hyper-masculine remark that "men will be men and boys will be boys", as well as his reference to the victim's knowledge of the implications of showing up to an arranged fight (Scully and Marolla, 1985), serve to introduce the listener to the appropriate cultural context (Copes, Hochstetler, and Forsyth, 2013) – that of the street code (Anderson, 1999; Brookman, Copes, and Hochstetler, 2011, Brookman, et al., 2011) – in making sense of what happened. It is through the lens of 'higher loyalties' (Sykes and Matza,

1957) that one is requested to interpret the given situation. His gendered talk achieves a situated masculine identity (Messerschmidt, 1993) and manages to diffuse some responsibility for the murder. The murder scene is located within the cultural narratives of the East London's gang-culture. This is further exemplified in the following passage, where he constructs a more intricate murder hierarchy, related to the weapon of choice:

Dan: The weapon of choice is important in the hierarchy.

Raul: Yeah, it is, I'd say it is. Not a massive difference, but it kind of shows the type of person you are. I mean, shootings, among the south London boys is seen as a big thing. In East London, it wasn't seen as anything special, because it's a gun, you can shoot someone from a mile away, you know, so for East London it was things like stabbing, and beating, if you beat someone to death with your own hands, it is a lot more visceral you know, because you know that guy, over there, he put in the work, that's what you call it, you know, so yeah (**Confrontational/Revenge murder**)

Raul's comparison with the 'Southern boys' *modus operandi* provides a glimpse into London's gang culture (Sandberg, 2009a), and positions Raul as a former 'hard working', true gangster, who was 'willing to put in the work'. The type of violence enacted by the East boys is portrayed as visceral and manly. He is unwittingly referring to a visceral habitus, inculcated in the social practices of industrial man, and re-enacted in the 'hard lad' cult and criminal economy of post-industrial East London (Hall, 1997). His connection to East-London emerged as crucial in constructing a sense of masculinity (Winlow and Hall, 2009), and offered some limited narrative resources in the way of constructing a territorial identity (Fraser, 2015). I have experienced (Presser, 2004) Raul's hyper-place attachment (Kintrea et al., 2008) and territoriality emerge first-hand, after we have concluded our interview and started walking together back to the train station:

> Raul pointed out to me every Romanian on the streets that he could identify. He didn't personally know these people; so, he only guessed with complete certainty that they were Romanians. This reminds me of the conversations we had before I started to record the interview; he said that the animal he identifies with the most is the eagle. He must look down on us, flying, he knows who the Romanians are, who the Asians are; he can spot this from miles, as he said. I was on his territory, and he wanted to make this clear.
> (Reflective Journal – 7/30/2019)

Raul managed stigma by situating our discussion of the murder within London's gang culture and positioned himself accordingly. His early resistance narrative may have been a consequence of his struggle to re-enter conventional society after release (Harding et al., 2017). As evidenced above, Raul has initially drawn from the seriousness of his crime to exclude any potential associations with petty offenders generally (sex offenders, burglars, etc.). Then, the hierarchy became more intricate, with specific hierarchies of moral worthiness being constructed. Interestingly, the discussion appeals to specific audiences rendering his stories as 'moving targets' (Maruna and Liem, 2020).

Nathaniel had been released for six years when I first interviewed him and had been recalled to prison on one occasion. The context of his killing had been kept silent to the extent to which he only mentioned killing a random man after breaking up with his girlfriend. Throughout the narrative, Nathaniel uses narrative tropes (Sandberg, 2016), "briefly [hinting] at shared stories that do not need to be fully articulated" (Laws, 2020: 11) to signal his 'hypernormality'. He pleads to 'generally accepted knowledge' to say that child killers experience 'most of the stigma': he does not directly refer to their abominable act/character, as it is implicitly inferred in the following interview.

Nathaniel: We all know that stigmas, like the child killers and all of them I think they always have the stigma, and it all goes to circumstance, how it happens, and stuff like that. It's weird to get your head around, because it's all about circumstance, why it happened, stuff like that. It's the longer you are out, the more you get on, the longer you are away from that type anyway, so the longer you out the more freedom you feel, the further you distance yourself from the past (**Random homicide**)

Through the informally used plural: 'we all know', Nathaniel underscores the sheer banality of stigma hierarchy, widely known to those in the 'lifer community' (Honeywell, 2015). He reinforces that 'child killers' experience the greatest share of stigma, although meaning is circumstantial to other murder types. Up to this point, the men have all used 'child killers' as a morality barometer against which they could construct their acceptability. All the men, except for Richard, who killed his fiancé, have constructed 'women killers' as being contemptible – perhaps second worse on the morality scale just after 'child killers'.

The callous and ruthless

To reiterate, Jacob's murder followed an 'execution style', as he described it, by shooting a person three times in the head. Jacob refers to his murder as 'callous, brutal, and ruthless'. He describes what seems to be a 'murder acceptability continuum', where those who kill their wife or girlfriend could find compassion. Then, on the righteousness axis, Richard placed petty killers and sexual murderers at one end, and terrorists alongside the most brutal,

180 *Life Beyond Murder*

fearsome murderers on the other. The latter are 'prisoners with solid convictions' (Ricciardelli, 2014, 2015: 179), who are given higher status in prison due to associated masculine characteristics. He also agrees with Richard, that 'child killers' are at the bottom of this constructed hierarchy (Crewe, 2009; Jewkes, 2005; Sapp and Vaughn, 1990; Winfree, Newbold, and Tubb, 2002). Having laid the coordinates of the discussion, Jacob then tacitly aligned himself alongside one of the two groups, whilst concomitantly, established a sense of uniqueness.

Jacob: But if you take for example, somebody who kills their wife or their girlfriend, I think society's perception of that kind of crime is different and more compassionate; if you take someone who has killed a child, then, that's if you like that's the farthest extreme in terms of … people's perception and horror and hate you know… if it involves sexual abuse and whatever; being at the other end of the spectrum there is the terrorist that puts a bomb in the pub or you know or a football stadium, or the twin towers or you know whatever that context is, it's a different kind of perception and horror and feeling, but I think that the nature of my kind, you know with the Home Office, that they saw it as particularly brutal and ruthless, aah, and there is no doubt that that has affected the way I was dealt with as well you know I was a maximum security prisoner for 10-12 years or something, and … and something else is that in the very early stages you know, every 15 minutes when I was in the segregation unit they would come and switch off the light, it will get movement and then it will switch it up, I was on suicide watch, so I never slept properly, I still don't sleep properly, I could exist on three hour sleep and … so, sleep deprivation and so on. But yes, there's definitely a stigma in terms of the way in which people are prepared to see things and I think there was a case recently where a wife killed her husband, she got guilty of manslaughter aa, and released because he had particularly brutalised her and you know driven her to the point, where you know, she killed him. You know, if you push and push and talk with somebody it's a little under that they will go [unclear]. It's a different kind of crime, it's a different kind of so yes (**Financial gain/Family feud murder**)

Whereas lifers who killed women occupy a contemptible position within prison culture, there seems to be compassion for these individuals outside of prison. In building his hierarchy, Jacob tacitly identifies with the special, dangerous type. Petty murderers sit at the other end of the spectrum. In fact, throughout his life story, Jacob constructs a strong individuality and sense of uniqueness, committed to a multiplicity of voices (Sandberg, 2009b; Sandberg, Tutenges, and Copes, 2015). He presents himself as both conventionally and unconventionally attached. Some of his stories of imprisonment serve to associate himself with well-known serial killers and gangsters, such as Peter Sutcliffe and the Kray twins. Other stories allow for the creation of a pious, devoted Christian who lives to give back to society – demonstrating the complexity of lived experience and identity negotiations (Sandberg, Tutenges, and Copes, 2015) for mandatory lifers. Jacob's murder is devoid of any extenuating circumstances compared with the context of other types of murder, such as Richard's 'crime of passion'.

Jacob: Many of the people that I know who served life sentences were unlike myself in some respects you know … my brother and I committed a horrendous crime, uhm, many of the life sentenced prisoners that I knew where people who on extreme emotional circumstances had overreacted and killed their girlfriend or their boyfriend or their wife or husband or whatever, the vast majority of life sentenced prisoners are domestic kinds (**Financial Gain Homicide**)

Jacob highlights the significance of having a prior relationship with the victim. In many cases murderers 'overreact' in heated argument with someone they know intimately, whereas the act of killing a stranger it generally more difficult to rationalise. Here, Jacob draws from the crime of passion discourse (Monckton-Smith, 2020) to create intimate partner femicide as unpremeditated and accidental and to distance himself from such rationalisations.

The crackheads

Peter murdered an elderly man during a robbery who 'turned out to be in the house that night'. Having asked him how this type of murder is perceived, he said:

Dan: Is it seen as if it would have been a woman, or a child.
Peter: It's seen like sort of crackhead, scummy.
Dan: There is a big stigma attached to the type of murder you committed.
Peter: A small stigma attached.
Dan: Still a stigma
Peter: A small stigma, but still the requisite amount of fear that people will be polite when they need to be, and you know what I mean. In prison yea, it matters, to a degree. But I definitely also think, after I got clean, it is your attitude that matters (**Financial Gain Homicide**)

Although a financially motivated murder (as was Jacob's) the financial purpose itself carries important meaning in this context. Peter recognised the 'crackhead' stigma (Copes, Hochstetler, and Williams, 2008) which accompanies the context of his murder. He drew from the prison code (Clemmer,

1940) to make sense of the question, but appealed to his identity – in the now post-prison and post-therapy (Stevens, 2012, 2013) to manage stigma. Heroin users are a stigmatised community in prison and Crewe (2009) found that heroin users are referred to with disdain because they imply contamination and moral decay. Evidently, Peter is resisting the narrative, but, unlike the other men does not engage with the hierarchy, perhaps evidencing the effect of his therapy in HMP Grendon. Peter situated our conversation about stigma post-release within the local culture of his workplace.

Peter: I guess … there's different ways you meet people innit? People that I meet at work, I talk to them, I just say. I've been in prison for a long time and they say … how long you've in jail for then mate … and I say 17 years … and they say fucking hell what did you do, and I say … well it wasn't graffiti, or colourful language it was something serious but it's done and they normally, if you lead them down that road, you know it's been done nearly 20 fucking years ago, they will go along with that, oh yah … they don't want to know … they don't really want to know, no. You get one or two who's gonna go and try to find it on the internet … and all of that … and when they do, they sort of … but I am there for work, communication is necessary for work and the way in which we interact with one another at work, that sort of thing is irrelevant. Someone came into work the other morning yeah, and said aa. this is how it is at work, the base level of its very black humour, same as prison yeah: say fucking hell, I nearly killed an old woman on my way here this morning! Ah really did ya? Yah, so I couldn't be bothered, so I just raped her. That's the base level that we are dealing with … and a few weeks ago, this notorious serial rapist got put back to prison, do you remember that, and it was on the news, and as I come into work, I walked into the canteen it was on the news and they said oh, we thought you was in jail, like its fucking making it like it's me, you know what I mean and that's alright, that's acceptance isn't it, that's trusting that they can say something out to me and I'm not gonna freak out (**Financial Gain Homicide**)

Evidently, Peter was ashamed of his stigmatising past and chose to avoid full disclosure as an initial post-release strategy and chose workplaces that subscribed to certain cultural logics to accommodate his past.

Discussion

As has been shown, the index offence has meaning for the perpetrator (Ferrito et al., 2012, 2020; Ferrito, Needs, and Adshead, 2017), and the men appealed to culturally derived and constructed meanings around what is acceptable killing to both make sense of their crime as well as to negotiate 'acceptable characters' in the interview context. Crucially, to negotiate acceptability, most of the men constructed themselves against the abominable and unacceptable killer. Compared to Becker's (1967: 239) 'hierarchy of credibility', where dominant voices are given legitimacy, here, the men construct hierarchies of moral worthiness by either accepting or negotiating with available master narratives. As Sarup (1996: 47) argues: "to maintain a separate identity, one has to define oneself against the Other" – and this was exactly what the men did with their reference to different typologies of killers. Further, through 'othering', the men were in fact defending against shame, whilst others internalised the label and accepted their own deficits. As Hoggett (2017: 376) remarked, "we often avoid shame by projecting it onto the 'other'".

Unlike guilt, which was explored in the previous chapters, shame is about our deficits and imperfections – it communicates something about us as individuals (Nussbaum, 2004). Nussbaum (2004) draws a sharp distinction between shame and guilt by arguing that the latter do not extend to the 'totality of the self', but rather it is constructed around the specific act of transgression. Ultimately, "we are held responsible for what we do in a way in which we are not held responsible for what we are" (Taylor, 1996: 60). A similar point was made by Keen (2023) who remarked how shame implies the existence of an audience that scrutinises a person, as opposed to guilt which centres on one's self-assessment. Although I agree to an extent with these definitions, in practice, this separation (what we are and what we do) seems too crude for these men. To commit murder is to ultimately be positioned into a new identity, that of a 'murderer'. In the Foucauldian sense, the word 'murderer' is used as a noun, creating a certain type of person, rather than simply an adjective relating to what someone might have done in the past (Burr, 2015). Stein (2007) characterised murder as possession and identity merger: 'to take a life' is to construct a shared identity between perpetrator and victim. This new identity is as much about the act as it is about the person; in the public opprobrium, as well as in the intricate hierarchies showcased above, only certain types of people are seen as capable to commit specific types of murders. The type of murder committed, the identity of the victim, and the circumstances surrounding it are all relevant in the identity reconstruction and stigma negotiation of these individuals. In other words, the type of murder committed often communicates something about the totality of one's identity which becomes their master status in prison and beyond.

The mandatory lifers drew from a multiplicity of voices to negotiate acceptable characters, thus evidencing the dialogic nature of their narratives (Frank, 2010). Also, the men revealed that stigma management is not unidimensional, but is continuously negotiated by appeals to a variety of local relevant cultural groups which are accepting of the lifer's past. Victims' identities were crucial in placing murderers on the hierarchy of moral abjection. In this sense, the men constructed categories of deserving and undeserving victims.

References

Anderson, E. (1999) *Code of the Street: Decency, Violence, and the Moral Life of the Inner City.* New York: Norton.

Bazemore, G. (1999) After shaming, whither reintegration: Restorative justice and relational rehabilitation. In G. Bazemore and L. Walgrave (Eds.), *Restorative Juvenile Justice: Repairing the Harm of Youth Crime.* Monsey, NY: Criminal Justice Press, pp. 155–194.

Becker. (1967) Whose side are we on? *Social Problems,* 14 (3), 239–247.

Brookman, F. (2022) *Understanding Homicide,* 2nd ed. London: Sage Publications.

Brookman, F., Bennett, T., Hochstetler, A., and Heith, C. (2011) The 'Code of the Street' in the generation of street violence in the UK. *European Journal of Criminology,* 8 (1), 17–31.

Brookman, F., Copes, H., and Hochstetler, A. (2011) Street codes as formula stories: How inmates recount violence. *Journal of Contemporary Ethnography,* 40 (4), 397–424.

Burr, V. (2015) *Social Constructionism,* 2nd ed. London: Routledge.

Clemmer, D. (1958[1940]) *The Prison Community.* 2nd ed. Holt, Rinehart & Winston: New York.

Copes, H., Hochstetler, A., and Forsyth, C. J. (2013) Peaceful warriors: Codes for violence among adult male bar fighters. *Criminology,* 51 (3), 761–794.

Copes, H., Hochstetler, A., and Williams, J. P. (2008) We weren't no regular dope fiends: Negotiating hustler and crackhead identities. *Social Problems,* 55, 254–270.

Crewe, B. (2009) *The Prisoner Society: Power, Adaptation and Social Life in an English Prison.* Oxford: Oxford University Press.

Ferrito, M., Needs, A., and Adshead, G. (2017) Unveiling of shadow of meaning: Meaning making for perpetrators of homicide. *Aggression and Violent Behaviour,* 34, 263–272.

Ferrito, M., Needs, A., Jingree, T., and Pearson, D. (2020) Making sense of the dark: A study on the identity of men who committed homicide. *Journal of Forensic Psychology Research and Practice,* 20 (2), 163–184.

Ferrito, M., Vetere, A., Adshead, G., and Moore, E. (2012) Life after homicide: Accounts of recovery and redemption of offender patients in a high security hospital – a qualitative study. *Journal of Forensic Psychiatry & Psychology,* 23 (3), 327–344.

Festinger, L. (1957) *A Theory of Cognitive Dissonance.* Evanston, IL: Row, Peterson [Database].

Fox, K. J. (2016) Civic commitment: Promoting desistance through community integration. *Punishment and Society,* 18 (1), 68–94.

Frank, W. A. (2010) *Letting Stories Breathe: A Socio-Narratology.* Chicago: University of Chicago Press.

Fraser, A. (2015) *Urban Legends: Gang Identity in the Post-Industrial City.* Oxford: Oxford University Press.

Garfinkel, H. (1956) Conditions of successful degradation ceremonies. *American Journal of Sociology,* 61 (5), 420–424.

Goffman, E. (1959) *The Presentation of Self in Everyday Life.* London: Penguin.

Goffman, E. (1963) *Stigma Notes on the Management of Spoiled Identity.* London: Penguin.

Hall, S. (1997) Visceral cultures and criminal practices. *Theoretical Criminology,* 1 (4), 453–478.

Hammack, P. L. (2008) Narrative and the cultural psychology of identity. *Personality and Social Psychology Review,* 12, 222–247.

Harding, D. J., Dobson, C., Wyse, J. J. B., and Morenoff, D. (2017) Narrative change, narrative stability, and structural constraints: The case of prisoner reentry narratives. *American Journal of Cultural Sociology,* 5 (1), 261–304.

Hochstetler, A., Copes, H., and Williams, P. (2010) That's not who I am: How Offenders Commit Violent Acts and reject authentically violent selves. *Justice Quarterly*, 27, 492–516.

Hoggett, P. (2017) Shame and performativity: Thoughts on the psychology of neoliberalism. *Psychoanalysis, Culture, and Society*, 22 (4), 364–382.

Honeywell, D. (2015) Doing time with lifers: A reflective study of life sentence prisoners. *British Journal of Community Justice*, 13 (1), 93–104.

Jenkins, R. (2004) *Social Identity*, 2nd ed. London: Routledge.

Jewkes, Y. (2005) Men behind bars: Doing masculinity as an adaptation to imprisonment. *Men and Masculinities*, 8, 44–63.

Keen, D. (2023) *Shame: The Politics and Power of An Emotion*. Oxford: Princeton University Press.

Kintrea, K., Bannister, J., Pickering, J., Reid, M., and Suzuki, N. (2008) *Young People and Territoriality in British Cities*. York: Joseph Rowntree Foundation. [Database]

Laws, B. (2020) Reimaging 'the Self' in criminology: Transcendence, unconscious states, and the limits of narrative criminology. *Theoretical Criminology*, 26 (3), 475–493.

LeBel, T., Richie, M., and Maruna, S. (2015) Helping others as a response to reconcile a criminal past: The role of the wounded healer in prisoner reentry programs. *Criminal Justice and Behaviour*, 42 (1), 108–122.

Lilgendahl, P. J. (2015) The dynamic role of identity processes in personality development: Theories, patterns, and new directions. In C. K. McLean, and M. Syed (Eds.), *The Oxford Handbook of Identity Development*. New York: Oxford University Press, 490–507.

Loseke, D. R. (2007) The study of identity as cultural, institutional, organizational, and personal narrative: Theoretical and empirical integrations. *Sociological Quarterly*, 48, 661–688.

Maruna, S., and Copes, H. (2005) What have we learned from five decades of neutralization research? *Crime and Justice*, 32, 221–320.

Maruna, S., Lebel, T. P., Mitchell, N., and Naples, M. (2004) Pygmalion in the reintegration process: Desistance from crime through the looking glass. *Psychology, Crime & Law*, 10 (3), 271–281.

Maruna, S., and Liem, M. (2020) Where is this story going? A critical analysis of the emerging field of narrative criminology. *Annual Review of Criminology*, 4, 125–146.

McAdams, D. P. (1993) *The Stories We Live By. Personal Myth and the Making of the Self*. New York: The Guildford Press.

McLean, K., and Syed, M. (2015) Personal, master, and alternative narratives: An integrative framework for understanding identity development in context. *Human Development*, 58, 318–349.

Messerschmidt, J. W. (1993) *Masculinities and Crime: Critique and Reconceptualization of Theory*. Lanham: Rowman & Littlefield.

Monckton-Smith, J. (2020) Intimate partner femicide: Using Foucauldian analysis to track an eight stage progression to homicide. *Violence Against Women*, 26 (11), 1267–1285.

Mullen, P. E. (1993) The crime of passion and the changing cultural construction of jealousy. *Criminal Behaviour and Mental Health*, 3, 1–11.

Nussbaum, M. C. (2004) *Hiding from Humanity: Disgust, Shame, and the Law*. New Jersey: Princeton University Press.

Plummer, K. (2019) "Whose side are we on?" Revisited: Narrative power, narrative inequality, and a politics of narrative humanity. *Symbolic Interaction*, 43, 46–71.

Presser, L. (2004) Violent offenders, moral selves: Constructing identities and accounts in the research interview. *Social Problems*, 51 (1), 82–101.

Ricciardelli, R. (2014) An examination of the inmate code in Canadian penitentiaries. *Journal of Crime and Justice*, 37, 234–255.
Ricciardelli, R. (2015) Establishing and asserting masculinity in Canadian penitentiaries. *Journal of Gender Studies*, 24 (2), 170–191.
Ryan, K. M. (2011) The relationship between rape myths and sexual scripts: The social construction of rape. *Sex Roles*, 65 (11), 774–782.
Ryan, K. M. (2019) Rape mythology and victim blaming as a social construct. In W. O'Donohue, and P. Schewe (Eds.), *Handbook of Sexual Assault and Sexual Assault Prevention*. Cham: Springer, 151–174.
Sandberg, S. (2016) The importance of stories untold: Life-story, event-story and trope. *Crime, Media, Culture*, 12 (2), 153–171.
Sandberg, S. (2009a) Gangster, victim, or both? The interdiscursive construction of sameness and difference in self-presentations. *British Journal of Sociology*, 60 (3), 523–542.
Sandberg, S. (2009b) A narrative search for respect. *Deviant Behaviour*, 30, 487–510.
Sandberg S., and Colvin, S. (2020) 'Isis is not Islam': Epistemic injustice, everyday religion, and young Muslims' narrative resistance. *The British Journal of Criminology*, 60 (6), 1585–1605.
Sandberg, S., and Fondevila, G. (2020) Corona crimes: How pandemic narratives change criminal landscapes. *Theoretical Criminology*, 26 (2), 224–244.
Sandberg, S., Tutenges, S., and Copes, H. (2015) Stories of violence: A narrative criminological study of ambiguity. *The British Journal of Criminology*, 55 (6), 1168–1186.
Sapp, A. D., and Vaughn, M. S. (1990) Juvenile sex offender treatment at state-operated correctional institutions. *International Journal of Offender Therapy and Comparative Criminology*, 34 (2), 131–146.
Sarup, M. (1996) *Identity, Culture, and the Postmodern World*. Edinburgh: Edinburgh University Press.
Scully, D., and Marolla, J. (1985) "Riding the bull at Gilley's": Convicted rapists describe the rewards of rape. *Social Problems*, 32 (3), 251–263.
Snajdr, E. (2013) Beneath the master narrative: Human trafficking, myths of sexual slavery and ethnographic realities. *Dialectical Anthropology*, 37 (2), 229–256.
Stein, A. (2007) *Prologue to Violence: Child Abuse, Dissociation, and Crime*. New York: Routledge.
Stevens, A. (2012) 'I am the person now that I was always meant to be': Identity reconstruction and narrative reframing in therapeutic community prisons. *Criminology and Criminal Justice*, 12 (5), 527–547.
Stevens, A. (2013) *Offender Rehabilitation and Therapeutic Communities: Enabling the TC Way*. Abingdon, Oxon: Routledge.
Sykes, G., and Matza, D. (1957) Techniques of neutralization: A theory of delinquency. *American Sociological Review*, 22, 664–670.
Taylor, G. (1996) Guilt and remorse. In R. Hare, and G. W. Parrott (Eds.), *The Emotions: Social, Cultural and Biological Dimensions*. London: SAGE Publications.
Ugelvik, T. (2012) Prisoners and their victims: Techniques of neutralization, techniques of the self. *Ethnography*, 13 (3), 259–277.
Winfree, L. T., Newbold, G., and Tubb, S. H. III (2002) Prisoner perspectives on inmate culture in New Mexico and New Zealand: A descriptive case study. *Prison Journal*, 82 (2), 213–233.
Winlow, S., and Hall, S. (2009) Living for the weekend: Youth identities in northeast England. *Ethnography*, 10 (1), 91–113.

11 Conclusion

The research emerged out of an initial interest in offender reintegration and desistance. A review of criminological literature on the topic demonstrated that people who committed murder are a neglected population in British desistance and resettlement literature. Most studies focused on populations who served short-term sentences, and perhaps this is reflective of their preponderance within the criminal justice system (Office for National Statistics, 2024). Of the limited research on this population, it was suggested by researchers, predominantly from the United States, that the 'usual' correlates of desistance do not apply to homicide offenders (Liem, 2016; Liem and Garcin, 2014). The only explanation available for some of their success was intra-individual, generally meaning that the 'successful group' had higher degrees of efficacy (they believed in their own capacities) than the 'unsuccessful group' (who returned to prison). This came as a surprise and warranted further research, in a UK context, especially when similar 'resonsibilisation of individuals', characteristic of neoliberalism, seems to have fallen on British criminology (Barry, Farrall, and France, 2022). The American studies were surprising specifically given the known deleterious effects of long-term imprisonment and the structural barriers faced by these individuals upon their release. Given the negative relationship between stigma, family formation, and employment after release from prison, I became interested in the ways constructed meaning around the index offence leads to specific resettlement pathways after release from prison. Given that we socially and culturally attribute distinct meaning to different forms of violence, I hypothesized that the type of murder committed (relationship to the victim and victims' identity) will have a significant impact upon Mandatory Life Sentence individual's pathways towards 'social rehabilitation' (McNeill, 2012). I mean social rehabilitation in the deep subjective sense as McNeill (2012) imagined it, as the informal social recognition and acceptance of the released mandatory lifer. The hypothesis was supported.

Murder, culture, and emotions: the splitting narrative

Let's return to the questions I posed to my students as outlined in the introduction to the book. Could the criminal career of a mandatory lifer influence their release trajectories? Is the type of murder committed important in this context? It seems that the answer to these questions is yes. Mandatory lifers draw from cultural, institutional, organisational, and personal narratives to construct their post-release identity (Loseke, 2007) and to justify (or not) their index offence. This is a complex task, considering the various expectations that they need to navigate within the cultural and institutional contexts that they inhabit (Chapter 7). The introjection (or investment in) of cultural and organisational narratives around acceptable and unacceptable killing leads to powerful experiences of self-conscious emotions such as guilt and shame (Chapter 8) (Kristjánsson, 2010). It seemed that certain discourses or stories provided a set of 'ready-made excuses' (Gadd and Jefferson, 2007: 44; Hollway, 1984) conveniently utilised by the men to justify their murder, defend against unbearable guilt, and to negotiate acceptability in interactions. This is important as narrative templates provide specific possibilities for post-hoc rationalisations of murder. This became evident when, for example, Richard drew upon a 'crime of passion' discourse (itself sharing knowledge with gender roles, heterosexual love, and expectations, see Monckton Smith, 2020) to frame his index offence as accidental and to showcase his acceptability outside prison walls. Also, Raul's hypermasculine remark that his opponent "lived by the sword and died by the sword" allowed the projection of blame fully onto his 'deserving victim' (Christie, 1986). In fact, Raul did not dwell on guilt for his crime as this emotion implies the transgression and breach of moral standards (Kristjansson, 2010) that were suspended in the cultural realms of his confrontation with the rival. This rationalisation radically influenced Raul's emotional repertoire and stigma negotiation strategy employed.

Peter, on the other hand, drew from psycho-medical insight to make sense of his index offence evidencing the organisational 'narrative reframing' that takes places in places such as HMP Grendon (Stevens, 2012) and in 12-steps programmes (Loseke, 2007). Interestingly, despite the extraordinary insight shown, the typical Grendon graduate is aware of needing to 'confront reality' (Shuker and Sullivan, 2010) and avoid excusing his crime (Sykes and Matza, 1957). This practice was evident in Peter's narrative. Perhaps this can also explain his difficulties in managing guilt in the first few years of his release (Chapter 5). The men's life stories are refashioned to provide coherence to these justificatory narratives. This was precisely the point behind the 'childhood-murder nexus' (Chapter 9). These discursive structures could represent what Farrall et al. (2014: 43) referred to as "slowly changing macro structures". What is considered acceptable violence subsumes a number of cultural aspects present in our society which do not change overnight, but which cast an important influence on the potential social rehabilitation of the men.

Despite these intricacies of identity work that are related to the type of murder committed, most men managed to tell the right type of story to showcase an 'appropriate level of remorse' as demanded by the probation system and the parole boards. Evidently, in most cases the men could not simply excuse their offence and project blame fully onto their victims. This would simply betray a lack of remorse and in turn could jeopardise their release prospects. In this sense, guilt is projected onto an ontologically insecure (Laing, 1960) murderous self. By engaging in this type of narrative labour (Warr, 2019) the men attempted to reconciliate a paradoxical position. This is the Splitting Narrative.

The Splitting Narrative (chapter 9) facilitated the negotiation of an acceptable, moral self despite the enormity of the index offence. The implication of this type of narrative is that a degree of agency problematisation could be considered as a natural step in creating a moral distance between a murderous self and the current self and not necessarily a criminogenic denial of harm or neutralisation of involvement (Sykes and Matza, 1957). The narrative serves three clear functions: (1) builds coherency between a murderous past and an ethical, moral self-present in a way which is not pathologically dissociative (guilt serves the role to link the story arc); (2) it defends against guilt and reconciliates the past with the present and the future (acting as an internal and external stigma management mechanism); (3) showcases acceptability and a minimal 'risk' to criminal justice agencies. The paradoxical nature of this narrative evidence its dialogic nature. These men live by 'multiple truths' (Frank, 2010), represented by a complex interplay of stories.

The achievement of successful resettlement and desistance may be dependent on the reconciliation of these paradoxes or extremes. Unbearable guilt as illustrated in Peter's case could possibly lead to self-flagellation via returning to prison (Chapter 5). Conversely, Raul's victim blaming of his 'deserving victim' (Christie, 1986) might raise concerns for the criminal justice system (Chapter 7). Interestingly, guilt emerged as a doubly edged sword in the men's narratives. A lack of clear meaning attached to the index offence resulted in what I referred to as 'unmetabolized guilt' which was potentially damaging. For others it represented the sublimated propelling force for good and generativity post-release (Chapter 8). The ways in which the men adapted to guilt was indicative of adaptive mechanism that requires further exploration (Chapter 8). Chiefly amongst these adaptations were taking on professional-ex roles which assisted with the performance of remorse, negotiate stigma, and sublimation of guilt (Chapters 8 and 10).

The men discussed at some length about the ways in which stigma operates post-release. For example, Richard acknowledged that society is much more forgiving of those who kill their partners out of 'passion' and was therefore much more 'relaxed' about disclosing what he has done. Thus, the men's experiences need to be understood psycho-socially (Gadd and Jefferson, 2007; Jones, 2019) linking affective states such psychological distress, with social power and discourse. The point has important implications for desistance research, particularly when viewed through symbolic interactionist lenses which consider one's identity to be created socially, via the looking glass of the other (Gålnander, 2020; McNeill, 2012). It was clear that the type of murder committed offered more 'difficult' or easier 'ways out' of internalising stigmatised identities. Constructing murder as a crime of passion was the most facile way to negotiate acceptability and gain sympathy from the public. This speaks volumes about our society as well as about perpetrators and their potential for 'moral' and 'social' rehabilitation (McNeill, 2012). In this sense, the identity of the victim emerged as significant in the construction of offenders (Chapter 10). In fact, Chapter 10 described the ethical battlefield occupied by the men who negotiated their acceptability by constructing murder hierarchies of moral abomination. So, it was not only guilt that was salient in the men's resettlement, but shame too as "one avoids shame in oneself or one's group by locating it in the other" (Hoggett, 2017: 376). We regard others with contempt to temporarily make ourselves look 'good' (ibid).

Despite these points, we need to acknowledge that not all people who commit murder will utilise the same narratives/discourses to justify their crime. One question that is left implicit in the research is why certain types of stories make sense to some men but not others? As Gadd and Jefferson (2007: 43) have put is "why for example, do some men identify with the 'hard man' or the Casanova?" It is often easy to overemphasise social structure (for example via dominant stories) at the expense of the personal, the biographical, and the emotional (Jones, 2019). To fully comprehend the men's experience and attachment to certain stories we need to explore their biographies in more depth.

Both guilt and shame are moral emotions (Haidt, 2003 in Eaton, 2024) that do not develop independently of early interactions with caregiver. For example, Schore (1994) found emotions such as shame (which he understood as intimately linked to guilt) to develop at around age two (Schore, 1994 in Jones, 2019). In this sense, it is suggested that more attention should be paid to the histories of individuals in discursive positioning (Hollway, 1984: 237–238 in Hollway and Jefferson, 2005: 149; for a critique see Wetherell, 2005). From a socio-narratological position the likelihood to be interpellated by a dominant justificatory story would be dependent on individual's' narrative habitus (the inner library that predispose us to hear certain stories at the expense of others). The concept of narrative ambush was developed by Frank (2010: 59) to explore precisely how stories sometimes break through and make themselves heard, creating 'new sections in the inner library'. It is difficult to say the extent to which the religious conversion narratives presented by the men in Chapter 9 were examples of narrative ambush or whether they were readily predisposed to them as dormant cultural stock. Early rearing practices, especially socialisation into certain values could potentially explain the predisposition towards certain adaptive behaviours later in life (Ellis, Winlow, and Hall, 2017).

Nevertheless, it was clear that the prison sentences represented turning points of identity reconstruction as discussed in Chapter 9. After release, the men's identities were influenced by a range of social structures that I referred to as the 'push-pull' factors.

Tug of war: push-pull forces in the liminal realm

In line with the socio-narratological and psychosocial perspectives that informed the analysis, the book focused on both the 'what's' and 'how's' of the men's resettlement stories. In other words, it explored the content of the stories as well as their function. The first few chapters drew from the 'tug of war' metaphor to evidence the 'push-pull' forces which interpellated the men to take on certain types of identities post-release. Following Loseke (2007: 661) it was argued that "narratives create identity at all levels of human social life". I have explored the ways in which mandatory lifers constructed narratives identities within the complex interplay of cultural, organisational, and individual stories that they encountered within prison and post-release. In this sense, the first part of the book explored the importance of social structure (Farrall, 2019; Farrall et al., 2014) at micro, meso, and macro level in shaping the post-release lives of five men who committed different types of murder. As F-Dufour (2022) also reminds us, the interaction between economic-political, institutional, and the psycho-neuro-biological is crucial when exploring desistance pathways. This is an immense desideratum which was only touched upon in this book. For example, the COVID-19 pandemic and subsequence lockdowns emerged as an important 'shock to the system' (Farrall, 2022: 347) that ultimately influenced the men's resettlement experience, but this discussion was scattered across different chapters.

Chapter 4 drew attention to the crucial importance of timing in accumulating 'reintegration capital', to ensure a smooth transitioning into a range of pro-social identities post-release. The men's organic/formed families, as well as employment status were important in providing social capital, and the necessary narrative resources to perform pro-social identities post-release (especially as 'family men'). This was an important resource which all men utilised throughout their early resettlement phase, and often acted as a protective mechanism in maintaining desistance from crime in times of exacerbated stress and confusion which was not slow to appear. Given this finding, the recommendation is that the criminal justice system – HMPPS, should continue to assist mandatory lifers in (re)building ties with families (Farmer, 2017), as well as new social relationships with pro-social groups whilst in prison. Further bridges between the voluntary sector and mandatory lifers need to be built to "foster the sort of ties and social contacts which allow the development of pro-social capital" (Farrall, 2011: 75; Kay, 2022). Most studies recommend that offenders should be given opportunities to receive visits from their families (Taylor, 2016), but very few discriminate between indeterminate sentenced prisoners, and those with fixed terms. The chapter demonstrated that indeterminate sentenced prisoners need as much support from their families (where this is possible) as possible to allow the accumulation of narrative resources to construct pro-social identities after release. Families and romantic relationships are critical in allowing the performance of these identities post-release, as well as to provide instrumental and emotional support. Best's (2019) research in this sense is timely. Prison-based programmes should encourage contact with families as the men approach the completion of their tariffs (or earlier), but this should be self-determined but guided, in line with Eglash's (1957) principles of restorative restitution. The 'hard timing' strategy (Kotova, 2020) employed so often by long-term prisoners, where relationships with families are severed to avoid emotional pain seems counterproductive. Interventions for mandatory lifers should aim at strengthening and enhancing protective factors, such as family integration and the development of resettlement capital in prison where this is possible. Alongside these measures, HMPSS in tandem with the voluntary sector should start considering this group of individuals as in need of measures to promote an expanding network and bridging capital outside of their existing network (Best, Musgrove, and Hall, 2018). One obvious difficulty in doing the above is that for indeterminate sentenced prisoners the "route map to freedom is by no means clear" (Crewe, 2011: 514). However, the recommendation is that the construction of bridging and bonding capital should start preferably before the men enter open prisons, and before the end of their tariffs.

It was also evidenced that cultural background was significant variable the men's resettlement process and desistance pathways. In this research, culture emerged as significant, especially in Raul's case who referred to his east-Asian heritage as significant in the way in which his family managed both the news of his crime and arrest, as well as his prison and post-prison journey (Calverley, 2013, 2019). Despite this, Raul spoke at length about experiencing stigma in his community, difficulties in finding a suitable partner for marriage, evidencing how social structure can hamper resettlement pathways (Farrall, 2019). Future research should consider larger samples of mandatory lifers from more diverse cultural and ethnical backgrounds in their analyses of life after a life-imprisonment. A further line of inquiry should focus on whether the type of murder committed has any influence in families' acceptance and willing to assist mandatory lifers' struggles to reconstruct their lives post release (see May, 2000 for a discussion around stigma and offenders' families). Although most of the men returned to their families, the research does not claim that this is a true representation of the experiences of mandatory lifers across the country. In fact, existing evidence points towards the opposite conclusion as discussed in the book.

Chapter 5 evidenced that the newly embraced family men identities were negotiated alongside a lingering 'prison voice'. In line with previous penological and criminological literature, the chapter evidenced that the coping mechanisms that are employed to 'survive' prison (physically and psychologically) are maladaptive for life post-release. Chiefly amongst these were issues such as hypervigilance and paranoia, especially acute in the period immediately after release. These adaptive personality traits did not easily fade with time but were rather incorporated into the men's developing identities. Despite this, the prison sentence served important emotional regulatory functions. I suggested that for some men punishment served to contain and regulate unmetabolised guilt that potentially stemmed from their index offence (if not from a more archaic source). In this sense, the chapter raises important questions around the ways in which mandatory lifers make sense of the index offence and the potential symptomatic relief that punishment via imprisonment can offer. It is thus important to realise that institutionalisation may be more complex that has been traditionally conceptualised by penological literature, and that 'recall' as a potential 'unconscious choice' can represent a symptom of a deeper underlying issue.

Moving on to 'macro-level influences' (Farrall, 2019) Chapter 6 explored the ways in which the most recently released mandatory lifers, Raul and Peter negotiated with master narratives of neo-liberal success (via conspicuous consumption) which interpellated them as consumers on their release. Interpellation is a process which teaches people who they are by inviting them to take particular identities (Frank, 2010). It was found that some people are more likely to respond to this invitation than others. As mentioned in Chapter 1, the narrative habitus (representing the collection of stories which make up one's identity), is crucial in deciding the success of such invitations. For Peter, his 'family man' identity acted as a protective mechanism against the forces that interpellated and attempted to render him as a 'flawed consumer'. He repudiated ornamental consumerism and thus constructed a resistance narrative stemming from an anti-capitalist moral position. Fatherhood equipped him with the necessary narrative resources to discard consumer culture as a mere distraction from the important things in life. It is also possible that Peter's narrative habitus was much more 'inhospitable' to these ideals. For example, we know that Peter had been stealing to feed his drug addiction prior to the murder. He never justified his criminal career as motivated by the pursuit of a luxurious lifestyle. There were no mentions of status, success, cars, or designers clothing (Jones, 2019) in his narrative.

Raul, on the other hand, had a more difficult trajectory in negotiating with this predominant discourse (and this was mainly because he was lacking in narrative resources to enact different identities). Soon after his release he experienced what I called 'consumption melancholia' as he failed to answer the 'cultural injunction to enjoy' (Žižek, 2002) and entered the 'battle for consumer significance' (Hall, Winlow, and Ancrum, 2008: 65). In the end, he managed to adapt to realities of his condition by slightly altering the set of values which stand at the heart of his narrative identity. In this way, he at times also resisted being positioned as a flawed consumer. The chapter showed the ways in which Raul managed to defend against shame and humiliation by drawing from alternative discourses and adapt to his circumstances. The adaptation of narrative identity to his structural position stemmed from his narrative habitus (see Fleetwood, 2016; Frank, 2010) – an internal, biographical source, intimately linked to ideals, and stories constructed around the father figure as well as competing ideologies (Stoicism).). To fully comprehend the differences between Raul's and Peter's investment in the consumerist discourse and ego ideal, I believe we need go beyond the men's surface level narratives and psychosocially analyse their biographies for any potential links (Gadd and Jefferson, 2007; Jones, 2019).

A few tentative suggestions and lessons can be learned from this chapter. Following the precepts of the Good Lives Model of offender rehabilitation (Ward and Stewart, 2003), practitioners of the criminal justice system should ensure that they identify released mandatory lifers' priorities, goals, and values as they make up their narrative identities before and after release. They should establish collaboratively on the most appropriate way of achieving these goods and values in ways which are manageable and adaptive to their situations post-release, in a Good Lives Plan (Ward and Fortune, 2013). For example, practitioners can focus on ways in which success can be reconceptualised, and secondary goods to achieving a reformed version of success can be constructed. In Raul's case, masculinity and success would have been important such sites of exploration. Although Raul has not proven ill-equipped to cope with his release, he evidenced the slow development of a cynical attitude towards the world outside. His narrative identities, evidenced in our conversations, are firmly built upon a set of ideological beliefs (McAdams, 1993) which suffered change throughout the years due to the structural constraints he faced. Probation officers, taking a strengths-based approach can identify MLS individuals' goals and value commitments and the secondary means used to achieve such goals. They then can assist mandatory lifers to harness energy in activities which deter them from developing such cynical attitudes that run the risk of finalising their enthusiasm and projections for the future. The chapter also raises an important point around the potential criminogenic effects of social media use. Social media can at times represent a punishing cultural superego leading to intense feelings of shame and humiliation in its users. We know from previous research that in specific situations these emotions can be criminogenic (Gilligan, 2000; Katz, 1988) and should be considered critically by future desistance research by incorporating the effects of social media and ego ideals into their analyses.

Moving at the meso-level of analysis, Chapter 7 showed how criminal justice agencies and probation services can act to constrain the development of pro-social identities for mandatory lifers due to their constructions of the men as responsible but risky, and fundamentally dangerous. This was evident from the men's internalisation of such constructions which emerged in our conversation. Criminal justice agencies were a vector that at times interpellated the mandatory lifers to accept dangerousness and risk identities (as evidenced in Paul's and Raul's case). Importantly, the type of murder committed had a significant effect on these constructions as well as expectations around performances of remorse. Critically, the men either resisted these invitations, or they tentatively accepted them. All the men experienced a lax and responsibilising supervision combined with episodes of acute risk assessment which betrayed an ideological schism in the way that the service works to construct and interpellate its subjects.

Peter's case draws attention to a problematic communication between different Multi-agency public protection arrangements partners and their inconsistent approach to the risk-management of mandatory lifers. In this sense, the probation system and social services have constructed Paul's dangerousness fundamentally differently. Whereas the parole board and his probation officer have not imposed any restrictions in communicating with and having children, the social services utilised a larger brush in painting Peter as a potential danger to his child, on account of his crime only (cf. Barry, 2021). In this sense, the social services acted to constrain Paul's development of a pro-social identity, that of the father, through spoiling this role by constructing him as a potential danger to his child. Fatherhood, as Opsal (2015) remarked, should be considered as an opportunity, and not a risk as it provides a perfect context for the development of pro-social identities. Raul's case drew attention to the importance of considering relational aspects to desistance as well as the importance of 'places' in imposing or avoiding stigma (Albertson, Philips, and Fowler, 2022). For Raul, the space-time rhythm which included routine visits to the probationer's office served as a reminder of his own riskiness (the alarm along the wall, the interview arrangements, the pen, and paper). Although these are necessary tools which serve to protect HMPPS staff, it is suggested that a psychogeography approach (Coverley, 2006) to improving the design of these places may be fruitful. Further interdisciplinary research should explore this possibility (Jewkes, 2018). By holding some of the meetings with Raul in his own environment rather than the office could possibly reinforce his 'community member' identity (Shingler and Stickney, 2024) as opposed to reminding of his own 'risk'.

The longitudinal nature of the data presented here demonstrated that this sample of MLS individuals had expected varied levels of probation involvement at different stages of their re-entry. The individualisation of probationers observed in some previous research was also evident here (Barry, Farrall, and France, 2022). In this sense, it is tentatively suggested that probation officers work together with probationers in setting the goals of their sentence plan of their collaboration more consistently, as the men's needs change with the stages of their resettlement. In this sense, the men should be constructed as individuals with complex needs and not merely subjects of supervision. As shown here, the men's needs change drastically in short spurs of time, which once more directs to the importance and complexity of the initial stages of resettlement for mandatory lifers.

Future research should employ an ethnographic approach in exploring how probation officers and mandatory lifers interact upon release; further, special attention should be placed on the importance of the murder type committed by the men in the ways in which they are constructed by their supervising officers. In turn, this will lead to a more nuanced understanding of the way in which mandatory lifers are governed in our communities and may inform important policy in improving the men's reintegration. This research is a first step in evidencing the importance of these elements.

Limitations?

The sample size consisted of five mandatory lifers who were at different stages of their resettlement and reintegration in the community. Three of the men were at (various) initial stages of their resettlement (Peter, Raul, Nathaniel) whereas the remaining two (Richard and Jacob) could be classed as 'veterans', having been released for over 20 years at the time of the first interview. This is as much of a limitation as it is a strength for the research. It is a limitation because the retrospective accounts of the more experienced mandatory lifers were at times used alongside the accounts of the early releases to construct themes around early resettlement. There are (at least) two risks in taking this approach: first, asking participants to reflect upon their experiences 20 years ago exposed the research to potential imagination inflation and post-event misinformation (Schacter, Guerin, and Jacques, 2011). Nevertheless, the men's experiences were remarkably similar to those who were experiencing early release and whose stories could be classed as 'in the now' (Brookman, 2015). This fact alleviated some of these fears. Second, as societies change, the men's early experiences were representative of a specific time and place. For example, Richard was taken aback by the prevalent use of phones after his release, which he would describe as walkie-talkies at that point. In this sense, narratives need to be historicised to a more significant extent by further researchers (Maynes, Pierce, and Laslett, 2008). Nevertheless, the exploratory nature of this book renders the approach as much a strength as it is a limitation.

The longitudinal approach allowed for the exploration of narratives at different stages at their resettlement stage. By combining these results cross-sectionally with the veteran's narratives I was able to cement these results and speculate on the long-lasting impact of imprisonment and the index-offence. Future research should (similarly to how penological research has already done so) identify barriers, hardships, and adaptations to different stages of the resettlement process for mandatory lifers. In this sense, research samples should include both cross-sectional designs based on groups of individuals at different stages of their release as much as longitudinal designs which spread over a significantly longer period.

To predict some criticism, the book was influenced by the Coronavirus pandemic. An initial face to face approach had to change in favour of phone interviews. Admittedly, this was not a limitation in the end, as the use of video-calls made up for lost paralinguistic elements which were important in making sense of data (but unfortunately, these could not be always used).

Further, the men's lives were influenced by lockdowns, and some of the narratives presented in this piece are representative of the hardships and struggles that turned to characterise the years 2020 and 2021. Some usual barriers to reintegration were exacerbated by the pandemic – some of my participants have lost their jobs, others, feared for their loved ones.

Critics of this book would naturally question the sample size. The sample consisted of 5 men, and it is therefore difficult to assume that the experiences presented here are representative for all mandatory lifers in the United Kingdom. Nevertheless, as discussed, qualitative research based on narrative inquiry do not aim at generalising their findings (Lewis et al., 2014). Such golden standards are reserved to the domain of hard sciences and positivist epistemologies with their insistence on the existence of universal truths. In a sense, each one of my participants' lives is unique and therefore representative generalisability or saturation is difficult to achieve. This limitation is one which stems from particular theoretical positions. It was not within the aspirations of this book to argue that the findings apply to all mandatory lifers in the United Kingdom. Thus, the statistical approach to generalisation is not consistent with the premises of the book; however, case studies involve 'generalisation to theoretical propositions' (Riessman, 2008: 13), or could represent inferential generalisations (Lewis et al., 2014). The book was interested in the worlds as they made sense to the participants. For Bruner (1991: 4), "narrative constructions can only achieve 'verisimilitude'". These are only "a version of reality whose acceptability is governed by convention [...], rather than empirical verifications". I was not guided by truth as understood in the ontological sense as a measurable or verifiable site, but rather, in what Spence (1982) coined 'narrative truth'.

In this sense, the book speculates that the findings (and most necessarily the recommendations) can be applied to other samples of mandatory lifers in the United Kingdom. Therefore, future research should explore whether the findings of this research apply to other mandatory life sentenced populations. Hopefully, the book can represent a heuristic guide to such researchers aiming at developing theory around the ways in which people who committed murder negotiate their identities post-release.

The demographics of the individuals can be subjected to criticism. The study focused solely on men who committed murder and therefore the experiences of women in similar position remain virtually absent from research. This is problematic given that we now know that women's desistance from crime and re-entry into society is highly gendered (Bachman et al., 2016). To my knowledge, the ways in which our society responds to calls for reintegration of women who killed remain virtually unexplored. Further, the narratives of secondary victims who lost their loves ones to murder are not given much voice in this book. However, research in this tradition has been carried out recently – see Brolan's (2022) doctoral study. Moreover, the research attempted to use an ethnically and culturally diverse sample to explore potential effects of culture and ethnicity on the ways in which MLS individuals experience resettlement and reconstruction/negotiation of identity post-release. Although this was achieved to an extent, future research can do a better job in exploring more diverse samples (including sexual minorities coming from Lesbian, Gay, bisexual, transgender, and Queer/Questioning Community [LGBTQ+] communities), and can devise interview schedules which have culture, gender, ethnicity, and sexuality at the forefront of the analytic interest. Another important variable that demands attention is participants' social class which had not been discussed to a significant extent here. For example, social class will most likely interact with levels of available social capital as well as with the adaptive response to consumer culture post release. Future research should consider these possibilities in their analyses.

In line with the theoretical framework of this research, it is suggested that individuals refrain from crime by enacting or by being guided by stories of their own selves. Nevertheless, as Laws (2022) mentioned, experience is not always storied. He drew from Kahneman's (2011) work on the 'experiencing self' to argue that much of our transformative experiences are difficult to verbalise (and thus transposed into stories). For example, an 'experiencing self' is found in accounts that can be called 'transcendental', or 'extensions of consciousness' after psychedelic experiences, which can rarely be transposed into words (Verde, 2021 for a response). In this book, one such example of transcendental experiences of the self were narrated by the men who experienced religious conversion in prison. Of course, narrative conceptualisations of identity are not without limitations, they are yet to "set out to present a complete theory of the self" (Laws, 2022: 8). In reality, as Laws (2022: 12) remarked, various positions on these issues "uncover deep epistemological fissures that are hard to reconcile". Such a reconciliatory project is beyond the scope and capacity of this book; it is sufficient to say that I had used a range of theoretical positions (not limited to narrative criminology, see use of concepts such as 'social capital', 'psychosocial criminology', and 'ultra-realism') to make sense of the data. Where possible, such fissures had been explored and attempted to be resolved.

Narratives do not just appear in a vacuum, but that they emerge within the specific socio-economic and symbolic architecture of our society and its underlying driving forces. Chapter 6 explored the men's negotiation of identities against master narratives of success within neo-liberal consumer capitalism. It was proposed that recently released mandatory lifers interact with ego ideals as proposed by consumer capitalism's prevailing consumerist culture (or master narrative). However, some questions were left unanswered: for example, what are the processes by which these subjectivities are generated? Recent theoretical developments in criminological thought, such as ultra-realism (Hall and Winlow, 2015) may be appropriate in making sense of this process by drawing from the transcendental materialist subject. In this sense, individuals' disposition to engage with ego ideals as constructed within neo-liberal consumerist capitalism may be conditional to individuals' immersion in a Symbolic Order which is characterised by individualism and competitiveness (Lloyd, 2018). Success on release is then intimately linked to specific patterns of consumption (Hall, Winlow, and Ancrum, 2008) characteristic of the Symbolic Order. Future research should consider utilising new criminological theory, such as ultra-realism and psychosocial criminology, to make sense of the rehabilitation and desistance in the context of prevailing ideologies in our society. Also, as Farrall (2019) argued, we should focus much more on the social, economic, and political context within which people desist from crime (Barry, Farrall, and France, 2022). It is precisely the effects of these broad systems that ultimately influence human subjectivity and available pathways out of crime. Also, the book reiterates the need to consider individuals' affective states as indispensable to the desistance process (Giordano, Schroeder, and Cernkovich, 2007; Hunter and Farrall, 2018). Moral emotions that are experienced negatively such as 'guilt' can be the sublimated propelling force for good. Or the very opposite.

Some final thoughts

I am often asked about my experience of meeting men who have committed murder and whether I was affected in any ways by what I heard during the research process. I've always replied with a certain level of bravado, conveying the message that this is 'what I do'. As criminologists, we work with individuals involved in various forms of criminality. I often dismissed my interlocutors by saying that the world seldom works in absolutes – we should not paint human experiences in black and white. I was not going to judge my participants for what they have done. This would simply betray an unprofessional attitude on my part. I realise now that I was in fact not allowing myself to feel much. Similarly, to Ellis' (2016) experience, I always felt I needed to be unphased by it all. I was aware that 'emotional labour' influences our interpretation of participants' lives and that it has deep 'epistemological significance' (Hubbard, Backett-Milburn, and Kemmer, 2001: 135). Despite this, I have often isolated my emotions from my intellect by unwittingly utilising a defence strategy that psychoanalysts refer to as 'intellectualisation' (McWilliams, 2011). Typically, this is healthy when used temporarily to avoid anxiety, but I sometimes still struggle to understand and verbalise how I felt during the research process.

Perhaps the enormity of the men's crime had at times been 'too much' for me to process, or, alternatively, I may have experienced some of their own numbness during our interviews. On few occasions some participants cried as they recounted their index offence. In such situations my anxiety regarding their potential re-traumatisation intensified. Other encounters had been truly peculiar. I remember sharing a laugh with one of the participants in the most inappropriate of contexts (during a conversation about wanting to swap places with his victim) – this made me feel uneasy and think about the ways in which we use humour to make sense of difficult situations and to build rapport. I have often witnessed striking incongruences between the gravity and seriousness of the conversation, our body language, and tone of voice. I remember feeling upset and powerless when some participants blamed their victims for their murders.

Some of the men regard me as a friend, having confided their most personal memories in repeated interviews over a relatively long period of time. I have often thought about the ways in which we, as qualitative researchers, reconcile research and developing friendships and whether I have unintentionally been exploiting these men. I often felt compelled to offer something in return for their time, although I have never really done so.

Perhaps the clearest message I received was from those potential participants who never made it to the interview. As an inexperienced researcher with a developing 'research self-esteem' I used to blame myself for each obstacle along the way. I now realise that their potential participation in this research represented a genuine risk of stirring long-buried memories. To go forward they really needed to forget and hopefully forgive the past.

I identified with my participants on different levels throughout the research. The men's accounts of their childhoods brought back several memories. I grew up in a small city in Eastern Romania and I often found myself on the 'wrong side' of the law. As an 'adolescent limited offender' (Moffitt, 1993), I was surrounded by violence, drugs, and alcohol. Many of my participants had similar childhoods as I did, and I could not help but think about my own early life as they were speaking about theirs. Some of these memories were shameful and others had simply led me to nostalgic reverie. This reminded me of Wengraf's (2001: 4–5) remark:

> The interview that you do or that you study is not an asocial, ahistorical, event. You do not leave behind your anxieties, your hopes, your blindspots, your prejudices, your class, race or gender, your location on global social structure, your age and historical positions, your emotions, your past and your sense of possible futures when you set up an interview, and nor does your interviewee […], (or) when you sit down to analyse the material you have produced.

All of this opens a discussion about the need to reflect upon the ways in which my own identity contributed to data and knowledge generation (Presser, 2005) and the emotional labour involved in conducting research such as this. My own background and emotional repertoire have undoubtably affected what stories I heard and which I may not have paid attention to (Frank, 2010). This has ultimately shaped the book in ways that are deeply personal to me. In social constructionist thought the observer, the observed, and interpretation are not separable (Riessman, 2015). Thus, the book caught a glimpse of the men's lives as I made sense of them and should not be treated as a final version of their story.

I often think about the ways in which I have navigated my responsibility in presenting the men's stories whilst respecting the dignity of their victims, and the impact on their families. I reflected upon O'Connell's (2023: 147) remark that we are often regarded as having a moral obligation to prioritise the story of the victims when discussing murder. Failing to do so, he remarked, means that we may risk reducing these people to mere visual representations of 'disembodied wounds'. Of course, this is not my intention, but the book focused exclusively on the narratives of those who perpetrated murder and has therefore 'silenced' the victim's perspective which was left untold. As I contemplate upon this point, I remind myself that I also have a duty to protect the privacy of the individuals who shared some of their most personal memories with me throughout the years. Every single one of the men I spoke to has been featured in the print media and any disclosure of their victims' identity or that of their families would invariably lead to their deductive disclosure. Nevertheless, despite their anonymity, these victims draw our attention once again to the wider structural forces that often create the conditions for their own victimisation (Wilson, 2007; Yardley, 2020) and ultimately serve as a mirror through which we can also discover something about ourselves.

References

Albertson, K., Philips, J., and Fowler, A. (2022) Who owns desistance? A triad of agency enabling social structures in the desistance process. *Theoretical Criminology*, 26 (1), 153–172.

Bachman, R., Kerrison, E. M., Paternoster, R., Smith, L., and O'Connell, D. (2016) The complex relationship between motherhood and desistance. *Women & Criminal Justice*, 26 (3), 212–23.

Barry, M. (2021) 'Walking on ice': The future of parole in a risk-obsessed society. *Theoretical Criminology*, 25 (2), 325–342.

Barry, M., Farrall, S., and France, A. (2022) Desistance and the state: Revisiting the individualization thesis in criminology and criminal justice. *Kriminologisches Journal*, 3/2022, 181–198.

Best, D. (2019) *Pathways to Recovery and Desistance: The Role of the Social Contagion and Hope*. Bristol: Policy Press.

Best, D., Musgrove, A., and Hall, L. (2018) The bridge between social identity and community capital on the path to recovery and desistance. *Probation Journal* 65 (4), 394–406.

Brolan, L. (2022) Making sense of murder abroad: Exploring the post-homicide experience of co-victims of murder which occurs in a foreign country. PhD Thesis. Birmingham City University.

Brookman, F. (2015) Researching homicide offenders, offenses, and detectives using qualitative methods. In H. Copes, and M. J. Miller (Eds.), *The Routledge Handbook of Qualitative Criminology*. Oxon: Routledge, 236–252.

Bruner, J. (1991) The narrative construction of reality. *Critical Inquiry*, 18 (1), 1–21.

Calverley, A. (2013) *Cultures of Desistance*. London: Routledge.

Calverley, A. (2019) Exploring the processes of desistance by ethnic status: The confluence of community, familial and individual processes. In S. Farrall (Ed.), *The Architecture of Desistance*. London: Routledge, 75–95.

Christie, N. (1986) The ideal victim. In E. A. Fattah (Ed.), *From Crime Policy to Victim Policy*. Basingstoke: Macmillan, 17–30.

Coverley, M. (2006) *Psychogeography*. Harpenden, Herts: Pocket Essentials.
Crewe, B. (2011) Depth, weight, tightness: Revisiting the pains of imprisonment. *Punishment and Society*, 13 (5), 509–529.
Eaton, J. (2024) *Apologies from Death Row: The Meaning and Consequence of Offender Remorse*. Abingdon, Oxon: Routledge.
Eglash, A. (1957) Creative restitution – a broader meaning for an old term. *Journal of Criminal Law and Criminology*, 48, 619–626.
Ellis, A. (2016) *Men, Masculinities, and Violence: An Ethnographic Study*. Abingdon, Oxon: Routledge.
Ellis, A., Winlow, S., and Hall, S. (2017) 'Throughout my life I've had people walk over me': Trauma in the lives of violent men. *The Sociological Review*, 65 (4), 699–713.
F-Dufour, I. (2022) A commentary on rethinking what works with offenders. In S. Farrall (Ed.), *Rethinking What Works with Offenders: Probation, Social Context, and Desistance from Crime*. Oxon: Routledge, 387–400.
Farmer, L. (2017) *The Importance of Strengthening Prisoners' Family Ties to Prevent Reoffending and Reduce Intergenerational Crime*. London: Ministry of Justice.
Farrall, S. (2011) Social capital and offender reintegration: Making probation desistance focussed. In S. Maruna, and R. Immarigeon (Eds.), *After Crime and Punishment: Pathways to Offender Reintegration*. Cullompton: Willan, 57–82.
Farrall, S. (2019) *The Architecture of Desistance*. London: Routledge.
Farrall, S. (2022) *Rethinking What Works with Offenders: Probation, Social Context, and Desistance from Crime*, 2nd ed. Abingdon, Oxon: Routledge.
Farrall, S., Hunter, B., Sharpe, G., and Calverley, A. (2014) *Criminal Careers in Transition: The Social Context of Desistance from Crime*. Oxford: Oxford University Press, Clarendon Studies in Criminology.
Fleetwood, J. (2016) Narrative Habitus: Thinking through structure/agency in the narratives of offenders. *Crime Media Culture*, 12 (2), 173–192.
Frank, W. A. (2010) *Letting Stories Breathe: A Socio-Narratology*. Chicago: University of Chicago Press.
Gadd, D., and Jefferson, T. (2007) *Psychosocial Criminology: An Introduction*. London: SAGE.
Gålnander, R. (2020) Shark in the fish tank: Secrets and stigma in relational desistance from Crime. *British Journal of Criminology*, 60, 1302–1319.
Gilligan, J. (2000) *Violence: Reflections on Our Deadliest Epidemic*. London: Jessica Kingsley Publishers.
Giordano, P. C., Schroeder, R. D., and Cernkovich, S. A. (2007) Emotions and crime over life course: A neo-median perspective on criminal continuity and change. *American Journal of Sociology*, 112 (6), 1603–1661.
Hall, S., and Winlow, S. (2015) *Revitalising Criminological Theory: Towards a New Ultra-Realism*. Oxon: Routledge.
Hall, S., Winlow, S., and Ancrum, C. (2008) *Criminal Identities and Consumer Culture: Crime, Exclusion, and the New Culture of Narcissism*. Cullompton: Willan Higate.
Hoggett, P. (2017) Shame and performativity: Thoughts on the psychology of neoliberalism. *Psychoanalysis, Culture, and Society*, 22 (4), 364–382.
Hollway, W. (1984) Gender difference and the production of subjectivity. In J. Henriques, W. Hollway, C. Urwin, C. Venn, and V. Walkerdine (Eds.), *Changing the Subject: Psychology, Social Regulation, and Subjectivity*. London: Methuen, 227–263.
Hollway, W., and Jefferson, T. (2005) Panic and perjury: A psycho-social exploration of agency. *British Journal of Social Psychology*, 44 (2), 147–163.
Hubbard, G., Backett-Milburn, K., and Kemmer, D. (2001) Working with emotion: Issues for the researcher in fieldwork and teamwork. *International Journal of Social Research Methodology*, 4 (2), 119–137.
Hunter, B., and Farrall, S. (2018) Emotions, future selves, and the process of desistance. *British Journal of Criminology*, 58 (2), 291–308.

Jewkes, Y. (2018) Just design: Healthy prisons and the architecture of hope. *Australian & New Zealand Journal of Criminology*, 51 (3), 319–338.
Jones, D. W. (2019) *Understanding Criminal Behaviour: Psychosocial Perspectives on Criminality and Violence*. Abingdon, Oxon: Routledge.
Katz, J. (1988) *Seductions of Crime: Moral and Sensual Attractions in Doing Evil*. New York: Basic Books.
Kay, C. (2022) Rethinking social capital in the desistance process: The 'Artful Dodger' complex. *European Journal of Criminology*, 19 (5), 1243–1259.
Kotova, A. (2020) The role of offenders' family links in offender rehabilitation. In P. Ugwudike, H. Graham, F. McNeill, P. Raynor, F. S. Taxman, and C. Trotter (Eds.), *The Routledge Companion to Rehabilitative Work in Criminal Justice*. London: Routledge, 835–843.
Kristjánsson, K. (2010) *The Self and Its Emotions*. New York: Cambridge University Press.
Laing, R. D. (1960) *The Divided Self: An Existential Study in Sanity and Madness*. Middlesex, England: Penguin Books.
Laws, B. (2022) Reimaging 'the Self' in criminology: Transcendence, unconscious states and the limits of narrative criminology. *Theoretical Criminology*, 26 (3), 475–493.
Lewis, J., Ritchie, J., Ormston, R., and Morrell, G. (2014) Generalising from qualitative research. In J. Ritchie, J. Lewis, C. M. Nicholls, and R. Ormston (Eds.), *Qualitative Research Practice*. 2nd ed. London: Sage, np.
Liem, M. (2016) *After Life Imprisonment*. New York: New York University Press.
Liem, M., and Garcin, J. (2014) Post-release success among paroled lifers. *Laws*, 3 (4), 798–823.
Lloyd, A. (2018) Serving up harm: Systemic violence, transitions to adulthood and the service economy. In A. Boukli, and J. Kotze (Eds.), *Zemiology: Reconnecting Crime and Social Harm*. Cham, Switzerland: Palgrave MacMillan, 245–264.
Loseke, D. R. (2007) The study of identity as cultural, institutional, organizational, and personal narrative: Theoretical and empirical integrations. *Sociological Quarterly*, 48, 661–88.
May, H. (2000) "Murderers' Relatives": Managing stigma, negotiating identity. *Journal of Contemporary Ethnography*, 29 (2), 198–221.
Maynes, M. J., Pierce, J. L., and Laslett, B. (2008) *Telling Stories: The Use of Personal Narrative in the Social Sciences and History*. Cornell University Press: Ithaca and London.
McAdams, D. P. (1993) *The Stories We Live By: Personal Myth and the Making of the Self*. New York: The Guildford Press.
McNeill, F. (2012) Four forms of 'offender' rehabilitation: Towards and interdisciplinary perspective. *Legal and Criminological Psychology*, 17 (1), 1–19.
McWilliams, N. (2011) *Psychoanalytic Diagnosis: Understanding Personality Structure in the Clinical Process*, 2nd ed. New York: The Guildford Press.
Moffitt, T. (1993) Adolescence-limited and life course persistent anti-social behaviour: A developmental taxonomy. *Psychological Review*, 100 (4), 674–701.
Monckton Smith, J. (2020) Intimate partner femicide: Using Foucauldian analysis to track and eight stage progression to homicide. *Violence Against Women*, 8, 476–494.
O'Connell, M. (2023) *A Thread of Violence: A Story of Truth, Invention, and Murder*. London: Granta Books.
Office for National Statistics (ONS) (2024) Proven Reoffending Statistics: July to September 2020. Available at: https://www.gov.uk/government/statistics/proven-reoffending-statistics-july-2022-to-september-2022/proven-reoffending-statistics-july-to-september-2022 [accessed on 19 August 2024].
Opsal, T. (2015) "It's Their World so You Just Gotta Get Through": Women's experience of parole governance. *Feminist Criminology*, 10 (2), 187–207.

Presser, L. (2005) Negotiating power and narrative in research: Implications for feminist methodology. *Signs*, 30 (4), 2067–2090.

Riessman, C. H. (2015) Entering the hall of mirrors: Reflexivity and narrative research. In Ana De Finna, and A. Georgakopoulou (Eds.), *The Handbook of Narrative Analysis*. Oxford: John Wiley & Sons, Ltd, 219–238.

Riessman, C. K. (2008) *Narrative Methods for the Human Science*. California: Sage Publication.

Schacter, D. L., Guerin, S. A., and Jacques, P. L. St. (2011) Memory distortion: An adaptive perspective. *Trends in Cognitive Science*, 15 (10), 467–474.

Shingler, J., and Stickney, J. (2024) "I can see freedom, but I can't have it": Supporting people in the immediate aftermath of release. In J. Shingler, and J. Stickney (Eds.), *The Journey from Prison to Community*. Abingdon, Oxon: Routledge, 21–43.

Shuker, R., and Sullivan, E. (2010) *Grendon and the Emergence of Forensic Therapeutic Communities: Developments in Research and Practice*. Oxford: Wiley-Blackwell.

Spence, D. P. (1982) *Narrative Truth and Historical Truth: Meaning and Interpretation in Psychoanalysis*. New York: Norton.

Stevens, A. (2012) 'I am the person now that I was always meant to be': Identity reconstruction and narrative reframing in therapeutic community prisons. *Criminology and Criminal Justice*, 12 (5), 527–547.

Sykes, G., and Matza, D. (1957) Techniques of neutralization: A theory of delinquency. *American Sociological Review*, 22, 664–670.

Taylor, C. J. (2016) The Family's role in the reintegration of formerly incarcerated individuals: The direct effects of emotional support. *The Prison Journal*, 96 (3), 331–54.

Verde, A. (2021) Whose narrative? The self as (also) an alien – for a complex concept of 'Self' in narrative criminology. *Tijdschrift over Cultuur & Criminaliteit*, 10 (3), 35–35.

Ward, T., and Fortune, C. A. (2013) The good lives model: Aligning risk reduction with promoting offenders' personal goals. *European Journal of Probation*, 5 (2), 29–46.

Ward, T., and Stewart, C. A. (2003) The treatment of sex offenders: Risk management and good lives. *Professional Psychology: Research and Practice*, 34 (4), 353–360.

Warr, J. (2019) 'Always gotta be two mans': Lifers, risk, rehabilitation, and narrative labour. *Punishment and Society*, 22 (1), 28–47.

Wengraf, T. (2001) *Qualitative Research Interviewing. Biographic Narrative and Semi-Structured Methods*. London: SAGE.

Wetherell, M. (2005) Unconscious conflict or everyday accountability? *British Journal of Social Psychology*, 44, 169–173.

Wilson, D. (2007) *Serial Killers: Hunting Britons and Their Victims, 1960 to 2006*. Winchester, Hampshire: Waterside Press.

Yardley, E. (2020) Serial killing. In N. Loucks, S. S. Holt, and J. R. Adler (Eds), *Why We Kill: Understanding Violence Across Cultures and Disciplines*, 2nd ed. Oxon: Routledge, 57–75.

Žižek, S. (2002) *For They Know Not What They Do: Enjoyment as a Political Factor*. London: Verso.

Index

abuser, identification of 157–160
adjustments, secondary 56
agentic split 151
Albertson, K. 77
alertness 90–94
anti-realist perspective, identity 31
anti-social capital 76
anxiety 90, 93–94, 96–97
Appleton, C. 7
Ashworth, D. 3
Asylums (Goffman) 53

Bangladeshi families 76
Bauman, Z. 102
Baxter, H. 7
Bottoms, A. 35–36
Brittan, L. 4
Brookman, F. 4, 16
Bucerius, S. 54
Burnett, R. 37
Bushway, S. 36

Caird, R. 52, 56
callous, execution style 179–182
Calverley, A. 36, 75
capitalist realism 62
capital punishment 4
Castle (Kafka) 18
Cernkovich, S. A. 38
Christianity 166–167
Clemmer, D. 55
cognitive-personality approach 33
Cohen, S. 53–54
Coker, J. B. 6
communication skill, risk-encoded 123
complicated redemption 135–138
confrontational fighter murder 11
confrontational homicides 134

confrontational/revenge murder 177, 178
consumer culture 61; mandatory lifers and 101–109
consumer obsolescence, negotiating 101–106
conversion process 164
Cook, F. 57, 60
Copes, H. 167
Cordess, C. 7
Cornwell, J. 14
countertransference 158
COVID-19 pandemic 11, 12, 20, 82, 106, 107, 118
crackhead stigma 181–182
Crewe, B. 53, 58
crime of passion 127, 152–155, 175
Criminal Justice Act 2003: Schedule 21 of 5
criminological research 17
culture, consumer *see* consumer culture
'Custody for Life' *see* mandatory life sentence (MLS)

death penalty 4
Death Penalty Act, 1965 4
'deep freeze' 55
Deppermann, A. 38
deprivation model of imprisonment 55
desistance 28–30; conceptualisation 76; defined 29; identity change and 33–34, 36–38; narrative criminology and 38–39; primary 29; relational 29; secondary 29, 30; sociogenic approaches to 34–36; tertiary 30; theoretical 33–34
desistance pains 61
discretionary lifers 7

disculturation 89
Dobson, C. 10
Doublethink 89, 136
Duggan, C. 7
Durnescu, I. 62

early re-entry narratives 101
elimination tournament 83
employment, as resettlement capital 77–80
equilibrium of equality 135
execution style 179–182
ex-murderer becoming 61–62

family feud murder 12, 157–160, 180
family formation, by offenders 71–77
Farrall, S. 29, 35, 76
felon label 41
financial gain murder 12, 180, 181, 182
Flanagan, J. T. 40, 55
flawed consumer 102, 193
Fortune, C-A. 106
Frank, W. A. 9
freedom pains 62–64

Gadd, D. 35
gang related murders 134–135
Garcin, J. 40, 41, 75, 78
Garfinkel, H. 143
generativity 38, 60, 132, 138, 145; stagnation *vs.* 145
Gill, A. E. 57
Giordano, P. C. 38
goal reframing 106–109
Goffman, E. 53, 54, 56, 61, 89, 95
Good Lives Model (GLM) perspective 106
Griffin, D. 70, 127
guilt 132–145; defined 133; experiencing 94–98; remorse *vs.* 133

Haggerty, K. D. 54
Hall, S. 61, 103
Hannah-Moffat, K. 122
Hanson, D. 113
Harding, D. J. 10, 93
Healy, D. 70
Herbert, S. K. 160
Her Majesty's Pleasure 5
hierarchies of murder acceptability 175–179
homicide: defined 4; financial gain 12; victims in 2022 5

Homicide Act 1957 4
Hulley, S. 58
Hyden, M. 14
hyper-normality 120–123
hypervigilance 90–94

identity 30–33, 56–57, 176; change, and desistance 33–34, 36–38; narrative conceptualisation of 8–9; perspectives 31; pre-prison 56, 95; reconstructing 164–165; of success 101–109; traditional sources of 103
importation model 56
imprisonment: deprivation model of 55; pains 52–55
inauthentic murderers 175–179
Indian families 76
inmate society 55–56
institutionalisation 55–56
interpellation, concept of 9
Intimate Partner Femicide 12
intimate partner femicide 175, 176
Irwin, J. 54, 165

Jacquelyn, B. F. 57
James, W. 167
Janus-Faced struggles 135
Jewkes, Y. 56
job market 61–62

Kay, C. 16, 35, 76
Kazemian, L. 57
Kemshall, H. 115
Kerley, K. R. 167
Kim, J.-H. 17
King, S. 29, 33, 37
Klaus, W. 55
Kunst, M. 60
Kvale, S. 17

Larkin, E. 7
Laub, J. H. 29, 34
LeBel, T. P. 61, 142, 143
Lemert, E. M. 29
Letting Stories Breathe (Frank) 9
Leverentz, A. M. 15
liberty 113
Liem, M. 38, 40, 41, 60, 75, 78
life imprisonment 4; life after 7–8
lifers 40; mandatory *see* mandatory lifers
longitudinal narrative interview 13–15, **16**

long-term offenders/prisoners 40; and disculturation 89; and imprisonment pains 52–55
long-term sentences/imprisonment 41, 52
loss of autonomy 53
Lucius-Hoene, G. 38

mandatory lifers 10–13, **11**; adapt to imprisonment and prepare for release 58–61; and consumer culture 101–109; as neglected population in desistance research 39–42; negotiating supervision ambivalence 112–117
mandatory life sentence (MLS) 3–5
Mann, L. 2–3
manslaughter 4
Martin, J. P. 6
Maruna, S. 29, 30, 37, 38, 142, 143
master narratives 174–175
maturation 160
McAdams, D. P. 13
McCarthy, L. 7
Mc-Jobs 62
McNeill, F. 63, 143
Mead, G. H. 32
meaning systems 160, 164
Mental Health Act 1983 7
Mishler, E. 13
Morenoff, D. 10
Morenoff, J. D. 93
'mortification of the self' 53
multi-agency public protection arrangements (MAPPA) supervision 116
murder acceptability, hierarchies of 175–179
murderer's condition 58
'murder for money' 11–12

narrative conceptualisation of identity 8–9
narrative criminology, and desistance 38–39
'Narrative Turn' 32
narratological desistance 33
National Association for the Care and Resettlement of Offenders (NACRO) 142
National Probation Service 6
negotiating consumer obsolescence 101–106

neuroimaging 31
nihilism 59
Nugent, B. 29
Nussbaum, M. C. 133

O'Connor, P. 151
ontogenetic desistance 33
O'Reilly, M. 17
orthodoxy of privatisation 127
Orwell, G. 89, 136
Owen, B. 54

Page, K. 7
Pager, D. 82
pains of freedom 62–64
pains of imprisonment 52–55
pains of probation/desistance 61
panoptic probation service 122
pareidolia 96–97
par excellence 112, 120
Parker, N. 17
Parker, T. 58
parricide 7
passion, crime of 127, 152–155, 175
Paternoster, R. 36
Perry, E. 117
personality: long-term imprisonment and 54; traits 60, 91
pessimism 105–106, 113
Pitchford, C. 2–3, 6, 113, 114
post-incarceration syndrome (PICS) 60
posttraumatic stress disorder (PTSD) 161–163
pre-prison identity 56, 95
primal wound 155–157
primary desistance 29
prisonization 55–56
probation pains 61
probation service 6, 113, 118; panoptic 122; role in interpellating 21
proportional remorse 123–127
Psalm 51 166

qualitative research 16–17
Quillian, L. 82

random homicide 179
Raymen, T. 102, 103
realists perspective, identity 31
recall 5–7
Recall, Review, and Re-release of Recalled Prisoners Policy Framework 6

recognition of interdependency 160
reconviction 5–7
redemption 139–145; complicated 135–138
re-entry narratives 89, 98–99, 101, 141
regret 134
Rehabilitation of Offenders Act (ROA) (1974) 61
relational desistance 29
release on temporary licence (ROTL) 74
religious conversion narrative 165–168
remorse: defined 133; guilt *vs*. 133; performing 132–145; proportional 123–127
resettlement capital, employment as 77–80
returning citizen status 143
Ricciardelli, R. 62
Rice, A. 113
Richie, M. 143
Ricoeur, P. 105
risk-encoded communication skill 123
risk reduction 123
ruthless, execution style 179–182

sampling 16–18
Sampson, R. J. 29, 34
Schiff, B. 17
Schinkel, M. 29
scholarly tug of war 33
Schroeder, R. D. 38
secondary adjustments 56
secondary desistance 29, 30
self, and society 36–38
self-appraisal 165
selfhood 31
Sentencing Act 2020: section 259 of 5
service-based economy 62
Shammas, V. L. 62
Shapland, J. 35–36
Sheffield Desistance Study 35
Sheppard, A. 62
sine qua non 52, 140
Smith, O. 102, 103
snares 55
social capital 34, 35–36, 73
social media 103, 104
social networks 36
social rehabilitation 187
social services 116
society, self and 36–38

sociogenic approaches to desistance 33, 34–36
socio-narratology 9
Somers, R. M. 32
splitting narrative 150–168, 188–191; abuser, identification of 157–160; crime of passion 152–155; goal of 151; murder nexus 152; primal wound 155–157; prison experience 160; reconstructing identities 164–165; religious conversion 165–168
stagnation 116, 119; generativity *vs*. 145
Stein, A. 7, 150
stigma 61, 82, 102, 103; crackhead 181–182; management of 174
stoicism 105
structural barriers 84
supervision: mandatory lifers negotiating 112–117
Sykes, G. M. 52, 53, 54, 58

'the tariff' 4–5
Taylor, L. 53–54
tertiary desistance 30
transference 158
Transforming Rehabilitation Policy 127
transition, offenders 70; employment as resettlement capital 77–80; family formation 71–77
trauma 160–163
TSM (Terrorism, Sex Offenders and Murderers) 82
Turnbull, S. 122

Verrier, N. N. 155

walking on eggshells sentiment 118–120
Ward, T. 106
Warr, J. 39, 53, 63
Weaver, B. 93
Western, B. 72, 74
Wilkinson, M. 57, 60
Winlow, S. 103
work ethics 106
Wright, S. 58
Wyse, J. B. 93
Wyse, J. J. B. 10

Young, J. 7, 61

Printed in the United States
by Baker & Taylor Publisher Services